Various Aspects of Mimesis in Selected Sea Novels
of Frederick Marryat, James F. Cooper and Richard H. Dana

Dis/Continuities
Toruń Studies in Language, Literature and Culture

Edited by Mirosława Buchholtz

Advisory Board
Leszek Berezowski (Wroclaw University)
Annick Duperray (University of Provence)
Dorota Guttfeld (Nicolaus Copernicus University)
Grzegorz Koneczniak (Nicolaus Copernicus University)
Piotr Skrzypczak (Nicolaus Copernicus University)

Vol. 3

Joanna Mstowska

Various Aspects of Mimesis in Selected Sea Novels of Frederick Marryat, James F. Cooper and Richard H. Dana

Bibliographic Information published by the Deutsche Nationalbibliothek
The Deutsche Nationalbibliothek lists this publication in the Deutsche Nationalbibliografie; detailed bibliographic data is available in the internet at http://dnb.d-nb.de.

Cover Design:
© Olaf Gloeckler, Atelier Platen, Friedberg

Reviewers:
Prof. Wiesław Krajka
Prof. Jacek Fabiszak

This publication was financially supported by
the Faculty of Languages and the Department of English,
Nicolaus Copernicus University, Toruń
(research grant No. 1169-FL).

ISSN 2193-4207
ISBN 978-3-631-62514-9
© Peter Lang GmbH
Internationaler Verlag der Wissenschaften
Frankfurt am Main 2013
All rights reserved.
Peter Lang Edition is an imprint of Peter Lang GmbH

All parts of this publication are protected by copyright. Any utilisation outside the strict limits of the copyright law, without the permission of the publisher, is forbidden and liable to prosecution. This applies in particular to reproductions, translations, microfilming, and storage and processing in electronic retrieval systems.

www.peterlang.de

In Memory of My Father
AIDG

Acknowledgements

I wish to express my gratitude to Professor Mirosława Buchholtz, who encouraged me to take an academic interest in sea fiction, for her scholarly guidance and valuable suggestions. I am also indebted to Professor Wiesław Krajka and Professor Jacek Fabiszak for their careful reading of this study, thorough reviews, and perceptive comments.

Table of Contents

Acknowledgements 7

Introduction..11

CHAPTER ONE
Mimetic Desire: Frederick Marryat's *The Phantom Ship* (1839)............................35

    1.1. The Flying Dutchman: Romantic Interpretations 37

    1.2. Variations on Triangular Desire..45

    1.3. The Flying Dutchman's Progress: A Christian Metaphor 62

CHAPTER TWO
Mimetic Form versus Spontaneous Life: J. F. Cooper's *The Red Rover* (1828) 73

    2.1. The History of the Topos of *Theatrum Mundi*..75

    2.2. The Red Rover: A Prisoner of Form...89

    2.3. The Rover Becomes Hamlet: Epiphany of Life..93

CHAPTER THREE
"Mimetic Mirror": R. H. Dana's *Two Years Before the Mast* (1840)....................103

    3.1. Sea Narrative: A Mirror of Maritime Life 104

    3.2. The Self and Sea Space: Reciprocal Mirrors 109

    3.3. Sea Voyage: A Reflection of the Journey of Life....................................116

    3.4. The Sea: A Mirror Reflecting Images From the Past 126

Conclusion..133

Bibliography 137

    Primary Sources 137

    Secondary Sources 138

Introduction

The sea has been depicted in English literature since its very origins, including such examples as *Beowulf, The Wanderer* or *The Seafarer*. If the Old English Period portrays sailors and the sea in an interesting and original way, the Middle Ages, with surprisingly scarce sea passages in literature of that period, may be characterized as neglectful. It is the Renaissance that generates a considerable widening of interest in maritime materials. Marek Błaszak enumerates a few authors who had some first-hand experience of the sea: Edmund Spenser, Sir Walter Raleigh or John Donne. A significant point in the evolution of English sea literature is the discovery of the New World. Columbus' momentous voyage of 1492 contributed to the immense popularity of the newly reached land and influenced the imagination of contemporary readers and writers with an unprecedented force. This may be illustrated by the fact that Columbus' letter depicting America had had twenty editions by the year 1500 (Błaszak 11–14).

The discovery had a tremendous influence on Richard Hakluyt, the first English author, editor, collector, translator and publisher whose great contribution to the development of English sea literature is undeniable. Educated at Oxford, he managed to master at least six foreign languages, including Greek, Latin, Italian, Spanish, Portuguese and French. Błaszak stresses the fact that after the defeat of the Spanish Armada, Hakluyt not only produced, but also financed the first edition of his influential work entitled *The Principall Navigations, Voiages and Discoveries of the English Nation made by Sea or over Land to the most remote and farthest distant Quarters of the earth at any time within the compasse of these 1500 yeeres* (1589). Classified by critics as "mercantilist propaganda in the service of Elizabethan rising imperialism" (Błaszak 17), Hakluyt's work, which was in fact well-ordered and at times highly creative, enjoyed great popularity among Shakespeare, Defoe, Coleridge, Tennyson or Thoreau (15–17). Błaszak underlines Hakluyt's influence on Shakespeare's *The Tempest* or on Coleridge's *The Rime of the Ancient Mariner* and *Kubla Khan* (18).

The second significant phase in the development of the English sea novel is connected with Daniel Defoe. As a merchant's son particularly interested in geography and having mastered Greek, Latin, French, Italian, as well as some Dutch, surprisingly Defoe travelled to the most remote parts of the globe above all in his library, making "the tour of the world in books" (Błaszak 19). His guidebook published between 1724 and 1726, *Tour Through the Whole Island of Great Britain,* provides meticulously detailed descriptions of almost all coastlines and regions of England, Scotland and Wales which he visited. It is, however, *Robinson Crusoe* (1719), his first literary production, for which he is famous today. Still, Błaszak points out that the narrative should not be regarded as a potential sea novel. Although the hero is referred to in the full title of the novel as a "Mariner," he resembles a landsman or a merchant rather than a sailor (21). Defoe's second literary production, *Captain Singleton* (1720), is not a sea novel either. Defined by Błaszak as a "pirate romance" or a "fictitious narrative of travel" (22), it presents the story of an orphaned boy who joins an international gang of pirates, then abandons the promising piratical career, and finally returns to England as a prosperous merchant. Błaszak admits that although Defoe is aware of "the enormous literary potential of maritime travel and adventure, exploration and discovery, exoticism and patriotism, as well as physical, moral and spiritual maturation and self-discovery" (25), he fails as a sea novelist. Regarding the sea merely as a travel channel for ships enabling them to move from one part of the world to another, he ignores the complexity of sea space and its impact on sailors. What is more, his protagonists are merchants interested in making profit ashore rather than real seamen, whose life is strictly connected with the sea. Błaszak concludes that Defoe, who lacked a first-hand maritime experience, seems to embody the essence of the eighteenth-century merchant and traveler (25).

The third important stage in the evolution of the English sea novel is marked by the works of Tobias Smollett. His first nautical production, *The Adventures of Roderick Random*, was published anonymously in 1748. Containing fascinating autobiographical material, the book enjoyed considerable success – eight editions were issued during the author's lifetime, as well as translations into French and German (31). Błaszak observes, however, that the marine section of the book is very limited, as only twelve chapters out of sixty-nine are set afloat, while Walker points out that 16.9 percent of all pages are those at sea, in contrast to one of Cooper's novels, *Homeward Bound,* where the proportion accounts for as much as 99 percent (Walker 68). Nautical passages are scarce also in Smollett's second novel entitled *The Adventures of Peregrine Pickle* (1751). As neither the sea nor ships are explored in his novels, Smollett's narratives can, according to Błaszak, but disappoint (Błaszak 31). Likewise, his protagonists are portrayed as so grotesque and, hence, so distant from reality that the reader does not identify with them. The fact that Smollett's sailors are not sufficiently convincing may be attributable to the novelist's lack of maritime experience. Not being a sailor himself and having spent in the navy only about a year as the surgeon's second mate, Smollett does not endow his fictional characters with the features of professional seamen. Often ridiculous, all his protagonists are secondary characters, presented outside their natural environment. Despite the fact that Smollett's caricatures of sailors are portrayed as significantly different from land-dwellers, they appear almost exclusively on land (33–34).

It is worth observing that Smollett's undeserved reputation as a marine novelist was established by Sir Walter Scott, his Scottish compatriot (36). Not acquainted with sea life, Scott stated in his *Lives of the Novelists* (1825) that the author of *Roderick Random* managed "to describe sailors with such truth and spirit of delineation, that from that time whoever has undertaken the same task, has seemed to copy more from Smollett than from nature" (Scott 75). Given the fact that this erroneous opinion was launched by a landsman, who in his *Pirate* sets at sea only 19 pages out of 444 (Walker 68), it is surprising that his inaccurate statement became definitive and was repeated by many later critics. Błaszak, whose opinion differs considerably from Scott's, is right in claiming that Smollett does not deserve to be called "a fully-fledged novelist of the sea" (37). Having no ambivalent feelings for the sea and perceiving the ship as a prison rather than a home, Smollett should not be referred to as a marine writer, but as "the creator of a sailor as an essentially distinct […] character in English prose fiction" (37).

Nautical references can be also found in Ann Radcliffe's Gothic romances. Surprising as it may seem, in her novels Radcliffe describes numerous mysterious seascapes or awe-inspiring coastal cliffs, on which she frequently situates her castles. Błaszak observes that while creating the settings of her masterpieces, such as *The Mysteries of Udolpho* (1794) or *A Sicilian Romance*, Radcliffe must have been influenced by Edmund Burke's aesthetic theory of the sublime, as described in his *Philosophical Enquiry into the Origin of our Ideas of the Sublime and Beautiful* (1756) (Błaszak 39). According to Burke, the sources of sublimity are associated with vastness and immensity of the space. He observes that sublimity is strictly connected not only with the fear of enormity, darkness and mystery, but also with all that rises beyond certain norms, for instance death, physical force or moral strength. It is admiration caused by awareness of pain, suffering and danger, as well as their overwhelming power over human that dominates in confrontation with sublimity. Stimulated by abyss, loneliness, silence, emptiness or enormity, the experience may be regarded as a mixture of pleasure and pain rooted in terror. The littleness of a human being contrasted with the magnitude of the universe frequently enhances the feeling of the sublime as well. If Smollett may be described as the creator of a peculiar sailor, then Radcliffe may be seen as the propagator of the nautical sublime.

Not only Radcliffe in her pre-romantic prose, but also many of English romantic poets utilized maritime motifs in their works. Among others, nautical metaphors can be traced in Coleridge's *The Rime of the Ancient Mariner*, Wordsworth's *Tintern Abbey*, Shelley's *Ode to the West Wind*, or Byron's *Don Juan* and *Childe Harold's Pilgrimage*. Other romantic authors who introduced sailors and pirates to their fiction include Jane Austen and Walter Scott. As both her brothers served in the navy, Austen, who corresponded with them and got to know many of their naval acquaintances, gained a considerable knowledge of maritime life. Błaszak claims that she was also influenced by the genuine admiration for the navy after the famous Battle of Trafalgar, as well as by the fact that her brother Frank served under Nelson (46). Sailors are presented both in Austen's *Mansfield Park*, published in 1814, and *Persuasion*, published posthumously in 1817. In contrast to Austen, Scott portrays a sailor hero only in one work, *The Pirate*, published in 1821. As its action takes place almost entirely on land and his sailors are not distinguishable from the land-living men, Scott's sentimental story is far from being a sea novel.

Still, it is important for two reasons. Firstly, it is the last book including marine motifs, issued by an eminent English writer before the advent of Frederick Marryat. Secondly, Scott's narrative irritated Cooper so greatly that he decided to write his own sea novel, which "if it had no other merit, might present truer pictures of the ocean and ships than any that are to be found in *The Pirate*" (Cooper's Preface to the 1849 edition of his first nautical romance, *The Pilot*) (Błaszak 38–49).

Arguing that Hakluyt, Defoe and Smollett fail to establish a canon of the sea novel, Błaszak proves in his study that it is Captain Marryat who should be regarded as the true originator of the genre in English literature. Błaszak delineates the generic matrix of sea fiction as composed of three constituents, including the sailor, his ship and the sea, which organize "the remaining elements in numerous other works belonging to the same generic category" (256). Applying the three dominants of sea fiction, Błaszak shows that none of the authors whose works he analyzes belong to the category of sea novelists proper, as their fiction only features marine motifs. Hence, his inspiring study is devoted to the founder of the genre in British literature, Captain Marryat.

Frederick Marryat was born in London in 1792. His father, Joseph, was a widely respected man of the City, and an author of several political pamphlets. Teenage Frederick ran away from school several times. Feeling an overwhelming desire to go to sea, he finally entered the Royal Navy at the age of fourteen in 1806. Young Marryat's willingness to become a seaman was first of all enhanced by Admiral Nelson's victorious Battle of Trafalgar in 1805 and, secondly, by his participation in the hero's state funeral in London. Błaszak observes that "Nelson's heroic victory and death must have been a powerful inspiration" (Błaszak 53). After the end of the war against Napoleon, Marryat was promoted to the rank of commander in 1815. Still younger than twenty-three years of age, he already had a nine-year-long experience gained in the Mediterranean and the Atlantic, soon to be explored in writing (59). The future writer not only invented a system of communication by flag signals and designed an unsinkable cork life-boat, but was also awarded a gold medal for saving many lives at sea, risking his own (60).

Having served for twenty-four years in the Royal Navy, Marryat decided to devote himself entirely to his family and "to try his luck as a writer of belles-lettres" (66). His first novel, the title of which was *The Naval Officer, or Scenes and Adventures in the Life of Frank Mildmay*, was published in 1829. His second novel, *The King's Own*, was issued in 1830 as a three-volume production. The book received glowing reviews in such prestigious periodicals as *The Spectator* or *The Edinburgh Review*. Enthusiastic about the novel was also Washington Irving, then at the peak of his popularity both in Europe and America, who, encouraging the Captain to continue his new career of an author, wrote in a letter dated August 25th, 1830:

> I hope you are busy with your pen, and that you intend to show up some of the old wreckers and rovers of the ocean. You have a glorious field before you, and one in

which you cannot have many competitors, as so very few write the author to the sailor. I think the chivalry of the ocean quite a new region of fiction and romance, and to my taste one of the most captivating that could be explored. (quoted in Błaszak 67)

Himself planning to run away to sea and fascinated by Lord Nelson, Irving was a competent reviewer of Marryat's first two novels and the first eminent writer to recognize the novelist's talent (67).

Establishing a new genre in contemporary prose fiction, Marryat relied on his nautical experience, as well as referred to native and foreign authors whose works he knew, including Homer, Milton, Coleridge, Cowper, Defoe, Austen and Cooper. Błaszak claims that "Captain Marryat's allusions to these authors show that he was entirely familiar with their works" (70). In 1832 Marryat bought the *Metropolitan Magazine*, becoming both its proprietor and editor. Therefore, he decided to publish almost all his subsequent works in periodicals, beginning with his third novel, *Newton Forster, or the Merchant Service* (1832). Engaged in cultural activity, Marryat became personally acquainted with contemporary novelists, among others Dickens and Thackeray (71). Marryat's next novel, *Peter Simple*, published in a three-volume edition in 1834, and *Jacob Faithful*, arousing enthusiasm both among critics and readers, confirmed his pre-eminent position among writers of sea fiction. Thackeray, impressed by the novel, referred to it as "my dearly beloved *Jacob Faithful*" (quoted in Błaszak 72). *Mr. Midshipman Easy*, yet another novel which was released in 1836, is nowadays the most often reprinted of all narratives created by the Captain in his heyday (74).

In 1837 Captain Marryat visited America, where he scored an immediate popularity. Marryat's success in the United States is attributable to at least two factors: his recognition as an eminent nautical novelist and his American roots, as the Captain's mother was of Bostonian origin (75). In 1838 Marryat's new novel, *The Phantom Ship*, began to be serialized in *The New Monthly* in England, and was published as a book in three volumes by Henry Colburn in 1839. The same year Longmans released the Captain's *Diary in America*, which, because of the author's critical remarks concerning the New World, made him extremely unpopular in America (76). Disillusioned and homesick, he wrote bitterly in a letter from New York in 1839: "If I were rather not in want of money I certainly would not write any more, for I am rather tired of it. I should like to disengage myself from the fraternity of authors, and be known in future only in my profession as a good officer and seaman" (quoted in Błaszak 76). Having come back to Europe, Marryat settled down in London again and had his next novel, *Poor Jack*, published in 1840. Edgar Allan Poe regarded *Poor Jack* as the Captain's best novel after *Peter Simple* (77).

In 1841, encouraged by his own children, Marryat composed *Masterman Ready, or the Wreck of the Pacific*, the publication of which marked the final period in his literary career – writing books for children. Marryat died in 1848, having written twenty-two novels, several novellas and tales, two diaries, two plays, as well as nonfictional writings, both published and unpublished (81). During his lifetime the Captain was immensely popular on both sides of the Atlantic, his productions being almost immediately translated into French and German (82). It is worth mentioning that all his private papers were destroyed after his death and his acquaintances were not allowed to write the Captain's biography (83). It was in 1872 that Florence Marryat published her father's *Life and Letters*, even today regarded as one of the most important documents concerning Marryat's maritime life and literary career.

In 1898 Joseph Conrad paid homage to the Captain in one of his essays, entitled "Tales of the Sea," confessing that his life and work had been influenced by Marryat's example. His nautical experience and writing impressed Herman Melville as well, who later admitted that his decision to become both a sailor and an author was "forced by the united influences of Captain Marryat and hard times" (quoted in Błaszak 87). Regarding the Captain as a great seaman who was able to transform his maritime life into fiction, Conrad wrote:

> To this writer of the sea the sea was not an element. It was a stage, where was displayed an exhibition of valour, and of such achievement as the world had never seen before. The greatness of that achievement cannot be pronounced imaginary, since its reality has affected the destinies of nations; nevertheless, in its grandeur it has all the remoteness of an ideal. (*Notes on Life and Letters* 53)

In Conrad's opinion, Marryat was then a realist, as opposed to Cooper, regarded by him as an idealist. What the famous author also stresses in the Captain's fictional output is his awareness of the demonic nature of the sea, surprisingly indifferent to the sailor's suffering. The author of *The Mirror of the Sea* observes: "He loved his country first, the Service next, the sea perhaps not at all. But the sea loved him without reserve. It gave him his professional distinction and his author's fame – a fame such as not often falls to the lot of a true artist" (*Notes* 55). Paying Marryat the highest compliment of a fellow author, Conrad states: "His greatness is undeniable" (54).

Similarly, Virginia Woolf praised Marryat's achievement in her essay entitled "The Captain's Death Bed," published in 1935. Like Conrad, she paid tribute to the novelist's realistic descriptions, announcing that "Captain Marryat had in embryo at least most of the gifts that go to make a master" (quoted in Błaszak 85). Yet another writer who extolled Marryat was Ernest Hemingway. In his "Monologue to the Maestro," originally issued in 1935, Hemingway enumerated the books that belong to the world's literary heritage. The first two masterpieces are Tolstoy's *War and Peace* and *Anna Karenina*, the next three are Marryat's *Midshipman Easy, The Naval Officer* and *Peter Simple*, followed, among others, by more works by Flaubert, Mann, Joyce, Fielding, Stendhal, Dostoyevski, Twain, Kipling, Turgenev and James (quoted in Błaszak 87).

Marryat, who was one of the most popular writers of the Victorian Era, faded into oblivion after World War II. It is surprising that only one monograph, written by Oliver Warner, devoted to him appeared between the end of the war and the last decade of the twentieth century. In his *Captain Marryat. A Rediscovery*, published in 1953, Warner concentrates on the Captain's career, reading his fiction through the prism of his life at sea. Since then, there has been no other comprehensive study of Marryat's writing in Britain (86). Błaszak observes that the Captain is not mentioned in Andrew Sanders' monumental *Short Oxford History of English Literature* (1994) and that Tom Pocock's recent biography of him, "written in the style of popular magazines," has hardly any literary value (87). In the United States the only comprehensive critical analysis of Marryat's narratives is Louis Parascandola's monograph entitled *Puzzled Which to Choose: Conflicting Socio-Political Views in the Works of Captain Frederick Marryat* (1997), in which the scholar investigates the Captain's life and work from social and political perspectives. Despite the scarcity of critical monographs, the number of Marryat's novels re-edited both in Great Britain and the United States has been growing. It should be noted that a new edition of *The Phantom Ship* was published in this century in the Fantasy Classics series by Wildside Press of Berkeley Heights, New Jersey (Błaszak 88–89). Three of the Captain's novels were issued in Polish translation: *Midshipman Easy* (between the two World Wars), *Peter Simple* and *The Phantom Ship* (both in 1973). Apart from Marek Błaszak's insightful monograph, *Sailors, Ship and the Sea in the Novels of Captain Frederick Marryat* (2006), no comprehensive critical analysis of Marryat's fiction has appeared within the last fifty years, either in Britain or in Poland.

If Błaszak investigates Marryat as the originator of the sea novel in British literature, then Thomas Philbrick explores James Fenimore Cooper, the author who established the sea novel in America almost simultaneously with Marryat. Cooper, like the Captain, did not create the canons of the genre *ex nihilo*, but exploited and developed the marine motifs introduced by his predecessors.

In his *James Fenimore Cooper and the Development of American Sea Fiction*, Thomas Philbrick observes that during the first half of the nineteenth century the sea had as powerful impact on the imagination of many Americans as the continental frontier after 1850. Offering adventure, a promise of quick profit and unlimited freedom from social conventions, the sea was regarded as an ideal testing-ground of human character, providing an opportunity to challenge man's strength and skill (1). Stressing the relevance of the sea to the past, present and future of the nation, Philbrick regards the element as the embodiment of liberty and political identity of people "so thoroughly maritime as the Americans" (58). Philbrick maintains that the development of American sea fiction runs parallel to the expansion of the American merchant marine and the new republic's naval successes of the War of 1812. It was, therefore, inevitable that this maritime activity should be mirrored in the introduction of the sea to American literature, its duty being "to keep the flame of maritime nationalism burning brightly" (2). Although in the first half of the nineteenth century the ocean was America's domain, as it had been England's in the eighteenth century, British nautical literature, dominated by Smollett, could not serve as an example to follow for American writers for at least two reasons (3). Firstly, Smollett restricted his portrayal of maritime life to descriptions of the daily routine of the Royal Navy, a huge organization which overshadowed all its individual members. Secondly, faithful to neoclassical canons, he regarded the navy as the instrument of British power and man as but a tiny part of little significance functioning in the colossal social machinery (4). By contrast, American writers at the beginning of the nineteenth century addressed their narratives to the nation which extolled heroic individuals rather than institutions and whose literary taste was strongly influenced by the romantic attitude towards external nature. A person's relation to society was beyond the scope of interest of the American audience. Finally, Smollett's most severe inadequacy was the tone of his fiction. Philbrick underlines that "[t]rue to the neoclassical dictum that heroism is incompatible with the realistic treatment of familiar materials," Smollett presented the life before the mast from a satirical perspective and portrayed his seamen as unconvincing caricatures (5).

Similarly, Smollett's portrayal of the sea and the ship was useless as a model for American writers. "Sharing the neoclassical distaste for the wild, primitive aspects of nature," he gave hardly any attention to the ocean, presenting it rather as a conventional background (5). Smollett did not associate the stormy sea with sublimity. He regarded the ocean as the embodiment of evil forces beyond human control, evoking nothing but terror. Similarly the ship, devoid of any grace and beauty, was a kind of a prison or a microcosm afloat, mirroring corrupt societies ashore (5–6). Captain Marryat, one of Smollett's imitators, expanded naval episodes, presenting them not in the narrative background but allowing them to serve as the principal setting. Unlike Błaszak, Philbrick claims that Marryat's fiction, like Smollett's, explores the seaman's relation neither to the sea nor to his vessel, but rather the sailor's function in a "segment of society," that is in the institution of the Royal Navy (6).

If British novelists were eager to follow in Smollett's footsteps, American writers felt obliged to move in a different direction. Aware of the inadequacy of Smollett's fiction for their purposes, American authors resorted to the ideal, regarded as an alternative to Smollett's satirical approach to life at sea. Cooper's seamen differ considerably from Smollett's grotesque and eccentric tars presented as stock characters, as well as from sentimentalized lonely and homesick sailors from Charles Dibdin's popular sea songs. Although sentimentalism delineated the sailor as a *pars pro toto* figure presenting his feelings and concerns as common, it reduced the capacity of maritime life to stimulate the sublime (8). Writing at the peak of romanticism in America, Cooper portrayed the sea as a source of the Burkean sublime, stimulating desires for transcendence. Emphasizing freedom and individuality, he presented life at sea as an escape from both the corruption and the oppression of civilized society. The American novelist's romantic sailor is capable of heroism, as he regards the immense sea as a stimulus for noble deeds, and the ship as a companion in the battle with the all-powerful element. Meeting the requirements of the romantic conception of maritime life, in his nautical romances Cooper fused the sublime with the heroic (9). Although he imitated some stock motifs typical of the Elizabethan romance, for instance demonized pirates, heroines disguised as sailors or dramatic rescues from shipwrecks, he combined marvels with realistic detail "convincing in its fullness, precision, and authenticity" (10). According to Philbrick, the artistic goal of Cooper and his contemporaries was to intensify Smollett's technique of realistic descriptions and to replace his satirical tone with that of "heroic seriousness" (11).

Moreover, Philbrick observes that it was William Falconer, both a British seaman and a poet, who in *The Shipwreck* (1762) first embedded nautical terminology in poetic descriptions of maritime life (11). Although the book was extremely popular not only in Great Britain, but also in America, Falconer's attitude towards the sea and the ship does not transcend neoclassical standards. Philbrick claims that the poet's innovation remains entirely a matter of diction, as, focusing on the seaman as "a product of civilization," regarding seamanship as a sophisticated technology and presenting the ship merely as a complex mechanism, Falconer is still far from the romantic preoccupation with the significance of the sublime aspect of the sea (12). In contrast to Falconer's "man-centered approach" (13) to life at sea, regarded in the eighteenth century as a norm, Byron's attitude presented in *Childe Harold* (1818) is sea-centered. In confrontation with the immense ocean, both beautiful and awe-inspiring, man, lost in deep contemplation, becomes aware of his insignificance within the system of the universe.

Philip Freneau, who in combining his poetic images with a practical knowledge of seamanship resembles Falconer, may be regarded as the pioneer in American literature, who reflected almost every aspect of the country's nautical history between the years 1776 and 1812, challenging English supremacy in nautical poetry (15). A journalist, a poet, and a master of a vessel in the West Indian trade, in his sea verse Freneau uses nautical materials more substantially than any American writer ever. *The British Prison Ship* (1781) is the first attempt in American literature to create a nautical narrative in verse (16). Unlike his contemporary authors, Freneau did not restrict his portrayal of maritime life to reportorial ballad-like descriptions. His serious nautical poetry is characterized by an ambivalent attitude towards the sea. Frightening in its lonely and monotonous vastness, the ocean poses a constant threat to seamen, reduced almost to nothingness in their impotence and fragility. Although Freneau perceives the sea both as fascinating and awe-inspiring, his admiration is not rooted in the combination of the element's beauty and terror. Freneau's portrayal of the sea differs considerably from the neoclassical notion of rough and dangerous water that can be mastered and exploited by the power of man's reason (18). Still, it is also different from the romantic conception of sublimity, as the sea serves in his human-centered poetry as a proving-ground of courage and strength.

The first example of a significant influence of romanticism on the portrayal of the ocean in American literature appeared in a brief sketch by Washington Irving (39). "The Voyage," published in the first number of *The Sketch Book* (1819), is significant not only for its originality, but "for the dominant influence it was to exert for many years on the tone and content of the American short sea story" (Philbrick 40). In Irving's sketch the ocean is no longer completely separated from humanity. As it is much more than a ferocious element against which man exhibits his power in order to achieve utilitarian purposes, the sea does not stimulate a revelation of the omnipotence of God. Philbrick claims that in Irving's prose, as in Byron's poetry, "the sea assumes a new significance through its effect on the human imagination and emotions; it becomes an aesthetic object to be savored for the capacity of its beauty to delight, its immensity to awe, and its danger to excite" (39).

The crucial phase in the development of the American sea novel is, however, associated with the person and works of James Fenimore Cooper. The future novelist was born in 1789. His father, Judge Cooper, was regarded as a considerable political power in New York State west of the Hudson River (Walker 2). At the age of thirteen young Cooper entered the Yale College, but was soon expelled for misconduct and sent home to Cooperstown. The Judge, foreseeing the future growth of the American Navy, sent his son to sea as "an ordinary seaman before the mast" in 1806 (6). Two years later Cooper received the midshipman's warrant signed by Thomas Jefferson (7). Warren S. Walker observes that the sea was the greatest love of Cooper's life: when travelling, he never missed the opportunity to go by water (10). Having inherited $50,000 after the death of his father, Cooper took furlough from Navy in 1810, never to return for active duty. Nine years later he became the *pater familias*, taking full responsibility for Cooper estates, which were heavily in debt (12). On the verge of bankruptcy, in 1820 he accepted his wife's challenge and began writing novels. Reading aloud to her from a current English novel, probably Jane Austen's work, Cooper found it boring. Hence, he wrote his own narrative, *Precaution* (1820), a sentimental novel set in England. Walker points out that Cooper's next three novels were also answers to challenges. Having awaited an American novel, critics, disappointed by *Precaution,* regarded the book as an imitation of English fiction. In response to attacks, Cooper wrote *The Spy* (1821) and *The Pioneers* (1823), both thoroughly American. *The Pioneers* was a runaway bestseller: 3,000 copies were sold on the first day and the author guaranteed a considerable sum of money. His first sea novel, *The Pilot* (1824), was also a great success. Annoyed by the praise of Scott's *The Pirate*, written by the author unacquainted with maritime life, Cooper created within a few months his own nautical romance (Walker 12–13).

In 1826 he offered the whole family the traditional Grand Tour of the Continent, which lasted for seven years. Although he visited Germany, Switzerland and spent almost two years in Paris, it was Italy that impressed him most (16). When he came back home, long before his death at Cooperstown in 1851, Cooper was regarded as America's master of the novel. During memorial services held in New York City, letters were read from, among others, Melville, Hawthorne and Emerson. Of Cooper's thirty-two novels, the *Leather-Stocking Tales* depicting the wilderness of the frontier, including *The Pioneers* (1823), *The Last of the Mohicans* (1826), *The Prairie* (1827), *The Pathfinder* (1840) and *The Deerslayer* (1841), have outweighed in popularity all his other works and are nowadays regarded as his major achievement (Walker 30). Creating the frontier myth, with his romances of the forest Cooper established a genre "indigenous to the new republic" (116). Walker observes that the author "brought to the printed page, however romantically, two epochs of American life that were soon to disappear forever – the day of the frontier and the day of the sailing ship" (117). It is remarkable that he achieved such a great success in a very short period of time, between 1821 and 1826 (22). Among eminent critics who extolled his art are Thomas Lounsbury, Brander Matthews and Wilkie Collins, to name but a few (121).

Not only a man-of-letters, but also a naval scholar and a historian of the Navy, Cooper published his monumental *History of the Navy of the United States of America* (1839), which became immensely popular as well. Within ten years three editions of the complete text of *The History* were published, making Cooper's two-volume book a standard reference work (Walker 84–85). His interest in maritime materials is reflected not only in the writer's non-fiction, but also in his sea narratives, in which he elevated the role of the sea, painting a picture of unforgettable seascapes and paying attention to nautical technicalities. Having many successors but hardly any forerunners in the American nautical novel as it is known today, Cooper may be viewed as genre founder (118). Among his eleven nautical novels, his early romances at sea including *The Pilot* (1824), *The Red Rover* (1828) and *The Water-Witch* (1831), which gained immediate critical approval, deserve a careful attention because of the original depiction of the sailor, the ship and the sea. As all sailors in Cooper's sea novels are detached from civilization, their characters and personalities have been shaped by maritime experience. Although Cooper presents the sea as an antagonist, his seamen love, admire and respect the ocean. It is its overwhelming vastness, unpredictability and changeability that is both fascinating and frightening. As the sailors perceive the sea as a force to define themselves against, they regard the ocean as the area of their achievement. Its tremendous power, affording a chance of success, encourages their longing for being tested and proving victorious. Extremely courageous, persevering and adventurous, Cooper's seamen fully realize themselves only in the constant battle with the sea, which enables them to live in absolute freedom, as well as to discover their limitless potential.

In his book devoted to Cooper, Philbrick claims that the American writer views the sea "not only as the arena of personal adventure but as the locus of national glory" (42). Philbrick claims further that a dominant aspect of Cooper's nautical romances is the awakening of the American national identity and the glorification of

America's independence (58). In *The Water-Witch* the crew's desire for liberating themselves from commercial restrictions imposed by English governors may be associated with their longing for political freedom. Similarly, in *The Red Rover* Cooper condemns blind loyalty to the British monarchy and projects a vision of the glorious future of America. The search for national consciousness, initiated in *The Red Rover*, is successfully completed in *The Pilot,* the novel that glorifies the birth of the American nation (58). Cooper's seamen, who associate sailing with liberty and autonomy, may be interpreted as *pars pro toto* figures standing for the whole nation, representing political identity and freedom of the new republic. In his nautical romances of the 1824–1831 period, mainly addressed to male audience, Cooper conforms to the existing codes of maleness, presenting the ideal seaman as a typical romantic hero. As the combination of romanticism and maritime nationalism constitutes for him the essence of masculinity, the ideal sailor is constructed not only as a daring, handsome man, but also as a great patriot who is motivated by a yearning for adventure and who does not hesitate to sacrifice his life in the interest of his beloved America.

Walker observes that it was *The Red Rover*, one of the novels combining romanticism with maritime nationalism and set during the American Revolution, that enjoyed enormous popularity in Cooper's own day (65). The central figure of the story, the eponymous Red Rover, is a Byronic hero-villain, who decides to move from the British to the Patriot side and resorts to piracy. At the end of the novel the Rover atones for his disgraceful conduct, sacrificing his life for the Republic in a naval battle. Following the established conventions of the sentimental comedy, with a pursuit-and-escape pattern or a sudden conversion of the protagonist, *The Red Rover* is highly theatrical. Walker points out that the novel's stage adaptation doubled its audience (65).

It is, however, not the novel's theatrical quality but the book's binding that Melville analyzes in his review of a new edition of the book for the New York *Literary World* in 1850:

> The sight of the far-famed *Red Rover* sailing under the sober hued muslin wherewith Mr. Putnam equips his lighter sort of craft begets in us a fastidious feeling touching the propriety of such a binding for such a book. Not that we ostentatiously pretend to any elevated degree of artistic taste in this matter; – our remarks are but limited to our egoistical fancies. Egoistically, then, we would have preferred for the *Red Rover* a flaming suit of flame-colored morocco, as evanescently thin and gauze-like as possible, so that the binding might happily correspond with the sanguinary fugitive title of the book. Still better, perhaps, were it bound in jet black, with a red streak round the borders (pirate fashion) – or, upon third thoughts, omit the streak, and substitute a square of blood colored bunting on the back, imprinted with the title [...]. (quoted in Jędrzejko 302)

Jędrzejko observes that in his reviews Melville tends to create his own, ontologically independent texts rather than investigate someone else's narratives. He defines Melville's critical analyses as "specific," as the author of *Moby Dick* reads through the prism of his own nautical experience, frequently shifting from a review towards a didactic digression (90). While Melville's remarks on the book as a physical object are excessive, the review proper is reduced to one paragraph:

> That we have said thus much concerning the mere outside of the book whose title prefaces this notice, is sufficient evidence of the fact that at the present day we deem any elaborate criticism of Cooper's *Red Rover* quite unnecessary and uncalled-for. Long ago, and far inland, we read it in our uncritical days, and enjoyed it as much as thousands of the rising generation will when supplied with such an entertaining volume in such agreeable type. (quoted in Jędrzejko 302)

Jędrzejko is right when he claims that Melville's analysis of the binding of *The Red Rover* may be regarded as a manifestation of his own dilemma concerning the arbitrary character of the relation between a visible *significant*, in this case the binding, and an invisible *signifié*, the content of the book. The problem will be later masterfully explored in *Moby Dick* (101).

Apart from Melville, Conrad was another author influenced by Cooper's nautical fiction who paid him tribute. In 1898 he wrote in his *Notes on Life and Letters*, commenting on the American writer's sea novels: "In his sea tales the sea interpenetrates with life; it is in a subtle way a factor in the problem of existence, and for all its greatness, it is always in touch with the men, who, bound on errands of war or gain, traverse its immense solitudes" (55). It is worth observing that Conrad not only stresses the existential dimension of Cooper's narratives, but also extols his idealistic, even if occasionally imperfect, approach towards the ocean:

> He knows the men and he knows the sea. His method may be often faulty, but his art is genuine. The truth is within him. The road to legitimate realism is through poetical feeling, and he possesses that – only it is expressed in the leisurely manner of his time. [...] In certain passages he reaches, very simply, the heights of inspired vision. (56)

The critics were of the same opinion; impressed by Cooper's romantic images of seascapes, they referred to him as "The Wizard of the North" or "the American Scott" (Walker 22). The term "romance," applied to Walter Scott's historical novels, was also used to indicate Cooper's idealism. Such a parallel drawn between Cooper and Scott, one of the most popular British prose writers of the day, is indeed not accidental: both used theatrical techniques, picturesque settings and mysterious characters, which contributed to their "removal from day-to-day realism" (Walker 22). Indeed, Cooper's exceptionality among other important American novelists was acknowledged long before his death, and some of his works have been translated not only into all Western European languages, but also into Persian (Walker 27). Unfortunately, the Polish edition of *The Red Rover*, entitled *Czerwony korsarz*, is an abridged version of Cooper's novel. It is probably attributable to the fact that in Poland his romances of the forest are much more popular than his nautical novels. In the first half of the nineteenth century, however, it was his nautical fiction that overshadowed his frontier novels. The author's friend, Samuel F. B. Morse reported that Cooper's novels "are published as soon as he produces them in thirty-four different places in Europe" (quoted in Walker 27). Schubert, dying in

Vienna in 1828, wanted to read Cooper's latest book in print, having been acquainted with *The Spy* and *The Pilot,* as well as with two *Leather-Stocking Tales.* When Cooper died, another composer, Berlioz, paid homage to the American novelist by renaming one of this overtures *Le corsaire rouge* after Cooper's most popular nautical romance in France (27–29). His novels were also praised by leading European writers: Scott, Thackeray, Balzac, Dumas and Goethe (28). What is more, a number of admirers imitated Cooper's narratives, especially the *Leather-Stocking Tales*, or wrote parodies of his works, for example Thackeray with his *Stars and Stripes* (121).

However, some of his contemporaries criticized his fiction severely. Twain's "Fenimore Cooper's Literary Offences" may be regarded as the fiercest attack on the novelist's idealistic approach towards reality and his style of writing. Walker claims that Twain's remarks, which concerned Cooper's romanticism viewed from the perspective of an embittered realist, should not be taken seriously (122). Still, his enumeration of the "offences" committed in *The Deerslayer* contains hilarious statements. Commenting on the novelist's creativity, Twain observes: "Cooper hadn't any more invention than a horse; and I don't mean a high-class horse, either; I mean a clothes-horse" (Twain 1459). Twain's remarks on the episodes presented in the novel are similarly sharp: "[A]s the *Deerslayer* tale is not a tale, and accomplishes nothing and arrives nowhere, the episodes have no rightful place in the work, since there was nothing for them to develop" (1457).

It is worth observing that it was Cooper who, with the publication of *The Pilot* in 1824, established the sea novel as a separate genre, setting a course for such successors as Melville or Conrad (Walker 67). Walker argues that pre-Cooperian nautical tales by Defoe, Smollett or Scott ignored the importance of the ocean, presenting only occasional and brief scenes set at sea. Cooper's innovation was therefore the emphasis put on the significance of sea space no longer regarded as a conventional background, but presented in his fiction as an arena for the sailor's theatrical existence aboard a ship, and the portrayal of an emotional relationship between man and the sea as "[transcending] mere physical proximity" (74). Later, both Melville and Conrad masterfully developed the existential aspect of nautical novels, that is the sailor's close relationship with the sea.

In the sea novel entitled *Homeward Bound,* published in 1838, Cooper's approach towards the sea is no longer idealistic, but moves rapidly "in the direction of the realism that Richard Henry Dana was soon to popularize" (Philbrick 121). Philbrick observes that the movement, which satisfied the expectations of the American audience, seems to have been the outcome of a fundamental change in Cooper's conception of the novel (121). Although the historical romance perfectly illustrated Cooper's doctrine of maritime nationalism, it failed to present the concepts of government and society which Cooper had defined during his stay in Europe (121). Hurt by the hostile reception of *The Bravo* (1831) and *The Heidenmauer* (1832), in 1832 Cooper was reluctant to write romances. In *A Letter to His Countrymen* (1834) he declared his intention to abandon the attempt "to illustrate and enforce the peculiar principles of his own country, by the agency of polite literature," and in the same year he announced that he might "return to Europe, and continue to write, for in that quarter of the world I am at least treated with common decency" (quoted in Philbrick 121). He neither abandoned his literary career nor moved to Europe, but he decided not to create historical romances any more.

Experimenting with various means of expression, Cooper resorted to direct exhortation in *The American Democrat* (1838) and satirical allegory in *The Monikins* (1835). Dissatisfied with both efforts and disillusioned with the historical romance, the author returned to the novel of manners, the genre with which he had begun his career of a man of letters (Philbrick 122). A prelude to the social satire, *Homeward Bound* is not characterized by the romantic perception of the sea. Depicting for the first time the nautical present, Cooper explores one of the most basic aspects of contemporary maritime reality, that is the packet service between London and New York, concentrating particularly on realistic descriptions of life at sea (123).

Having flourished in the 1920s and 1930s, in the second half of the twentieth century, critical interest in Cooper's narratives significantly decreased. The titles of the volumes including essays on Cooper published in the first quarter of the twentieth century suggest his leading position among American novelists: W. C. Brownell's *American Prose Masters*, Brander Matthews' *Gateways to Literature* or Henry Canby's *Classic Americans*. It is worth noting that D. H. Lawrence was the first important critic to speak of Cooper's works in terms of mythmaking in *Studies in Classic American Literature* published in 1923. In his essay Lawrence analyzes the *Leather-Stocking Tales*, praising Cooper as an explorer of the frontier. Other critics followed in Lawrence's footsteps, for example H. N. Smith or R. W. B. Lewis, concentrating mainly on Cooper's romances of the forest (Walker 124–125). Overshadowed by frontier novels, his nautical narratives seem to be ignored by critics. Thomas Philbrick's monumental work, *James Fenimore Cooper and the Development of American Sea Fiction,* published in 1961, has been by far the most extensive and insightful monograph on the writer's achievement in the realm of sea fiction.

The next stage in the development of post-Cooperian sea fiction is marked by Edgar Allan Poe. His novella, *The Narrative of Arthur Gordon Pym* (1838), occupies an important place in the evolution of American nautical fiction, as it represents an interesting variant of the treatment of marine motifs. Exemplifying the Gothic tendency of the short sea stories published before 1835, *Pym* presents the ocean as a mysterious setting evoking terror. Contrary to the neoclassical conception of maritime experience, Poe, unlike Smollett, does not condemn the sea's capacity to cause suffering and death (Philbrick 168). His attitude is similar to Marryat's, who in *The Phantom Ship* explores the ocean's hostility and brutality. In contrast to Poe, Marryat emphasizes also the purgatorial qualities of oceanic waters, whereas the author of *Pym* stresses only their destructive properties. Philbrick underlines that Poe's achievement lies not only in his meticulously detailed descriptions, but above all in the vividness of the depiction of horror (170). According to Philbrick, Poe overshadows his predecessors, as even in portraying nightmarish images the writer concentrates on *vraisemblance* (171). The scholar, analyzing Poe's attempt to give his novella the appearance of a documentary, pays special attention to the preface, in which Gordon Pym explains that it was him who had allowed Mr. Poe to publish the first few chapters of the story in the *Southern Literary Messenger*. As the "fictionalized fact" provoked the readers' favourable reaction, Mr. Pym has decided to continue the narrative in his own words in order to add credibility to the story. Although the journey he presents is a pseudo-voyage, Poe, like the authors of authentic narratives, acquaints his readers with the topography of the remote islands, serving, apart from the sea, as a setting for his fiction (171–172). Nevertheless, Philbrick observes that the realism produced by Poe is superficial, as it fails to give a truthful picture of life at sea. Written by a resident of the Atlantic Seaboard whose maritime experience was limited, *Pym* is not devoid of "several glaring nautical anomalies of the kind that would make Cooper snort with contempt" (172).

Contrasting Cooper's fiction with Poe's narrative, Philbrick emphasizes that while the former's treatment of the materials of maritime life is idealized, the latter's shifts towards the grotesque (173). A fundamental difference between the two writers lies, however, in their portrayal of the sea. Cooper presents the ocean as a stage on which his theatrical novel is performed. Poe, by contrast, reduces the importance of the ocean, treating it only as a source of terror and horror, frequently irrelevant for these emotions. Although *Pym* does not adhere to the convention of realistic narrative, Poe "pointed the way to the greatest achievement of American sea fiction" (175). It is worth noting that *Pym* mirrors Poe's interest in the maritime frontier. Supporting the views of Jeremiah N. Reynolds, who stressed the importance of the exploration of the South Pole, Poe deliberately sets his novel in Antarctica (175). Responding to the public interest in the United States Exploring Expedition and satisfying the readers' demand for verisimilitude in nautical literature, Poe manages to combine "Gothic romanticism and documentary realism, scientific discovery and mystic revelation" (176). Hence, in spite of its inadequacies, *The Narrative of Arthur Gordon Pym* is, according to Philbrick, a great achievement. The researcher places Poe's sea novella between Cooper's early nautical romances and Melville's *Moby Dick* (176).

In the 1830s the portrayal of the sea in American literature changed drastically. No longer satisfied with the glorious images of the maritime life of the War of 1812 introduced by Cooper, the American reading public demanded a more realistic vision of the ocean. Accustomed to the sea as a setting for fiction and interested in discovering facts concerning present life at sea, the Americans began to re-evaluate Cooper's early nautical romances. Philbrick claims that the majority of Cooper's readers in the 1820s and early 1830s considered the author of *The Red Rover* to be, above all, a realistic writer. In 1829 the *Edinburgh Review* attacked him for being too faithful to technical details in his direct copying from nature. As a result, Cooper mistakes "the province of the artist for that of the historian," as "by considering truth or matter-of-fact as the sole element of popular fiction, our author fails in massing and in impulse" (quoted in Philbrick 120). However, in the 1840s the conventions established by Cooper began to conflict with the realistic interpretation of the sea. Some of his fellow seaman-writers, for example Nathaniel Ames, severely criticized Cooper's nautical romances. Ames claimed that the author of *The Red Rover* failed to give a real picture of maritime life. According to him, Cooper's nautical romances can be praised only by "exquisites and boarding school girls, who do not know salt water from fresh, or at least which end of a ship goes foremost" (quoted in Philbrick 116). Similarly, a writer for the *Gentleman's Magazine* complained in 1837 that "we are tired of nautical tales; the sea is positively worn out" and that "novelty is a thing to be desired, but not expected in maritime delineations' (quoted in Philbrick 116).

In the 1840s the American book market was dominated by cheap nautical novels which parodied Cooper's romances. Deprived of any nautical or historical authenticity, the novels "warped Cooper's characters and incidents in the direction of either the absurdly ideal or the sensationally grotesque" (Philbrick 191). Philbrick stresses that although the cheap novels were worthless as literature, they indicated the power with which the American myth influenced the popular imagination. Their appearance also serves to present the damage to the romantic conventions established by Cooper. Philbrick points out that after 1842 no respectable publisher would be interested in printing *The Red Rover* (192).

The demand for a realistic approach was indeed satisfied in 1840, with the publication of Richard Henry Dana's *Two Years Before the Mast*. The vast majority of critics immediately began to extol Dana's book, perceiving it as an alternative to the idealization of Cooper's nautical romances. The *Democratic Review* and the *North American Review* were enchanted by the author's realistic treatment of maritime life; the *Knickerbocker* called *Two Years* "one of the most striking and evidently faithful pictures of the 'real life' at sea, that has come under our observation," and the *New York Review* referred to Dana's novel as "a picture drawn wholly from nature – from beginning to end," in which "there is not a touch, or a trait, or a color, of the ideal" (quoted in Philbrick 117). However, Philbrick underlines that *The Southern Literary Messenger* was not particularly enthusiastic about Dana's book. An anonymous reviewer, venturing a statement that *Two Years* was written in order to promote the author's legal practice among seamen, emphasized that the book "contains little that is new or striking" (quoted in Philbrick 305).

It is worth noting that Dana regarded his novel as the first account of life at sea written by a common sailor. Aware of the small documentary value of Ames' fiction, Dana stated in his preface to *Two Years*: "With the single exception, as I am quite confident, of Mr. Ames' entertaining, but hasty and desultory work, called *Mariner's Sketches,* all the books professing to give life at sea have been written by persons who have gained their experience as naval officers, or passengers, and of these, there are very few which are intended to be taken as narratives of facts" (Dana 6). Although Dana was acquainted with Cooper's nautical tales, he erroneously regarded the author of *The Red Rover* as a gentleman, "with his gloves on" (7) who had no idea whatsoever about maritime life viewed from the perspective of a common sailor. Ignorant of Cooper's service in the merchant marine as a foremast hand, Dana claimed that the author of *The Red Rover* never experienced "real life" at sea. It was Richard Henry Dana, Sr., Dana's father, who sent a copy of *Two Years Before the Mast* to Cooper, at the same time apologizing for his son's ignorance (Philbrick 306).

Disapproving of Cooper's idealism, Dana adopted realistic techniques, his aim being to show life at sea as seen from the forecastle. Even before the publication of *Two Years*, the once extremely popular nautical Gothicism was no longer sought after because of a growing interest in the folklore of the sea and Washington Irving's comic treatment of the supernatural. The serious stories about ghost ships were replaced by comic yarns stemming from the legends of the forecastle, describing for example a Yankee's encounter with the Flying Dutchman. A good illustration of literary exploitation of folk materials is Reynolds' story *Mocha Dick; or the White Whale of the Pacific* (1839), which has been regarded as a source for Melville's masterpiece (Philbrick 194). Commenting on the new tone employed by Dana, which differs considerably both from Cooper's idealism and Irving's comic treatment of Gothic, Melville observed in the *Literary World* in 1847:

> From the times immemorial many fine things have been said and sung of the sea. And the days have been, when sailors were considered veritable mermen; and the ocean itself, as the peculiar theatre of the romantic and wonderful. But of late years there have been revealed so many plain, matter-of-fact details connected with nautical life that at the present day the poetry of salt water is very much on the wane. The perusal of Dana's *Two Years Before the Mast,* for instance, somewhat impairs the relish with which we read Byron's spiritual address to the ocean. And when the noble poet raves about laying his hands upon the ocean's mane (in other words manipulating the crest of a wave) the most vivid image suggested is that of a valetudinarian bather at Rockaway, spluttering and chocking in the surf, with his mouth full of brine. (quoted in Jędrzejko 300)

Jędrzejko claims that the juxtaposition of the poet's romantic image and the realism of the perceived analogy may be interpreted as a baroque conceit. Playing with the reader, Melville suggests in a subtle way that although he is impressed by the reportorial technique applied in *Two Years*, he praises the artistic value of Byron's poetic visions much higher than Dana's realistic descriptions (Jędrzejko 92–93). Influenced by Coleridge, Melville believed that the artist should operate on symbols in order to explore *natura naturans* rather than produce mimetic images of nature. Approving of the documentary quality of *Two Years,* the author of *Moby*

Dick seems to admit at the same time that, in comparison with Byron's visions, the book lacks symbolic depth and intrinsic literary value of works of art.

Encouraged by Dana's imminent success, other seaman-writers presented their accounts of real life at sea, "putting Dana to shame by the length of their service and the extent of their sufferings" (Philbrick 119). Written by sailors who had firsthand experiences of maritime life and were therefore able to portray it with reportorial exactness, Samuel Leech's *Thirty Years from Home, or A Voice from the Main Deck* (1843), Nicholas Isaacs' *Twenty Years Before the Mast* (1845), or William Nevens' *Forty Years at Sea* (1845) fully satisfied the American public's demand for novelty of the image of the sea (119). However, not all seaman-writers praised Dana's portrayal of the dreariness of the merchant marine. John Codman, who issued *Sailors' Life and Sailors' Yarns* (1847) under the pseudonym of "Captain Ringbolt," referred to *Two Years* as one of those books which "have had too extensive a circulation, and which, purporting to be narratives of personal experience, have obtained a great deal more credit than they deserve" (quoted in Philbrick 196). Codman emphasizes that his account of life at sea is "not the result of 'one cruise,' or of 'two years before the mast,' but of thirteen years in various stations from the hawse-hole to the quarter-deck" (quoted in Philbrick 196). Disapproving of Dana's idealized portrayal of seamen, Codman argues that sailors are neither noble nor generous, as presented by the author of *Two Years,* but highly degenerate, deprived by prostitutes and addicted to alcohol.

Dana's realistic sea diary reflects the first-hand experience of the future lawyer. Born in Cambridge, Massachusetts, Richard Henry Dana, Jr., came of a line of Colonial ancestors, whose patriotism was commonly recognized. His father, Richard Henry Dana, Sr., was widely known as a poet, critic and lecturer (Keyes 1). Young Dana, who regarded himself as destined for "memorable accomplishments" (Gale 164), and was therefore nicknamed "The Duke of Cambridge," decided to attend the Harvard College. However, at the beginning of his third year, he was forced to cease studying due to a severe attack of measles. Suffering the after-effects of measles, which significantly weakened his eyesight, Dana hoped that his eyes would improve at sea. As his father could not afford to send him on the Grand Tour, the young Dana decided to experience maritime life as a common sailor. He later wrote: "When I recall the motives which governed me in this choice, I can hardly tell which predominated, a desire to cure my eyes, my love of adventure & the attraction of the novelty of a life before the mast, or anxiety to escape from the depressing situation of inactivity & dependence at home" (quoted in Gale 28). In his introduction to *Two Years,* H. E. Keyes points out that the voyage was calculated to kill or to make stronger (Keyes 2). As Dana's myopia was gone within a week, it had the latter effect. Healthy and vigorous, he reentered Harvard in 1836, and graduated with honours in six months.

Analyzing the sea diary, Gale points out that the title of Dana's book is inaccurate. Out of his twenty-five months as a sailor, he spent at sea only a little less than ten months. During his almost sixteen months in California, Dana travelled mainly on coastal voyages between San Diego and San Francisco (Gale 31). In *Two Years* Dana describes his 150 days on the way from Boston to Santa Barbara, his experiences along the California coast and his 135 days on the journey back home to Boston (108). Never wanting to become a writer, the author of *Two Years* throughout his life craved for being an influential politician. Keyes observes that Dana's longing for political and juridical career was characterized by unfulfilled dreams, unrealized ambitions and thwarted hopes because he lacked "the tact, the personal magnetism, or the business sagacity to make a brilliant success before the bar" (Keyes 2). Still, extremely proud of his distinguished family, he decided to follow in his ancestors' footsteps and in 1840 opened his law office in Boston. In 1876 Dana felt the deepest disappointment of his life, when his nomination for an ambassador to England was blocked in Senate by his political and personal enemies. Although he was appointed United States District Attorney, elected to represent Cambridge in Massachusetts Legislature, and granted the degree of a Doctor of Laws by Harvard in 1866, Dana perceived his life as a "failure" (Shapiro VIII). Samuel Shapiro points out that he dreamt not only of a senatorship, but also of the White House (Shapiro X). Keyes suggests that instead of being a lawyer, Dana should have become a scholar or a man of letters, as it is only *Two Years*, called late in his life "a boy's work," that brought him recognition (Keyes 1). Disillusioned and tormented by health problems, Dana vacationed in France, Switzerland and Italy before his death, dedicating himself to the preparation of a treatise on international law. He died in Rome in 1882 and was buried there in the Protestant Cemetery (3).

Two Years Before the Mast appeared in 1840, when its author, "the man of one book," was still a student (Shapiro 188). Immediately after its publication the book was favourably received in America, soon to be recognized as an American classic of the sea in England as well. Harper's, who bought the original copyright for $250, earned $50,000 on the book. Houghton Mifflin sold one hundred thousand copies between 1911 and 1961, and fifty-four other publishers issued seventy-seven different editions in this period. There were twenty-three separate editions in England within these five decades, as well as translations into many foreign languages (187–188). Initiating a vogue for realistic sea narratives, *Two Years* helped to create an audience for Melville's fiction. Shapiro notices that Melville had read and extolled Dana's novel long before he became a writer himself. As Melville felt impressed by his factual account, Dana was one of the Bostonians the author of *Moby Dick* wanted to meet. In the 1840s the two men did meet, and spent several evenings discussing their adventures at sea (190–191). Strikingly enough, it was Dana who urged Melville to describe whaling realistically and with exactness. Although Dana probably never read *Moby Dick*, as the men lost contact with each other before its publication in 1851, he considered Melville his inferior (65). Paradoxically, today *Two Years* seems to be just one of the references in a Melville bibliography (192). Regarded among other works as the source material for *Moby Dick*, nowadays Dana's novel is read, for example by Paweł Jędrzejko, through the prism of Melville studies. Dana's perception of the sea as a merely physical space is contrasted with philosophical depth attributed by Melville to the ocean. Although *Two Years* is classified by Philbrick as belonging to the mainstream of American Realism (118), due to having been referred to as juvenile and therefore of little literary value, it is ignored by critics, such as Maud Bodkin, Joseph Campbell or Richard Chase (Gale 130). Gale observes that apart from Dana's biography by Charles F. Adams, Jr. published in 1890, two unpublished doctoral dissertations, written in 1936 and 1958, and Samuel Shapiro's 1961 biography, comprehensive studies of Dana's writing are non-existent (8).

Hence, the aim of this study is to fill the gaps in Marryat's, Cooper's and Dana's criticism, as well as to offer a comparative analysis of their sea fiction. Hardly ever read in colleges and frequently dismissed in surveys of British and American literature, the three novelists deserve more attention and a closer consideration than they have received so far. All highly regarded during their lifetimes, in the second half of the twentieth century they fell into oblivion. I have chosen Marryat, Cooper and Dana for at least two reasons. Firstly, judged by the generic constituents of marine fiction provided by Błaszak, all three writers belong to the category of sea novelists proper, as sailors featured in their narratives constitute a dominant element, ships are endowed with autonomous existence, and the sea is not reduced to a conventional background, but elevated to an arena of the drama of human life. Secondly, all three fictionalized their authentic first-hand experience of maritime life. Still, I would argue that in their narratives, Marryat, Cooper and Dana not only copy from nature, but also go beyond the concept of *mimesis*, as defined by Aristotle.

In his preface to a recent English edition of *Poetics*, John Baxter delineates some of the intricacies of the concept of *mimesis*. First of all, he notices that the term has at least two linguistic equivalents in English: "imitation" and "representation." However, Mirosława Buchholtz observes that scholars such as Stephen Halliwell and George Whalley disapprove of perceiving the concept through the prism of stasis and product, underlining the dynamism and process involved in *mimesis* (Buchholtz 59). In her analysis of the concept, Buchholtz observes that Gerald Else provides yet another interpretation of Aristotle's use of the term. According to Else, *mimesis* "becomes the closest neighbour to creation: not out of nothing – no Greek ever believed in creation *ex nihilo* – but out of carefully observed 'universal' human tendencies to thought and action" (quoted in Buchholtz 59). Another problem is associated with various relations between *mimesis* and *catharsis* or *mimesis* and *praxis* (60). Stephen Halliwell notices that if it had not been for Plato, Aristotle would not have been aware of "a whole set of suggestions, issues and challenges which were superimposed on the intricacies of existing non-philosophical uses of the word" (60). Despite certain doubts raised by Aristotle, some points are clearly illustrated. Buchholtz argues that Aristotle stresses two causes of the poetic art: imitation, "deep-rooted in the very nature of man," and penchant for images, that is "the pleasure we all take in copies of things" (quoted in Buchholtz 60). Significantly, Aristotle observes that what connects both of these habits is the willingness to learn (60).

This observation is crucial and applicable to sea novels in general. It helps to explain their immense popularity in the first half of the nineteenth century among male and female audience, as well as the reading public's growing demand for accuracy. Sea narratives, regarded as an imitation of authentic life at sea, by meeting the reader's expectations for images, satisfied the inexperienced audience's eagerness to learn in order to be initiated into the mysteries of maritime life. It is worth observing that Plato's understanding of mimesis is much broader than Aristotle's, as he uses the notion of the concept in reference not only to poetics, but also to many other aspects: linguistic, visual, philosophical, or musical (61). Halliwell, like Plato, places Aristotle's *mimesis* in a wider context, developing his own doctrine of mimetic arts perceived as the "representation of general truths" rather than the "reproduction of particulars" (61).

Halliwell's commentary on Aristotle's *mimesis* makes the concept applicable to Marryat's *The Phantom Ship* (1839), Cooper's *The Red Rover* (1828) and Dana's *Two Years Before the Mast* (1840). Although the three novels may be regarded as simulacra of reality imitating the then extremely popular literary conventions of the Gothic sea novel, the nautical romance and the sea diary, respectively, this study seeks to prove that the reading of these texts involves interpretations of allegories and symbols, as they combine the reproduction of maritime experience with the representation of general truths concerning human existence. The critic Martin Green wrote that "[t]he sea novel in general has not been a high genre" (quoted in Błaszak 258), which seems largely true of Marryat's, Cooper's and Dana's narratives. Still, although their sea novels cannot be equated in value with Conrad's and Melville's masterpieces, the authors can be regarded as "serious" writers, who, combining in the above-mentioned texts both *mimesis* and *creatio,* paved the way for the future great literary masters of the sea. The significant influence their sea novels exerted on the works of other writers, among others Conrad and Melville, who expressed their indebtedness to Marryat, Cooper and Dana, provides further justification for a revival of interest in them. Hence, the study seeks to demonstrate that the reading of the selected nineteenth-century sea novels through the lens of twentieth-century theories, regarded as variations on the concept of *mimesis*, may lead to re-evaluation of the long forgotten texts, which proved inspiring to some of the most prominent nautical writers.

Chapter One explores mimesis perceived as an insatiable desire for what someone else either has or craves for. Informed by René Girard's theory of mimetic desire, the analysis investigates the protagonist of Marryat's *The Phantom Ship*, Captain Vanderdecken, presented as an incarnation of Faust, overwhelmed by his desire for God's omnipotence and omniscience. In his triangular model, Girard views

Aristotle's concept of *mimesis* from the perspective of desire, insisting on the presence of the third party, the mediator, between the subject and the object of desire (Buchholtz 62). As the relationships between Vanderdecken, his son, God and Satan described in Marryat's Gothic sea novel are far too complex for Girard's theory, as outlined in *Deceit, Desire, and the Novel*, I present my variation on Girard's triangular model, enriching his theory with the Christian aspect of purifying suffering. Captain Vanderdecken, an incarnation of the Flying Dutchman, is sentenced by God to everlasting wandering at sea for his staggering *hubris*. Although regarded as unbearable, the Captain's eternal sea voyage purifies him of both his enormous pride and his desire for God's attributes. Hence, the ocean portrayed in *The Phantom Ship* resembles purgatory.

Chapter Two investigates mimesis as an imitation of established social conventions, leading to a more or less conscious role-playing on the stage of the *theatrum mundi*. It is shown that Luigi Pirandello's form/life dichotomy, defined by the Italian critic and writer in his famous essay entitled *L'umorismo*, bears directly upon *The Red Rover*. The protagonist of Cooper's nautical romance, the Red Rover, is presented as a prisoner of mimetic form imposed on him both by himself and the society. Playing the role of a bloodthirsty pirate and living in a masked world of illusion, the Rover is no longer able to distinguish between fictitious form and authentic life. Chapter Two explores also the role of the carnival which takes place aboard the protagonist's ship, stressing its demystifying function. In Cooper's sea narrative the piratical masquerade is presented as an epiphanic moment, revealing the Rover's true nature, carefully hidden under the mask of form. In contrast to Marryat's purgatorial waters, Cooper's sea is portrayed as an arena of human theatrical existence.

Chapter Three is devoted to the examination of mirror reflection and its role in Dana's *Two Years Before the Mast*. Applying Meyer Abrams' famous metaphor of the mirror and the lamp, it is argued that Dana's narrative is not a mere reportorial account regarded as a copy of authentic maritime life, but, rather, that it illustrates the author as torn between *mimesis* and *creatio*. A comparative analysis of *Two Years* and Joseph Conrad's collection of essays entitled *The Mirror of the Sea* concentrates on the portrayal of the sea and a lonely seaman, examining his reflection in the mirror-like surface of the water. While the interpretations of both texts are mainly based on Abrams' dichotomy, other critical views are noted as well, such as Gaston Bachelard's phenomenological attitude towards "intimate immensities" or Piotr Domeracki's statements on existential loneliness, offering broader, philosophical perspectives on various mimetic aspects examined in this chapter.

CHAPTER ONE
Mimetic Desire: Frederick Marryat's *The Phantom Ship* (1839)

In her introduction to the Polish edition of *The Phantom Ship*, Maria Janion defines Marryat's Gothic sea novel as a romantic tragedy of fate having its roots in ancient tragedies. Characterized by pessimism and fatalism, Janion argues, the British novelist's work focuses on *ananke* inherent in the protagonists' acts. She claims that in *The Phantom Ship* Marryat concentrates on the problems typical of Greek tragedies: firstly, whether or not man is to be blamed for circumstances that are not under his control, and, secondly, whether or not it will ever be possible for man to conquer and master the overwhelmingly powerful force which orchestrates his life, be it fate, fortune, destiny, *ananke*, or *fatum*. Janion maintains that in ancient tragedies all efforts to master one's fate, to reject the role of a puppet, and to act in accordance with one's own scenario are futile. The researcher claims further that all protagonists are devoid of free will, and hence presented in *The Phantom Ship* as toys in the hands of omnipotent fate (5–22).

Although Janion's claim that Marryat illustrates human condition applying the topos of *theatrum mundi* is justified, I would like to argue that while presenting his protagonists as actors on the stage of the theatre of the world, Marryat does not emphasize the lack of free will and illusion of moral independence. On the contrary, he seems to suggest that human beings are not puppets unable to show any initiative whatsoever, but they are able to act freely and independently in the performance of life. In my opinion, Marek Błaszak is right in stressing an "overt religious message" of the book (Błaszak 160) and reading the novel as a manifestation of "fundamental truths of the Christian faith" (202). Indeed, I would argue that Marryat's protagonists are not victims of coincidence, whose apparently meaningful actions turn out to be deranged in a universe governed by an ungraspable force. I would venture a statement that Marryat places his characters in the contexts which transgress the generic boundaries of both a Gothic novel and a tragedy. Presenting God as the director of a Gothic *theatrum mundi*, the novelist not only obeys popular conventions of fiction, but also pursues more ambitious goals. According to Błaszak, "in *The Phantom Ship* nautical adventure assumes the form of a parable of a seafaring mortal who dares to challenge God" (258). Extending beyond the domain of Greek *fatum* and the topos of *theatrum mundi*, the novel seems to require more complex instruments of analysis.

As *The Phantom Ship* suits the Biblical paradigm of crime, punishment and atonement, Marryat's work appears to fit into the Old-Testament representation of reality, as defined by Erich Auerbach in his remarkable book entitled *Mimesis. The Representation of Reality in Western Literature.* It seems to me that the reality presented by Marryat resembles the Biblical world described by Auerbach. The author of *Mimesis* argues that unlike legends, which portray "only clearly outlined men who act from few and simple motives and the continuity of whose feelings and actions remains uninterrupted" (Auerbach 19), the figures of the Old Testament are "so much more fully developed, so much more fraught with their own biographical past, so much more distinct as individuals" (17). In my opinion, Auerbach's statement may be applied in the interpretation of the Flying Dutchman of *The Phantom Ship* who, being considerably different from other legendary heroes, resembles several Old-Testament figures. "Fraught with [his] development" and marked by "a distinct stamp of individuality" (18), the doomed captain expresses himself through silence: the externalization of his thoughts and feelings is in Marryat's novel almost non-existent. Characterized by indeterminacy, the Captain constantly calls for concretization and interpretation. Claiming that God "continues to work upon them, bends them and kneads them" (18), Auerbach defines major Old-Testament figures as those who finally achieve greatness through humiliation. Likewise, the Flying Dutchman, who is no longer alive but not yet dead, and, therefore, he is ever becoming and never being, perfectly suits Auerbach's definition. Additionally, in the story of the doomed captain, similarly to Biblical narratives, there is no legendary simplification of events. On the contrary, in his Gothic novel, dark and full of spots of indeterminacy as it is, Marryat conveys what Auerbach calls "a second, concealed meaning" (15). Stressing the relation between the material and the spiritual, the novelist, like Biblical authors, progresses *per visibilia ad invisibilia.* Hence, the aim of this chapter is to explore the legend of the Flying Dutchman from a Christian perspective, as a modern version of the Biblical archetype of the fall of man as a result of succumbing to Satan's temptation. As both the Adamic myth and the legend of the doomed captain are marked by the presence of the devil, I elaborate as well on the relation between Captain William Vanderdecken, Satan and God, applying René Girard's model of mimetic desire, enriching however its psychological and anthropological aspects with a religious dimension, as defined by Auerbach. Informed by Girard's theory, my analysis of the protagonist's crime and punishment reveals a similarity between Auerbach's and Marryat's understanding of mimesis. I argue that Marryat's Flying Dutchman is in his eternal wandering strikingly similar to Wagner's *Fliegende Holländer,* Coleridge's Ancient Mariner and Bunyan's Pilgrim. The present chapter also examines the nature of Captain Vanderdecken's desire for God's omnipotence and omniscience not only in reference to British or American literary masterpieces, but also in a broader European context. A comparative analysis of Marryat's novel, Goethe's *Faust,* Melville's *Moby Dick* and Dostoyevsky's narratives focuses on the characters' deviated transcendence leading some of them to self-destruction.

1.1. The Flying Dutchman: Romantic Interpretations

According to folklore, the Flying Dutchman is a ghost ship doomed to sail the seas forever and to fight with the ferocious sea. It is also the name of the Dutch Captain, a daring and courageous traveller who is condemned to be eternally tossed about by the waves around the Cape of Good Hope, willing death to bring an end to his suffering. He cannot reach salvation and escape his fate, as other seamen seeing the ghostly ship on the horizon are petrified and quickly change their course in order to avoid its fatal influence. The legend of the doomed Dutch Captain was already a well known tale with numerous versions in nautical folklore before Frederick Marryat incorporated it into his text.

The legend of the Flying Dutchman is one of the most widely known sea stories in the world. Zofia Drapella stresses that its main theme, an eternal problem of crime and punishment, is extremely attractive to artists. It fascinates not only novelists and poets, but also musicians and painters, who in their works develop the story, giving a new meaning to the original version of the legend. A prototype of the Flying Dutchman is a sixteenth-century story of a pirate ghost ship commanded by Captain Noir, which was seen by travellers at warm and misty seas (Drapella 235). Interestingly, Elizabeth Frenzel in *Stoffe der Weltliteratur* refers to the figure of a seventeenth-century captain Fokke, who agrees to sell his soul to the devil in order to reach the West Indies as quickly as possible. Because of the pact, Fokke is eternally condemned and doomed to ceaseless wandering round the Cape of Good Hope. However, according to Drapella, it is Augustine Jal's story presented in his *Scènes de la vie maritime* in 1832 that constitutes the basic romantic version of the Flying Dutchman. The protagonist of Jal's story is a Dutch Captain, an atheist, who during a raging storm decides to round the Cape of Good Hope, ignoring desperate pleas of his fellow seamen and risking the lives of the crew. In Jal's version it is God himself who in the form of a white-bearded old man appears aboard the Captain's ship in order to prevent the bold Dutchman from realizing his plan. Outraged, the Captain tries to kill the visitor by firing a gun. When it proves impossible, since the Dutchman's hand becomes paralyzed and the fired bullet bounces off the old man, wounding the Captain, he curses the stranger and, thus, blasphemes against God. The old man punishes the Dutchman, condemning him to eternal wandering and constant seeking of the peace of death. What is more, calling the Captain the Devil of the Sea, he announces that at the end of time the daring commander will be doomed forever.

In England, the legend of the doomed sea captain first appeared in printed form in 1821 as an anonymous short story in the then extremely popular *Blackwood's Magazine*. The narrator of the story entitled "Vanderdecken's Message Home: or the Tenacity of Natural Affection," with which Marryat was probably familiar, navigates his ship in the vicinity of the Cape of Good Hope. Aboard the ship the seamen are narrating the legend of the Flying Dutchman. One of the narrators recalls that seventy years earlier, the captain of a Dutch ship tried to round the "Stormy Cape" at any cost, despite adverse winds and a raging storm. In his enormous pride and stubbornness, Vanderdecken swore against God and expressed his readiness to fight with the sea until the Day of Judgement in order to perform his task. Taken at his word, he was doomed to sail the seas forever, always bringing unfavourable weather and bad luck to any ship that encounters him. All seamen are frightened of him, as the Captain always hails other ships and asks the sailors to take bundles of letters for his family and friends in Holland. Hardly anyone is ever courageous enough to communicate with him, as he is generally regarded as a harbinger of misfortune and death. Soon after the conversation between the seamen, the Flying Dutchman's ship indeed appears with a pile of letters from the Captain. Having glanced at the letters, the English sailors refuse to take them to Holland. Petrified, they explain that the Captain's family died many years ago. Despite the crew's reluctance, the letters are left aboard their ship, but they are blown into the sea. After a while the ghost ship vanishes and the weather immediately improves, to the great relief of the English sailors (Barker 36–39).

In this version of the legend it is neither the supernatural nor the Captain's pact with the devil that is emphasized. Unlike in other variations on the legend, in the story printed in the *Blackwood's Magazine* it is the Captain's affection for his family that is stressed. The subtitle, "the Tenacity of Natural Affection," may suggest that the author of the story is deeply impressed by Vanderdecken's attachment to his beloved ones, which is illustrated by the Captain's writing to his family for seventy years. The motifs of a letter and of number seven seem to be crucial in the story and will appear also in Marryat's version of the legend. However, as it is demonstrated later in this study, in *The Phantom Ship* both motifs will acquire a symbolic meaning.

Marryat's variation on the Flying Dutchman is thoroughly original. According to Marek Błaszak, *The Phantom Ship* is remarkable for "the highly dramatic treatment of the sea legend" (Błaszak 76). Only in Marryat's version there appears Vanderdecken's son, named Philip, whose mission is to avert his father's destiny. In the final chapter of the book, Philip accomplishes his task, atoning for the Captain's blasphemy with self-sacrificial death. The problem of sacrifice central to the legend is also accentuated by Richard Wagner. Frederick Marryat's full-length novel is one of the most interesting and extensive realizations of the legend of the Flying Dutchman, whereas Richard Wagner's opera entitled *Der fliegende Holländer* (1843) constitutes a brilliant musical illustration of the well-known motif. Although Wagner made no use of Marryat's version, the number of similarities between *Der fliegende Holländer*, an opera which is performed even nowadays especially during the Richard Wagner Festival in Bayreuth, and *The Phantom Ship*, a Gothic novel which is now completely forgotten, is striking.

In both works the legend, much older than the European nineteenth-century Romanticism, acquires a deeper meaning when confronted with the romantic perception of life. Surprising as it may seem, there are numerous correspondences between Marryat's novel and Wagner's opera, existing on the level of both the genesis of the works and the autobiographical aspects presented in them. However, what makes the two works so remarkably similar is, above all, the fashioning of the Flying Dutchman as a Faustian figure.

Marryat's Gothic sea story, *The Phantom Ship*, began to appear in *The New Monthly* in 1838 and a three-volume book edition was published by Henry Colburn in 1839 (Błaszak 76). The novel plays an important part in the Captain's career as a writer. Using an extremely popular genre in all English-speaking countries, which the Gothic novel was at that time, Marryat tried to spread major Christian ideas, that is fall, contrition, penance and absolution. In Marryat's novel Captain William Vanderdecken becomes a *pars pro toto* figure. Marryat identified himself with the weak and sinful protagonist who in falling and overcoming his weaknesses becomes a representative of the whole humanity. According to Marek Błaszak, Marryat's novel is his artistic reaction to Samuel T. Coleridge's lyrical ballad, *The Rime of the Ancient Mariner*, which the author of *The Phantom Ship* found deeply inspiring (41). Coleridge's poem, published in a volume from 1798 entitled *Lyrical Ballads,* constitutes a romantic realization of the legend of a doomed sea captain. The poem explores the voyage of the Ancient Mariner, which abounds with unusual phenomena. The Mariner's fate becomes determined by the act of killing an albatross, which may symbolize man's violation of the natural law, and by the supernatural consequences of this crime. All phenomena occurring during the voyage have a symbolic sense and contribute to the formation of the Ancient Mariner's morality. Janina Kamionka-Straszakowa claims that in *The Rime of the Ancient Mariner* the plot follows a scheme of crime, punishment, penance and expiation. After almost unbearable suffering the sin is forgiven, but the wrong-doer has to roam around the world for the rest of his days, narrating his story in order to warn others (Kamionka-Straszakowa 32). Highlighting ethical aspects of Coleridge's poem, Kamionka-Straszakowa focuses on the problem of man's transgression of the moral law and on the necessity to perform penance, only after which will the ethical order be restored and the union with nature will be recreated. She observes that the figure of the Ancient Mariner has some features of the Wandering Jew and that his voyage, that is an attempt to cross the frontiers of what is permissible and attainable, may be regarded as a "quest for limitless experience" (Vaughan 28). The Ancient Mariner, wandering ceaselessly from one country to another and preaching love of all creation, resembles the Wandering Jew in his being an eternal wanderer who will never reach his destination (Kamionka-Straszakowa 33). Central to the medieval legend of the Wandering Jew, like to that of the Flying Dutchman or to the Adamic myth, are the motifs of sin and eternal wandering, regarded as a punishment for being disobedient to God. The Jew taunts Jesus on the way to Calvary, the Dutchman blasphemes against the divine Creator, and Biblical Adam wants to usurp God's omniscience. Having committed a sin, all are sentenced to roaming the world: the Jew and Adam on land, whereas the doomed captain at sea. William Vaughan underlines in his article that the Ancient Mariner, travelling ashore and afloat, incarnates both the legend of the Wandering Jew and that of the Flying Dutchman (Vaughan 29). Accentuating the moral aspect of the crime, Coleridge's Gothic lyrical ballad, presented in the form of a dream vision, conveys an ethical message. It stresses the necessity to distinguish between what is permissible and what is not, warning against crossing the boundary between the two too recklessly.

Just as Marryat was inspired by Coleridge's poem, Wagner drew his inspiration from Heinrich Heine. Having read some of Heine's works, the composer decided to write an opera based on themes taken from the German poet. Wagner worked on the music to *Der fliegende Holländer* for three months. In the summer of 1841 he finished the sketch of the libretto and in November he completed the score. The opera premiered on the 2nd January 1843 in Dresden, conducted by the composer. Even today the composition of the then thirty-year-old Wagner is regarded by critics as a manifestation of a wonderfully spontaneous young talent (Pociej 77). According to Bohdan Pociej, the opera was inspired by two sources. The first is a first-hand experience of the power of the sea during a nightmarish sea voyage from Riga to London made by the composer and his wife, Minna, in July 1839. The second source is Wagner's reading of Heine's humorous and autobiographical *Memoirs of Herr von Schnabelewopski* (1833). In his work, Heine describes a performance of the play *Der fliegende Holländer* which he watched in a theatre in Amsterdam. The main character, a Dutch captain, is destined to eternal seafaring, as he promised the devil that he would round a certain reef, even if the navigation should last till the end of time. Interestingly enough, the devil, before condemning the Captain, offers him a possibility of redemption: he can be released from his fate by a faithful wife. The Dutchman, known under the name of "the Wandering Jew of the Ocean," comes ashore every seven years in quest for a woman who would be able to lift the curse from him. When the daughter of a Scots sea captain falls in love with the Dutchman and vows to remain faithful to him until death, the doomed sailor is so touched by her feeling that he chooses a lonely life at sea to save her the fate of a "Flying Dutchwoman."

In his narrative, Heine treats the motif of the Flying Dutchman not seriously, but ironically. By contrast, in Wagner's adaptation of Heine's satire, the composer removes the romantic irony and views the story with pathos. Joachim Köhler observes that Wagner's opera of a wandering seaman has its sources in the composer's soul, as he gave Heine's ironic story "a highly personal spiritual form" (Köhler 177). Zdzisław Jachimecki also claims that the Dutchman can be regarded almost as Wagner's double, a character with whom the artist strongly identified. Unlike Marryat, who in *The Phantom Ship* individualizes what is general, in *Der fliegende Holländer* Wagner generalizes what is individual.

Both the British novelist and the German composer present in their works a romanticized legend of the Flying Dutchman, adding new elements to the original version. Captain Vanderdecken, the protagonist of Marryat's novel, is portrayed as a daring and self-confident sailor, for whom taking part in dangerous expeditions in order to explore the extremes is the essence of his existence. In *The Phantom Ship*, Marryat supplements the figure of the Captain with a religious dimension. Vanderdecken is presented as a believer who in a moment of weakness blasphemes against God. Swearing on the relic of the Holy Cross, which he has worshipped for years, the Captain challenges God and expresses a willingness to satisfy his desire even against the Creator's will. As it happened in Jal's version as well, in Marryat's novel it is not Satan but God that condemns the Captain to ceaseless wandering. Strikingly enough, in *The Phantom Ship* everlasting seafaring is not equated with eternal condemnation.

Wagner also transforms the legend of the Flying Dutchman. However, unlike Marryat, he does not supplement the original version with a religious dimension, but enriches it with a psychological aspect. The Wagnerian Dutchman constitutes a figure fully developed psychologically, sensitive and ennobled, in which the composer found his own features. For Wagner the Flying Dutchman became an incarnation of a romantic artist, due to his being a doomed wanderer condemned to everlasting homelessness, craving for a permanent settlement ashore, but at the same time aware of his non-belonging to any place whatsoever. The composer, perceiving himself as an outstanding individual, tired with freedom and with his life of an exile, treated "the Wandering Jew of the Ocean" as his *alter ego*. It is also worth noting that the figure of the hunter Erik, Senta's fiancé, comes from Wagner, not from Heine. In the concluding moment of Act III, Erik and Senta have a bitter argument about the cursed sea captain. The Dutchman, listening to their conversation, is convinced that he has been betrayed once again. In a gesture of despair, he rushes to his ship and immediately goes to the open sea. Wagner, like the Dutchman, felt betrayed: his wife, Minna, was unfaithful to him and finally decided to leave the composer for her lover. Tormented by life and completely alone, the Dutchman mirrors Wagner's suffering and his sense of loneliness. Comparing Wagner's opera with his life, Piotr Kamiński is convinced that *Der fliegende Holländer* should be regarded as a form of autobiography. He holds that in this composition Wagner expresses his innermost emotions, which makes the work so egocentric or, as Kamiński puts it, "so Wagnerian" (646).

Another aspect connecting Marryat's Gothic novel with Wagner's opera is the figure of the Flying Dutchman portrayed as a Faustian character. Extremely talented and proud, the legendary scholar represents both individual and universal features. Although his limitations are typical of all human beings, Faust's cognitive insatiability and his desire for knowledge raise him above mediocrity. Filled with all-consuming passion, the scholar wants to know the unknowable and to rebel against his weaknesses resulting from the imperfections of human nature. Faust is also characterized by inexhaustible energy and by his willingness to sell his soul to the devil in order to satisfy his greatest desire: to find the ideal.

Similarly to Faust, Vanderdecken in Marryat's novel is also extremely gifted. The Captain, aware of his exceptional nautical abilities, perceives himself as an outstanding individual, ready to challenge the raging sea and able to emerge victorious over nature. The Faustian cognitive insatiability and desire for knowledge are manifested in Vanderdecken in the form of a passion for discoveries, which the Captain views as the essence of his existence. Defying any limitations when it comes to fighting with adverse winds and unfavourable tides, in his attempt to round the Cape of Good Hope Vanderdecken does not hesitate to sacrifice the lives of the crew or to give his soul to the devil in order to master the sea. What is more, the Captain craves for the ideal which is for him a participation in God's omnipotence and omniscience. In Marryat's novel rounding the Cape of Good Hope at any cost has a symbolic meaning and can be interpreted as a desire for reigning over the ocean and taking control of the forces of nature.

The main character in Wagner's *Der fliegende Holländer* has Faustian features as well. A rebel and an adventurer who wants to explore the extremes, the Dutchman does not hesitate to collaborate with evil forces in order to satisfy his desires. Interestingly, Köhler stresses the fact that before Wagner composed the opera, he wanted to write a Great Symphony entitled *Faust*. In his composition the German artist wanted to present a drama of an outstanding individual whose desire is to extend the boundaries of human knowledge and to find satisfaction in the company of an ideal woman. Unfortunately, the writing of *Faust*, planned as a four-part composition, resulted in failure: only the last part was performed. Not only did Wagner neglect to introduce the figure of Gretchen into the plot, but also his Faust turned out to be a flat character devoid of any power of expression. It is worth noting, however, that the projects that were not brought to completion in the symphony of Faust, were fully realized in *Der fliegende Holländer*, perfectly illustrating Wagner's unquestionable talent. Connecting the main principles of the symphony, an elaborate musical composition for full orchestra, with some elements of the stage drama, Wagner managed to create a new conception of the music drama based on operatic music, giving a strong emanation of intensity and unprecedented power of expression. According to Köhler, "a dumb Faust was transformed into a poetically talented Dutchman, flowing on the melancholy melodic line" (Köhler 179 – my translation). Vaughan also underlines in his article that Wagner drew his inspiration for creating the figure of the Flying Dutchman from Goethe's *Faust*, seeing a parallel between the ending of *Faust* and the culmination of Wagner's opera. In Goethe's masterpiece, the suffering and death of Gretchen contribute to the redemption of Faust's soul. Similarly, in Wagner's opera *ewig Weiblichkeit*, represented by Senta, is presented as a redemptive force, powerful enough to release the Flying Dutchman from his curse (Vaughan 28). The word *senta*, which is an imperative form of the Italian verb *sentire* denoting both "to listen to" and "to feel," may illustrate the woman's attitude towards the condemned captain: she listens to his story and feels sorry for him. Therefore, in Wagner's romantic treatment of the theme, the Dutchman is viewed with sympathy, not with irony, as was the case in Heine's interpretation.

Despite numerous similarities, *The Phantom Ship* and *Der fliegende Holländer* differ considerably in certain respects. One of the essential divergences between the two is the portrayal of the figure of the Flying Dutchman. Although in both works the life of the doomed captain and sea space are inseparable, Marryat's Flying Dutchman seems to be presented as *il penseroso*, while Wagnerian *Holländer* is constructed as *l'allegro*.

Created by the power of the word, Vanderdecken is portrayed as capable of performing analyses, as his long-lasting wandering on the seas stimulates reflection and self-examination. The immensity and vastness of the sea are awe-inspiring for the Captain and make him feel insignificant in confrontation with the power of the element. Reflecting on his adventurous past, the Captain discovers that God's presence is indispensable in his life. He shows signs of genuine repentance for the committed blasphemy and wants to kiss the relic of the Holy Cross, which is now in his son's possession. In Marryat's novel, the ceaseless wandering illustrates man's fight with his own weaknesses on the way to *sacrum*. Marryat adds a religious aspect to the *peregrinatio vitae* metaphor, showing God both as the beginning and the end of wandering characterized by contemplation. It is the divine Creator who reigns over oceanic waters; in his hands the sea no longer constitutes a *locus horridus*, but belongs to the sphere of *sacrum* and acquires purgatorial features. An apparently senseless seventeen-year-long voyage has in fact a deeper meaning. The monotony of continuous wandering gradually purifies the proud Captain of egoism and opens his eyes to his fragility and insignificance in confrontation with the all-powerful sea. Oceanic waters, being a manifestation of God's omnipotence, are similar to baptismal water in their bringing purification and absolution of sins. After a long-lasting wandering, the Captain falls on his knees aboard his ghost ship, and in a gesture of humility kisses the relic of the Holy Cross, against which he swore seventeen years before. Finally, he finds the peace of death and reaches the land of never-ending happiness.

In the Wagnerian opera there is a parallel drawn between the Dutchman and the sea as well. Not only the figure of the Flying Dutchman, ever becoming and never being, but also the ocean, characterized by continuity in time and shapelessness in space, are created in *Der fliegende Holländer* by the power of music. Therefore, portrayed by the means of sounds, rather than words, the Wagnerian Dutchman does not constitute a reflective character. Apart from the protagonist, the grimly roaring sea is also continuously "illustrated" by the orchestra in the analyzed opera. According to Jachimecki, Wagner's "exceptional attempt to paint with sounds gives rise to a number of musical pictures of nature and various elements, whose colouring, delineation and the power of expression are absolutely outstanding" (Jachimecki 57 – my translation). It is musicality that makes the Dutchman unaware of possible consequences of his actions and unable to reflect on his adventurous life. As an ideal character devoid of the power of words, he lacks self-awareness and self-examination. Therefore, the Wagnerian *Holländer* cannot be judged in terms of good and evil. Indeed, the amoral Flying Dutchman in Wagner's opera is not an individual, but a universal character, remaining in the realm of aesthetics. By contrast, it is self-reflection that implies in Marryat's novel the idea of sin, leading to a transition from the aesthetical phase, through ethical, to religious.

Yet another difference between Marryat's novel and Wagner's opera is the fact that different forces triumph at the end of the two analyzed works. In *The Phantom Ship* Captain Vanderdecken attains salvation thanks to his son's heroic self-denial. Of his own free will, Philip decides to sacrifice himself in the name of saving his father from eternal condemnation. Sailing the seas of the world in search of the ghost ship commanded by the doomed captain, Philip acquires Christ-like features, his mission on earth being to obey his father's will. Due to his obedience, Philip does not hesitate to sacrifice his life in order to perform the task. When in the final scene he brings the relic of the Holy Cross to his father, the Captain is released from the curse. He finally finds the peace of death, as his ghost ship, gradually immersing in purgatorial sea waters, eventually sinks. The father, tightly embracing the son, is filled with joy, and so is the surrounding nature. This image creates an atmosphere of reconciliation, forgiveness and renewal. In the final chapter of the novel, Marryat stresses the redemptive power of sacrifice, presenting a triumph of sacrificial love over the sin committed in the past.

In contrast to Marryat's novel, a gloomy atmosphere prevails in Wagner's opera. Since his youth, the composer associated the spiritual world with bare fifths opening Beethoven's Ninth Symphony (Köhler 183). According to John Deathridge, it is likely that Wagner "deliberately converted the mysterious bare fifths of Beethoven's opening into the rasping sound of the open fifths at the beginning of the *Dutchman* Overture [...] – the 'salty breeze' which Franz Liszt claimed to hear in the piece" (Deathridge 15). Analyzing the demonic aura of the opera, Deathridge notices that the interval of diminished fifth was defined by medieval theorists as the "Devil in Music" [*diabolus in musica*] (16). Wagner probably applied such an interval in his opera to indicate the protagonists' *discesos ad inferos*. In *Der fliegende Holländer*, Senta flings herself from the rock to unfathomable sea depths, thus confirming her oath of faithfulness to her beloved until her death. At the same time, the doomed captain's ship sinks and the embraced figures of the lovers appear on the horizon. Committing suicide, Senta is finally united with the Dutchman and accompanies him on his way to eternal condemnation. Despite the triumph of demonic forces and the perdition of the main characters, in the final scene of the opera Wagner celebrates *Liebestod*, that is the culmination of love in death (Vaughan 32). According to Wagner, it is Senta's love that makes her feel fulfilled in the role of a self-sacrificing woman and contributes to the doomed captain's victory in finding the desired death. In the turning point of the opera, both protagonists may symbolize a paradoxical union between Eros and Thanatos.

The number of similarities between Marryat's novel and Wagner's opera is really intriguing. The central theme of both, namely a mysterious contact of the human and the spiritual world, and a constant interpenetration of the two inexplicable and ungraspable realities, contributes to the fact that the discussed works perfectly enrich the original version of the legend with typically romantic elements. Not only *The Phantom Ship*, but also *Der fliegende Holländer*, both taking place in the sphere of supernatural order and exuding a strong emanation of evil, constitute very interesting variations on the well-known legend. The romantic rendition of the motif of the Flying Dutchman intensifies the tragedy of the doomed captain, allowing him to influence the audience's imagination with an unprecedented force.

1.2. Variations on Triangular Desire[1]

In his sea novel, Marryat not only presents one of the most extensive versions of the legend, but also explores in great detail the Dutch Captain's crossing of both the geographical and the moral frontiers. In his enormous pride and enthusiasm for discoveries, William Vanderdecken wants to usurp the Absolute's demiurgic power in order to discover lands, cross frontiers, and stake out new territories in an imitation of God's creative acts.

As has been outlined in the previous section of the present chapter, Captain William Vanderdecken of *The Phantom Ship* may be regarded as a Faustian figure representing both individual and universal features. Extremely gifted and enormously proud, Faust is beyond any doubt an exceptional individual who rises above mediocrity. On the other hand, his cognitive insatiability and his desire to know, rather than be lost in conjecture, are common to many humans. Overwhelmed by his passion and unable to accept the limits of cognition resulting from the weaknesses of human nature, Faust wants to touch the intangible and to know the unknowable. This active and dynamic genius, whose life is characterized by constant eagerness to explore, does not agree to accept his helplessness and insignificance within the system of the universe. Rejecting the limitations of human condition and rebelling against the inscrutability of knowledge, Faust lives on the verge of normality and insanity, convinced in his enormous pride that he is able to scrutinize the inscrutable and to be God's equal. The Renaissance legend of Faust becomes the myth of human sin characterized by usurping God's rights. In his book devoted to the fall of man as presented in Genesis, Marian Grabowski states that in Eden the serpent promises Adam participation in divinity, that is in God's omnipotence and omniscience. The serpent's lie is tempting for Adam, as it presents the absurd assurance of achieving perfection, which is in fact inaccessible, as being within hu-

---

1   Some fragments of this section will be published under the title "The Flying Dutchman's Mimetic Desire. Crossing Geographical and Moral Frontiers in Frederick Marryat's *The Phantom Ship*" in PASE 2010 post-conference volume.

man reach (Grabowski 217). The serpent always takes advantage of the feeling of lack, as well as of the fact that for each person the desired object is a mixture of what is real and what is imagined. Constituting the source of negative inspiration, the serpent presents the illusory and the impossible as reachable and possible, causing a human being to become overwhelmed by desire and hardly able to resist the temptation. Faust's pact with the devil may be regarded as a repetition of Adam's fall in Eden. The talented scholar rejects his helplessness and desires to manifest his unusual power; much like Adam, he wants to try the fruit from the tree of knowledge, to gain wisdom in order to unravel all the mysteries of the world, as well as to decide what is definitely good and what is not. Mephistopheles makes Faust an unfulfilable promise to satisfy his desires for the price of his soul.

The legend of the Flying Dutchman as presented by Marryat may also be interpreted as a romantic version of the Biblical archetype of the fall of man as a result of succumbing to Satan's temptation. The desires and temptations of William Vanderdecken are similar to Faust's constant eagerness and his cognitive insatiability. Vanderdecken's blasphemy against God, which took place seventeen years prior to the action of *The Phantom Ship*, is not presented by a third-person omniscient narrator, but appears as a recollection on the part of his wife, Catherine. In a flashback, she describes the tempestuous and horrifying night when the ghost of her husband suddenly appeared in front of her eyes to confess his dreadful deed. Catherine's story carries with it a sense of credibility, as she heard the account of the fatal cruise directly from her husband and also saw his recollections written down in the form of a letter, left by the ghost of the Captain.

In a short retrospection, William Vanderdecken is depicted as a bold sailor who resembles typical romantic heroes. During a cruise to India with valuable cargo, he attempts to round the Cape of Good Hope. Prevented by adverse winds and currents, he is not able to fulfill this daring plan. Not discouraged by misfortune and continually overwhelmed by passion for discovery, Vanderdecken strikes a mutinous pilot, who then falls overboard and drowns. His irresistible desire to round the "Stormy Cape" at any cost, which soon becomes a kind of obsession, may be compared to Ahab's quest for the white whale. In his analysis of *Moby Dick*, Michael T. Gilmore investigates Ahab's aversion to inscrutability and his desire to eliminate all that is beyond his understanding, at the same time stressing the fact that the quest for knowledge may be seen as both fascinating and having associations with unimaginable destruction (Gilmore 87–94). For Ahab, the search for knowledge has a touch of obsession much like the idea of extermination of Moby Dick, the whale which from Ahab's point of view represents everything that is evil in the world, and becomes the *raison d'être* of his existence. Similarly, Vanderdecken, another fanatical truth-seeker, hates inscrutability and cannot accept the fact that some lands and territories still have the status of an enigma for him. The Captain's insatiable passion for discovery also turns into an obsession, as he is ready to risk his life and to destroy himself in quest for scrutability. Regarding the sea as a malicious adversary, preventing him from going round the Cape of Good Hope and testing the limits of his power, Vanderdecken wants to emerge victorious from the battle with the powerful ocean at any cost.

Not only the Faustian archetype and the Adamic myth, but also the legend of the Flying Dutchman are marked by the presence of Satan, who is the source of negative inspiration. In *The Phantom Ship,* Satan takes advantage of Vanderdecken's frustration as well as his readiness to risk his life or to give up his soul to satisfy his desire for conquering at all costs and being powerful enough to master nature. It is Satan who kindles the Captain's passion for discovery to an enormous extent and tempts him with the promise of achieving God's perfection. As Vanderdecken refuses to accept his powerlessness and insignificance in confrontation with the Almighty and remains convinced of his own greatness, he gives credence to Satan's empty words. At the moment of committing blasphemy, the Captain rejects God and, like Adam, reaches for the fruit of the tree of knowledge. In other words, he resorts to Satan as the mediator who will help him to satisfy the desire for God's omniscience and omnipotence.

René Girard's controversial idea of mimetic desire may be applied here in order to interpret the nature of Vanderdecken's pact with the devil. Girard's theory of the triangular nature of desire, in which he utilized Plato's and Aristotle's investigations of *mimesis* and combined them with his critical outlook on Sigmund Freud's and Jacques Lacan's analyses of desire (Buchholtz 62), was presented in *Deceit, Desire, and the Novel* (1965). However, some weaknesses of Girard's theory were pointed out by Mirosława Buchholtz. First of all, she observes that Girard does not investigate the mechanism of choosing the model. What is more, he takes the situation of the existence of the personified mediator for granted. Buchholtz also claims that Girard "needs to personify the mediator for the sake of his next move, which is to expatiate on the rivalry between the mediator and the person who desires [...]" (Buchholtz 62). If the mediator is no longer regarded as the model but rather as an obstacle, the subject is "torn between two opposite feelings towards his model – the most submissive reverence and the most intense malice" (Girard 10). Furthermore, in her analysis Buchholtz underlines Girard's objection to Freud's tendency to flatter the illusion of spontaneity of desires which in fact always appear through the mediation of the third party (Buchholtz 63). She also evokes Gavriel Reisner's history of the concept of desire in which he stresses the fact that Lacan enriched Freudian "wish" and "desire" with the reference to the quest for what cannot be found. Buchholtz sees a correspondence between Reisner's reading of Lacan's concept of desire, on the one hand, and his focusing on the object of desire and Girard's theory of mimetic desire, on the other. Lacan's regarding of the reachable signifier as a representation of the unreachable signified, the object that is desired for but will never be possessed, is very close to the idea of the mediator representing the model expressed by Girard (Buchholtz 64).

Although Girard's model does not accurately reflect the mimetic aspects of Marryat's novel, his idea of the triangular nature of desire, however slightly modified, is applicable to Captain Vanderdecken's relationship with Satan and God, neither of whom is explicitly named in the novel. The fact that the ultimate object of Vanderdecken's desire is purely metaphysical, as he does not want to have God's attributes but to be his equal, is an essential but lacking element in Girard's theory. What the Captain desires is not possessing an external object, but discovering the enormous divine potential within himself. He is convinced that the better he imitates God, the closer to perfection he comes. Vanderdecken's desire to be God's equal is spontaneous only to a certain extent; it occurs as a result of his enormous pride and his conviction of being exceptional. To a greater extent, however, his desire is initiated by Satan, who tempts Vanderdecken with illusory promises of power and knowledge. As Satan also imitates, or rather mocks, God, and desires His omniscience and omnipotence, he becomes the Captain's mediator, having a profound influence on his actions. Nevertheless, Vanderdecken is convinced that his relationship to the object of desire is independent of the mediator. Experiencing the illusion of autonomy and spontaneity, the Captain believes that his desire to be God's equal is thoroughly original and certainly not rooted in someone else. In his self-centeredness and unawareness of any mediation, Vanderdecken does not realize that he places his faith in a false promise from the outside. The hero's illusion of the possibility of possessing God's omnipotence is only partially created by his imagination; to a large extent it is fostered by Satan, who maintains the Captain's illusion of spontaneous desire. Vanderdecken borrows his desire from the other (Satan), completely confusing it with the will to be oneself. Blinded by illusory autonomy, he does not realize that behind his seemingly spontaneous desires, there is someone else's suggestion.

Vanderdecken would never reach for God's power if he were not imitating Satan and succumbing to his suggestions. Much like Emma Bovary and Don Quixote, the characters analyzed by Girard in his book, the Captain "obey[s] the suggestion of an external milieu, for lack of an auto-suggestion from within" (Girard 5). Unlike the characters of Flaubert and Cervantes, the Captain does not imitate the desires of the model he has chosen, namely God, but the model itself. Yet, having no idea about the real nature of God, he copies the imaginary characteristics of the model. The distance between the desiring subject and the mediator is in Marryat's novel even greater than in the works of Flaubert and Cervantes. In this case it is not physical space that measures the gap between the mediator and the subject; the distance between the two is primarily spiritual and will always remain insuperable. Therefore, there is no rivalry with the mediator. In *The Phantom Ship* the mediator, that is Satan, being a spiritual creature not only much more intelligent and perfect than a human being, but also capable of transcending the boundaries of time and space, remains beyond the universe inhabited by the hero. Based on the distance between the hero and the mediator, Girard groups romantic works into two fundamental categories: external and internal mediation. External mediation appears in those works in which "the distance is sufficient to eliminate any contact between the two spheres of possibilities of which the mediator and the subject occupy the respective centres" (Girard 9). Girard claims further that the hero of external mediation admits the truth about his desire. Although Vanderdecken does not worship his model, but rather openly desires to imitate His power and knowledge, the divergence between God's transcendence and the Captain's limited nature makes the latter's mimetic desire as absurd and grotesque as that of Don Quixote and Emma Bovary. By contrast, internal mediation occurs when the distance between the spheres of the subject and the mediator is reduced and makes it possible for them to influence each other more or less profoundly, permitting the rivalry of desires.

Philip Vanderdecken, unlike his father, does not copy God, whose power he desires, but, as a Christian, he wants to imitate Jesus Christ. Much like his father, Philip experiences triangular desire marked by the presence of the mediator. However, as the distance between the subject and the mediator is reduced, and the spheres of their possibilities penetrate each other, Philip's desire is not characterized by external, but rather by internal mediation. The mediator is no longer a model, but a rival who hates the subject and acts as an obstacle. Girard's theory of internal mediation should be modified to describe the nature of Philip's desire, as he is torn between two opposite mediators, a negative and a positive one. Unlike in Girard's theory, it is the negative mediator who copies the subject's desire, which serves for him as an example. As there is no insuperable spiritual gap between the two, the distance is small enough to enable a fierce rivalry of desires. Pilot Schriften, the negative mediator, desires the same object as Philip, the desiring subject, that is William Vanderdecken's soul. A crucial difference between their desires, however, lies in the fact that Philip wants to save his father at any cost, whereas Schriften, pretending to act as a mediator and to serve as an ally, imitates Philip's actions in a negative way and is his fierce enemy.

Pilot Schriften, a seemingly diabolical figure who wants to possess the soul of William Vanderdecken, carefully hides his efforts to imitate Philip and never proclaims aloud the true nature of his desire. His profession deserves attention as well; being a pilot, that is a person with expert local knowledge qualified to take charge of ships entering or leaving a harbor, Schriften is supposed to lead seamen. However, what the Pilot does is the exact opposite: he constantly misleads young Vanderdecken. In his naivety, Philip is not aware of the Pilot's real intentions and remains convinced that they are united by the common goal. In Marryat's novel it is Schriften, not the subject, as is the case with Girard's theory of internal mediation, who is torn between the admiration for Philip's readiness to make sacrifice for his father and the most intense malice. For Schriften Philip is an object of hatred, as he prevents the Pilot from satisfying his desire. Schriften regards the subject, whom he scrupulously imitates in a negative way, as "a shrewd and diabolical enemy; he tries to rob the subject of his most prized possessions; he obstinately thwarts his most legitimate ambitions" (Girard 11). The Pilot hates Philip so much because he sees the futility of his negative imitations and is overwhelmed by the feeling of impotence. Schriften feels the imperative need to imitate Philip's actions by transforming them into their opposite. Using Girard's words, Philip may be called a passionate person who "is distinguished by his emotional autonomy" and by "the spontaneity of his desires" (19). The Pilot's imitated desire is just a negative reflection of Philip's spontaneous and passionate desire.

The mimetic behaviours of Captain Vanderdecken, a typical romantic hero are yet another exact opposition of Philip's spontaneity. J. A. Cuddon defines "romantic" as "emotional," "exuberant," "mysterious," "adventurous," "daring," "extraordinary," and "passionate" (Cuddon 768). Cuddon further claims that Romanticism may be characterized by "emphasis on the need for spontaneity in thought and action, increasing importance attached to natural genius [...] and a tendency to exalt the individual and his needs" (769–770). In his article J. H. Stape also accentuates that all romantic desires convey "a yearning for transcendence, a desire to evade compromise, and a longing for the release that can be found only in death" (Stape 77). Beyond any doubt, Captain William Vanderdecken is a daring and adventurous sailor who overshadows his fellow seamen and exalts himself. As a romantic hero, Vanderdecken is also overwhelmed by a burning desire for transcendence, defined by Girard as metaphysical desire.

When analyzing "symbolist" desire, René Girard underlines that for the proud symbolist subjectivity, the external world is of hardly any value. He also emphasizes that "symbolist" desire would not exist if it were not for the power of imagination. Vanderdecken is a man of extremes who often experiences overwhelming emotions and becomes a subject of flights of imagination. Blinded by his immense pride, his youthful ardour and his imaginative nature, the Captain perceives himself in an unrealistic way. Vanderdecken's conviction of his greatness, uniqueness and exceptionality is the source of the his strength and exhilaration in the face of danger and the unknown. Unfortunately, the vision of himself that the Captain projects lacks any basis in reality and this distorted image of himself has a destructive influence on Vanderdecken's actions. In his analysis, Girard claims further that although a proud individual turns away from the uninterested world, it happens sometimes that the subject of desire perceives some object which "slips into the consciousness like a grain of sand into the shell of an oyster; a pearl of imagination forms around this one small atom of reality" (Girard 28). The Captain's pride and boldness make him so prone to Satan's temptations that the devil's suggestion of the possibility of Vanderdecken's being God's equal slips into the Captain's consciousness. It is his powerful imagination that transforms Satan's false promise into a passionate desire for transcendence and makes Vanderdecken similar to demonic protagonists of Dostoyevsky's novels.

In the chapter entitled "Men Become Gods in the Eyes of Each Other," Girard explores a metaphysical aspect of desire in Dostoyevsky's novels. He stresses that

1.2. Variations on Triangular Desire 51

the desire for transcendence is usually initiated by an individual's faith in a false promise from the outside. In Dostoyevsky's novels the false promise is associated with the possibility of replacing God, as in the world presented in the fiction of the Russian novelist God no longer exists. The protagonists of Dostoyevsky's novels desire to absorb the being of the mediator, as they are convinced that only the mediator is able to help them achieve the divine inheritance, from which they feel excluded (Girard 57). However, the protagonist's desire for transcendence becomes deviated, as it is based on a lie. The mediator, toward whom the hero passionately turns, does not, in fact, enjoy the divine inheritance, but only pretends to participate in it. Girard argues therefore that "[s]o great is the disciple's faith that he perpetually thinks he is about to steal the marvellous secret from the mediator. He begins to enjoy his inheritance in advance. He shuns the present and lives in the brilliant future. Nothing separates him from divinity [...]" (Girard 58). The vast majority of the protagonists of Dostoyevsky's novels are unable to ignore the infinity, despite the fact that they do not believe in God. Directing their existence toward other people, not toward the non-existent, in their opinion, God, they choose human models and treat them as substitute gods (Girard 65). The denial of God leads to the imitation of the model who seems to have God's attributes and to the deviation of transcendence. As a consequence, "[t]he positive mediation of the saint is replaced by the negative mediation of anguish and hate" (Girard 60). Girard also claims that the characters who obey the suggestion from the outside and begin to regard themselves as gods, usually are aware of their nothingness and their inability to equal the God they desire to substitute. However, he points out that Dostoyevsky's heroes are too proud to admit their failure: "Blinding their judgement, [their vanity] puts them in a position to deceive themselves and to identify themselves in their own eyes, with the image which they have substituted for their own personality" (Girard 63). Although the protagonists of Dostoyevsky's novels are bitterly disappointed with the deviation of the desire for transcendence, hiding this disillusionment becomes the essence of their existence. Girard calls their idea of transcendence "deviated in the direction of the human" (Girard 80).

Girard's statements concerning Dostoyevsky's fiction may also be applicable in an interpretation of the nature of William Vanderdecken's metaphysical desire. The Captain's craving for transcendence is also deviated but, to paraphrase Girard's words, in the direction of Satan. Like the protagonists of Dostoyevsky's novels, Vanderdecken gives credence to a false promise from the outside. In Marryat's novel it is arguably Satan who tempts the Captain with the promise that divinity is within his reach. Satan's idea of transcendence is also based on a lie, as he is not God's equal and does not enjoy God's omnipotence and omniscience: he only wishes and pretends that he does. Vanderdecken, like the heroes of Dostoyevsky's narratives, chooses a mediator and becomes convinced that Satan is able to help him achieve divinity. However, unlike Dostoyevsky's protagonists, the Captain lacks awareness. In his self-centeredness, he is not aware of the existence of the mediator whose suggestions he follows. What is more, he is so blinded by pride that he is not able to realize his insignificance within the system of the universe and his nothingness in confrontation with the Almighty. Furthermore, he does not accept the present situation and constantly looks into the future, hoping for his final triumph and his participation in divinity. Another difference between the Captain and the characters investigated by Girard lies in the fact that the heroes presented in Dostoyevsky's narratives consciously reject God and resort to the human mediator, whereas Vanderdecken wants to imitate God at any cost, even following Satan's deviated suggestions. In other words, he does not choose substitute gods as models but his model is the Almighty.

Yet another striking difference between the protagonists of Dostoyevsky's novels and the Captain is associated with the way they are punished for their desire to participate in God's transcendence. While Dostoyevsky underlines that in the world portrayed in the vast majority of his novels God no longer exists and, hence, the Russian author confronts his heroes with an ungoverned universe, the world presented in Marryat's novel is marked by the Almighty's presence. In consequence, in Dostoyevsky's fiction the non-existent God is not able to punish the protagonists for their pride and their deviated perception of themselves as substitute gods. For them, the punishment is a bitter confrontation of the imagined divinity with their obvious nothingness. As Girard puts it, "in [splendid palaces of imagination] the Self entertains itself, indescribably contented, until the day when the treacherous magician – reality – brushes against the fragile dream buildings and reduces them to dust" (Girard 28). Extremely disappointed as the heroes of Dostoyevsky's novels are, in their pride they are not able to admit their failure and they suffer throughout their lives pretending to be perfectly satisfied with the deviated transcendence.

By contrast, Captain Vanderdecken is punished severely by the Almighty against whom he has trespassed for his enormous pride and his desire to be God's equal. Both in his pride and in his final failure, Vanderdecken resembles the Old-Testament king, Belshazzar. The fragment of the Bible describing the King's sin reads as follows:

> 1 King Belshazzar gave a great banquet for a thousand of his lords, with whom he drank. 2 Under the influence of the wine, he ordered the gold and silver vessels which Nebuchadnezzar, his father, had taken from the temple in Jerusalem, to be brought in so that the king, his lords, his wives and his entertainers might drink from them. 3 When the gold and silver vessels taken from the house of God in Jerusalem had been brought in, and while the king, his lords, his wives and his entertainers were drinking 4 wine from them, they praised their gods of gold and silver, bronze and iron, wood and stone. (Dn 5: 1–4)

Much like his father, Nebuchadnezzar, Belshazzar feels powerful enough to equal God. Extremely proud and self-confident, Belshazzar, the Chaldean king, regards himself as having God's attributes and the right to judge what is good and what is bad. The fact that during a great banquet the king allowed his lords, wives and entertainers to drink from the vessels stolen from the temple in Jerusalem is significant, and may be interpreted as an act of initiation. Up to this point the king has felt excluded from full participation in divinity, and convinced that there are certain mysteries that God reserved only for Himself. Having drunk the wine from the vessels that belonged exclusively to God, Belshazzar believes that he managed to wrest all secrets from the Almighty. The act of profanation of the vessels can be interpreted as the King's symbolic transition from partial exclusion to full inclusion in God's omnipotence and omniscience.

Similarly, Captain Vanderdecken also equals God in his own eyes. He swears by the fragment of the Cross that is in his possession that he will circle the Cape of Good Hope against God's will "in defiance of storm and seas, of lightning, of heaven, or of hell, even if [he] should beat about until the Day of Judgment" (Marryat 11). Vanderdecken is convinced that going round the Cape will prove his godlike mastery over nature. The Captain's blasphemy, like Belshazzar's profanation, can be regarded as a symbolic satisfaction of the desire for penetrating all God's mysteries and for participating in His divinity.

In both cases, God does not remain indifferent to the transgressions which Belshazzar and Vanderdecken commit against Him but immediately reacts and inflicts punishment. The fragment from the Old Testament continues:

> 5 Suddenly, opposite the lampstand, the fingers of a human hand appeared, writing on the plaster of the wall in the king's palace. When the king saw the wrist and hand that wrote, 6 his face blanched; his thoughts terrified him, his hip joints shook, and his knees knocked. (Dn 5: 5–6)

The mysterious inscription that appears on the wall consists of three words: MENE, TEKEL, PERES. As nobody is able to decipher the meaning of the writing, the prophet Daniel, who knows "how to interpret dreams, explain enigmas and solve difficulties" (Dn 5:12), is asked by the King to resolve the mystery. Daniel interprets God's handwriting as a harbinger of imminent punishment for the King's appropriation of God's attributes and as a warning against Belshazzar's impending fall. Indeed, God keeps His promise and that same night the King is killed.

Likewise, in *The Phantom Ship* it is God's handwriting that announces the punishment. The words UNTIL THE DAY OF JUDGMENT are written in flame and appear in the centre of a huge cloud surrounded by immense darkness: "The hurricane burst upon the ship, the canvas flew away in ribbons; mountains of seas swept over us, and in the centre of a deep o'erhanging cloud, which shrouded all in utter darkness, were written in letters of livid flame, these words – UNTIL THE DAY OF JUDGMENT" (Marryat 11). Unlike Belshazzar, the Captain is not punished with death, but, rather, is sentenced by God to go round the Cape of Good Hope until doomsday. For the adventurous and daring seaman, such eternal and monotonous seafaring always in the same direction is the greatest suffering imaginable.

The severity of such a punishment is masterfully described by Joseph Conrad in one of his essays from the collection entitled *The Mirror of the Sea*:

> But I know that there is no harder trial for a seaman than to feel a dead ship under his feet. There is no mistaking that sensation, so dismal, so tormenting, and so subtle, so full of unhappiness and unrest. I could imagine no worse eternal punishment for evil seamen who die unrepentant upon the earthly sea than that their souls should be condemned to man the ghosts of disabled ships, drifting for ever across a ghostly and tempestuous ocean. (64)

As all romantic heroes, Vanderdecken is characterized by "a longing for the release that can be found only in death" (Stape 77), the state of living death being unbearable for him. In order to punish the bold Captain, God transforms Vanderdecken into the Flying Dutchman, a character whose ontological status is uncertain, as he is neither a human being nor a ghost. It is striking that the Flying Dutchman is the exact opposite of what Captain Vanderdecken used to be. Once enormously proud and bold, the Captain has regarded the discovery of new lands and active fighting with the sea as the essence of his existence. Vanderdecken's pride is now stifled and his passion for adventure is replaced by overwhelming passivity, similar to the deadly calm sea, which is for him unbearable.

In view of the Flying Dutchman's suffering resulting from metaphysical desire, Girard's theory appears particularly incomplete. Analyzing the metaphysical aspect of mimetic desire, the researcher concentrates on its initial and final stages, that is self-deification and disillusionment or even self-destruction, respectively, giving hardly any importance to the in-between phase – suffering. As it is a potentially significant aspect which can be seen as missing from Girard's theory, I want to supplement his theses with an analysis of the connection between metaphysical desire and the problem of suffering, as presented by one of the leading critics of American literature of the first half of the twentieth century, Francis Otto Matthiessen. I would argue that Matthiessen's statements on *Moby Dick* are worth examining, as they appear to bear directly upon Marryat's novel. Indeed, another reference to Melville's masterpiece, perfectly illustrating a relation between the three stages, may be quite illuminating in the interpretation of the figure of Captain Vanderdecken, obsessed with his metaphysical desire. What is striking to me is the fact that Matthiessen's theses presented in his essay "The Fate of the Ungodly God-Like Man," originally published in 1941 in a volume entitled *American Renaissance: Art and Expression in the Age of Emerson and Whitman*, not only contributed to the revival in the United States of the then entirely forgotten Melville, but are also remarkably applicable to *The Phantom Ship*. The year of the publication of *American Renaissance*, 1941, deserves attention too. Interestingly enough, in the same year Melville was rediscovered in Italy thanks to Cesare Pavese's translation of *Moby Dick*, which has been regarded by critics as a work of art in itself.

Presenting Melville as one of canonical American writers, Matthiessen underlines that the author of *Moby Dick* was responsive to the nineteenth-century "alteration in the object of [...] belief from God-Man to Man-God, and to the corresponding shift in emphasis from Incarnation to Deification" (70). The researcher argues that in his masterpiece Melville presents Ahab as a self-appointed God, immersed in evil forces. Rising above mediocrity and exalting himself excessively, the self-deifying Captain may be regarded as a monomaniac who, because of his aforementioned fixed idea and hatred of inscrutability, enters into a pact with the devil. Therefore, Matthiessen argues that "[t]he contrasting halves of his nature cannot be summed up better than in the 'ungodly, god-like' of Captain's Peleg's description" (76). The author of *American Renaissance*, pointing out that the God-like desire to eliminate the source of evil becomes an obsession leading to unbelievable *hubris*, concludes that the protagonist's *hubris* inevitably entails *nemesis*, and describes Ahab's career as "a tragedy of pride" (72).

In his article Matthiessen also observes that it is not without significance that in the characterization of Ahab's obsessive desire, Melville stresses the protagonist's suffering. M. O. Percival, who explores the problem of suffering in *Moby Dick* referring to Søren Kierkegaard's analysis of the concept, claims that for each sufferer there are two possibilities: he will either become "demonic" or "essentially religious" (Percival 110). As the initial reaction to suffering is despair, the sufferer can accept infinite resignation, and, in consequence, find peace, or resort to defiance, which inevitably leads to destruction. Percival points out that due to his being too proud to humiliate himself in any gesture of infinite resignation, Ahab is turned demonic. Investigating the irreligious attitude of the character, the researcher accentuates that the hatred of suffering always results in despair, only exacerbated by desperate attempts to eliminate it. Since the sufferer strongly hates his impotence in confrontation with suffering, he exalts himself infinitely, the result being that the increasing despair increases both self-deification and self-hatred. Percival concludes that the vicious circle set in motion by a rebellion against suffering has a disastrous outcome: the sufferer becomes diabolic (111). Likewise, Matthiessen emphasizes that Ahab, a suffering Faustian figure who is not able to look his impotence in the face, is not purified by his suffering. On the contrary, it precipitates Ahab's perdition (Matthiessen 77).

Strikingly enough, the contrasting terms "ungodly" and "god-like" seem to perfectly characterize yet another sufferer, Captain Vanderdecken. Perceiving himself as a Man-God powerful enough to challenge the Almighty and overwhelmed by the slavery to his metaphysical desire for omnipotence and omniscience, Vanderdecken may be described as "ungodly." Like Ahab, the Captain is obsessed with his fixed idea to master the sea, which is "god-like," as it represents human desire for the Creator's mastery over nature. Similarly to Ahab, Vanderdecken is punished for his colossal *hubris*. However, there is a significant difference between the two sufferers: while the demonic Ahab is eternally condemned, the suffering caused by Vanderdecken's eternal seafaring, regarded as *nemesis*, leads to his purgation and reconciliation with God. As the "ungodly, god-like" being, the Captain resorts to "the Christian way of resignation, the only way [...] whereby a morbid nature, passionate and self-willed, can encounter despair and conquer it" (Percival 110), Vanderdecken is transformed into a deeply religious character, the Flying Dutchman. The religious aspect of suffering is also explored in Percival's analysis. The researcher underlines that only if the sufferer, renouncing his pride, resorts to God and begs for help, will he be able to bear the burden of suffering (Percival 110). It is during his never-ending and apparently senseless seafaring as the Flying Dutchman that the Captain loses his pride and frees himself from the slavery to metaphysical desire.

In one of the chapters of *Deceit, Desire, and the Novel*, Girard stresses the fact that metaphysical desire inevitably leads to "the metaphysical disappointment" (Girard 88). What the humiliated subject of desire tries to do is hide his or her metaphysical failure by going "from desire to desire, as one crosses a stream, jumping from one slippery stone to another" (89). Girard continues: "Two possibilities present themselves. The disillusioned hero can let his former mediator point out another object for him, or he can change mediators" (89). William Vanderdecken resorts to the second solution. Deeply disappointed with Satan's empty promises and sentenced to suffering by God, after the seventeen-year-long seafaring the Captain decides to choose another mediator, who this time is not the devil, but Vanderdecken's only child, Philip. When the Captain returns as a ghost to his wife, Catherine, in order to deliver a letter, the boy is an infant. About twenty years later, when Philip is already a young man, the dying Catherine reveals to her son the terrifying story of her husband's blasphemy and informs him about the Captain's letter which reads as follows:

> To CATHERINE
>
> One of those pitying spirits whose eyes rain tears for mortal crimes has been permitted to inform me by what means alone my dreadful doom may be averted. Could I but receive on the deck of my own ship the holy relic upon which I swore the fatal oath, kiss it in all humility, and shed one tear of deep contrition on the sacred wood, I then might rest in peace. How this may be effected, or by whom so fatal a task will be undertaken, I know not. O Catherine, we have a son – but, no, no, let him not hear of me. Pray for me [...].
>
> VANDERDECKEN (Marryat 26)

Beyond doubt, the subsequent disappearance of the letter and the fact that its content becomes engraved in Philip's mind is not without significance. After a moment of hesitation and doubt, Philip realizes "that it was only in the letter that there was hope, hope for his poor father, whose memory he had been taught to love, and who appealed for help" (26). Philip is aware that his father, who remains "IN LIVING JUDGMENT" (26) chooses him in the letter as the mediator of his desire for eternal peace. Philip willingly accepts his role, which is expressed in his solemn oath:

> Hear me, dear father, if thou art so permitted, and deign to hear me, gracious Heaven – hear the son who, by this sacred relic, swears that he will avert your doom, or perish. To that will he devote his days; and having done his duty, he will die in hope and peace. Heaven, that recorded my rash father's oath, now register his son's upon the same sacred cross, and may perjury on my part be visited with punishment more dire than his! Receive it, Heaven, as at the last I trust that in thy mercy thou wilt receive the father and the son! And if too bold, O pardon my presumption. (Marryat 26)

The oath is remarkable at least for two reasons. Not only does it symbolize Philip's acceptance of the role of his father's mediator, but it also indicates that young Vanderdecken becomes the subject of his own spontaneous desire, only partially stimulated by the letter. What his father asks for is bringing him the holy relic so that he could worship it. Vanderdecken's tentative suggestion expressed in his letter, initiates Philip's passionate desire. He regards the task as a kind of mission, in the name of which he is ready to sacrifice both his own happiness and his life. However, when he marries his beloved Amine, Philip feels so blissfully happy that he almost forgets about his mission: "Strange as it may appear, from the first day which put him in possession of his Amine, Philip had no longer brooded over his future destiny: occasionally it was recalled to his memory, but immediately rejected, and, for the time, forgotten" (Marryat 48).

The scene of the arrival of Pilot Schriften, who appears in Chapter Seven, is significant due to the wealth of meanings accumulated therein. What strikes the reader immediately is the Pilot's unusual, if not demonic appearance:

> [Schriften] was a little meagre personage, dressed in the garb of the Dutch seamen of the time, with a cap made of badger skin hanging over his brow. His features were sharp and diminutive, his face of a deadly white, his lips pale, and his hair of a mixture between red and white. He had very little show of beard – indeed, it was almost difficult to say what his age might be. He might have been a sickly youth early sinking into decrepitude, or an old man, hale in constitution, yet carrying no flesh. But the most important feature, and that which immediately riveted the attention of Amine, was the eye of this peculiar personage – for he had but one; the right eye-lid was closed, and the ball within had evidently wasted away; but his left eye was, for the size of his face and head, of unusual dimensions, very protuberant, clear and watery, and most unpleasant to look upon, being relieved by no fringe of eyelash either above or below it. (Marryat 49)

It should also be underlined that both Amine and Philip feel chilly when Schriften sits next to them, which may suggest that he is a ghostly figure. Although Schriften introduces himself as one of the pilots of the *Ter Schilling*, a ship on which Philip is about to become second mate, the tone of his voice, his facial expression and especially his unnaturally huge left eye, seem to indicate that the Pilot is acquainted with the supernatural world: "There was an evident malignity in the words and manner of the one-eyed messenger, an appearance as if he knew more than others" (50). It is also striking that Schriften carefully scrutinizes Philip with his one eye and wants to know if he is a Catholic. Philip's association of the Pilot with his father's letter is also crucial for the interpretation of the scene. Indeed, the Pilot's name, Schriften, which derives from German *Schrift,* that is "a written sign," indicates that Philip's connotation is perfectly right. As he regards Schriften as a messenger of God's will, Philip decides to leave his newly-wed wife and to set out for his mission, with the holy relic hanging round his neck. Aboard the *Ter Schilling,* the name of which connotes making money and seeking profit, Philip ponders on the nature of his mission, which differs considerably from acquiring financial wealth: "Do I seek a fortune? No! [...] I seek communion with the dead" (56). The Pilot Schriften also appears on the *Ter Schilling.* Endowed with unusual capacities, Schriften knows that Philip carries a piece of the Holy Cross and tries to steal it. He is also aware of Philip's reasons for sailing near the Cape of Good Hope and does not hesitate to reveal this knowledge to young Vanderdecken: "Pray did you bring [the relic] on board, in case we should fall in with the Flying Dutchman?" (65). Apart from alluding to Philip's mission, the Pilot criticizes him and tries to undermine his authority. Young Vanderdecken wonders: "Strange [...] that the man should feel such malice towards me. I never injured him" (65).

It is worth emphasizing that Schriften imitates Philip's actions in a negative way. When the ship sails near the Cape of Good Hope, there is a serious danger of it being crushed on the rocks because of the silence at sea. While Philip performs all actions possible to avoid the catastrophe, the Pilot remains overwhelmingly passive and is delighted by the idea of the ship's destruction. Similarly, when the phantom ship suddenly appears, and after a while vanishes, Philip prays and is deeply moved; Schriften, by contrast, remains untouched. As the disappearance of the Flying Dutchman is followed by a ferocious storm, Philip begs the crew to stay sober and obey his orders. Schriften does exactly the opposite, encouraging the sailors to drink heavily and to be disobedient to the words of young Vanderdecken: "Schriften, the pilot, appeared to be the leader of the ship's company. With the can of liquor in his hand, he danced and sang, snapped his fingers, and, like a demon, peered with his one eye upon Philip [...]" (Marryat 75). Despite all odds, Philip is full of hope: "This wreck then must not be for me, I feel that it is not, that I have a charmed life, or rather a protracted one, to fulfill the oath I registered in heaven" (75). What he senses by intuition turns out to be true, as he is indeed the only person to be rescued from the shipwreck. Not discouraged by misfortune, Philip comes back to Amsterdam and embarks on the *Batavia.* Hence, he can be interpreted as the exact opposite of "ungodly, god-like" Ahab, who tries to be faithful to his oath at any cost. Due to his altruism, Philip differs considerably from the protagonist of *Moby Dick,* a monomaniac who does not hesitate to sacrifice the lives of the *Pequod's* crew in order to fulfill his egoistic promise of seeking revenge upon the white whale.

During his second voyage, Philip experiences a growing sense of anxiety and remorse for risking the lives of other sailors in order to save his father: "He felt like a criminal; as one who, by embarking with them, had doomed all around him to death, disaster, and peril" (94). He sighs with relief when the *Batavia* goes round the Cape of Good Hope without coming across the Flying Dutchman. The name of the ship, the *Batavia*, possibly deriving from the Italian word *battaglia* meaning "battle," is important, as it may connote Philip's going into battle and his readiness to fight with dark forces for his father's soul. When young Vanderdecken comes back home to his wife, it is Pilot Schriften who visits them once again in order to deliver a letter. To Philip's great surprise, the Pilot explains that he did not die in the *Ter Schilling*'s catastrophe, but was thrown up by the waves. This time not only does Schriften allude to Philip's mission, but he says explicitly that he knows the reason for young Vanderdecken's sea voyages. Amine is convinced that "[t]he hateful messenger appears to have risen from the grave that he might deliver [the letter]" (118). From that moment Philip is almost certain that the Pilot is an unearthly messenger, mysteriously connected with his fate. In the letter from the company, Philip finds out that he has been appointed as first mate on the *Vrow Katerina*.

During a horrible storm, the *Vrow Katerina* comes across the phantom ship, but the vessel immediately disappears. Philip instinctively feels that the catastrophe of the *Vrow Katerina* is inevitable, and he begs God for mercy. His premonition turns out to be true, as suddenly the ship starts to burn and quickly transforms into a huge mass of fire. Only thirty-six people out of three hundred are saved. Full of grim forebodings, Philip continues his mission as a captain on the *Dort*. The name of the ship, which may derive from the German word *dort* meaning "there," can suggest the final stage of Philip's mission and his approaching meeting with someone from "out there," that is from the other world. Indeed, this time he meets his father's ship as well, which brings bad luck on the *Dort*: the vessel is mysteriously run aground. When after several months Philip is appointed as captain on the *Utrecht*, he decides to take his wife on board. One day the *Utrecht* rescues a shipwrecked man. Philip is horrified when he realizes that it is the Pilot Schriften. Now young Vanderdecken has no doubt that the Pilot is inseparably connected with his mission. In a conversation with Amine, Schriften tries to convince her that Philip's task is senseless, and encourages the young woman to steal the holy relic from her husband. The Pilot also reveals that Philip's mission is soon going to end with his death. Schriften's words turn out to be true, as not only does Philip during his fifth voyage notice the phantom ship, a harbinger of death, but also the ghost of his father. When the *Utrecht* is possessed by the doomed vessel and Philip meets his father, he is so excited and moved that he faints. This time Schriften also reacts in the opposite way: he is furious and shakes his fist at the ghost of Captain Vanderdecken.

As the mimetic relations outlined by Marryat are too complex for Girard's model of triangular desire, I want to enrich his theory with Zofia Mitosek's statements on "unifying" and "antagonistic mimesis," which seem crucial in my further analysis of *The Phantom Ship* from a religious perspective. In her article entitled "Mimesis i religia" ["Mimesis and Religion"], Zofia Mitosek analyses an *exemplum* written by Thomas à Kempis circa 1427 entitled *De imitatione Christi*. According to Mitosek, in his book à Kempis does not present the Gospel as *Vita Christi*, that is an idealistic image of Jesus Christ and His life, but, on the contrary, he emphasizes the pursuit of the ideal, manifesting itself in following Christ's way of life. In other words, Mitosek argues that in his book à Kempis explores *Via Christi*, presenting Jesus not as a static model which should be imitated, but rather as a dynamic God-Man who should be followed. Importantly, the researcher also stresses the opposition between two Latin terms: *imitor* and *sequor*. The word *imitor*, deriving from Greek *mimeisthai*, means "to imitate," "to regenerate," "to mimic," "to be similar to" and "to be equal to." *Sequor*, by contrast, derives from Greek *akoloutheo* and does not belong to the semantic field of mimesis. *Akoloutheo* means "to follow somebody" or "to accompany somebody." In the New Testament the word *akoloutheo* is understood as following in Christ's footsteps and imitating His way of life. Hence, Mitosek claims that it is Jesus Christ who may be regarded as a figure establishing a connection between *akoloutheo* and *mimeisthai* (175). She emphasizes a number of similarities between the two terms, and maintains that both Plato and Aristotle were aware of the threats caused by spontaneous mimesis, that is pure practical behaviours devoid of any theoretical background, inevitably leading to the transgression of certain borders established between practice and theory (177). Both Plato, in life, and Aristotle, in poetry, wanted to provide the rules of good imitation and regarded mimesis neither as pure practice nor as sheer theory, but rather as a practical application of theory, that is action. Indeed, it is practical behaviours that are stressed not only in the notion of *mimeisthai*, but also in that of *akoloutheo*. According to Mitosek, the two concepts are also similar to each other in that in both cases a relationship between the model and the imitator has a personal character. What is more, in the Greek mythology the term *mimeisthai* and in the Bible the word *akoloutheo* frequently refer to the relationship between a human being and god(s) (173–192).

However, despite pointing out certain similarities between them, Mitosek perceives the two concepts as significantly different. Firstly, mimesis is a representation of a model that is not present; in other words, it is a replacement of the model based on illusion. *Akoloutheo*, by contrast, is always associated with either real or spiritual presence of a master. Secondly, while the category of similarity is fundamental for Greek mimesis, Biblical *akoloutheo* refers to a final goal: salvation. Finally, although *akoloutheo* is strictly associated with the sphere of *sacrum*, it is rooted in everyday experience. Unlike *akoloutheo*, *mimeisthai* remains separated from reality, which inevitably leads to the creation of illusion and substitutes of real life. In Greek culture imitation doubled life; in the Bible following God was regarded as the essence of human existence. Mitosek maintains further that for Thomas à Kempis being a Christian means listening to Christ's voice and following in His footsteps (179–180). À Kempis presents a human being as *homo viator*, at the same time stressing the fact that the journey of life, which is marked by hardships, difficulties and suffering, resembles the Way of the Cross. The author of *De*

1.2. Variations on Triangular Desire   61

imitatione Christi also emphasizes the importance of words, praising them much higher than visual images. He perceives images as imitations of God and contrasts them with the symbolic significance of words, regarded as the emanation of divinity. His book is therefore an artistic collection of various quotations from the Bible, in which each word is a manifestation of God's presence and should be viewed as His footstep. Thus, imitating Christ means listening to His words, acting in accordance with them and, as a result, following in His footsteps throughout one's whole life in order to attain salvation. Both in the Bible and in *De imitatione Christi*, words serve as visible signs of the invisible presence of the Guide, helping human beings not to get lost during their journey of life. In her article, Mitosek also points out that à Kempis reduces the importance of sight and highlights the audible contact (185), claiming that listening is strictly associated with being obedient.

In the final part of her article, Mitosek describes the imitation of Jesus Christ as "unifying mimesis" [*mimesis jednocząca*]. She argues that in the Christian mimesis there is neither rivalry nor antagonism; on the contrary, the whole community that follows Christ is united by the common goal, attaining salvation, and by constant being on the way in search of Christ's footsteps (192). She juxtaposes "unifying mimesis" with "antagonistic mimesis" [*mimesis antagonistyczna*], as defined by Girard in his book entitled *The Violence and the Sacred*. According to Mitosek, in Girard's theory there is no bond with others in common admiration of the model, but only the essential mimetic rivalry, which can be described as a desire to eliminate all rivals and to appropriate the model that is imitated (192). Hence, Girard's model differs considerably from the Christian dogma.

The theses posed by Mitosek may be applied in the interpretation of the nature of Philip Vanderdecken's and Pilot Schriften's internal mediation. Both of them are subjects who desire for Captain Vanderdecken's soul and choose Jesus Christ as their mediator. Philip, who is ready to sacrifice himself in order to fulfill his father's will, wants to live in accordance with the Gospel. His imitation of Christ should be regarded as Biblical *akoloutheo,* that is following in Christ's footsteps. The nature of Schriften's imitation is completely different. As a demonic character, the Pilot does not know Christ; therefore, he seeks His presence in young Vanderdecken. As Philip is for him a Christ-like figure, Schriften constantly observes the young man with his left eye (an action which can be regarded as a mockery of God defined by Marsilio Ficino as the *oculus infinitus*) and tries to imitate, or rather mock, Philip's actions. The Pilot's imitation of Christ is then Greek *mimeisthai,* as investigated by Mitosek in her article. Schriften's imitation of the mediator, who is not present, is a representation based on illusion. By contrast, Philip follows the mediator who is spiritually present in his life. In order not to get lost on the way, Philip reads Christ's signs and tries to comprehend them. He regards written words, for instance his father's letter or, metaphorically, Schriften himself, as visible footsteps of the invisible mediator. Pilot Schriften, a "misleading" written sign, is therefore to be read and interpreted by Philip; young

Vanderdecken, by contrast, is to be observed but never comprehended by the Pilot. Schriften, who is described as a huge watery eye with the rest of the small body attached to it, is a voyeur, who wants to look without being seen. As he is capable only of looking and unable to make any profound analysis, Philip's self-sacrificial actions, which the Pilot tries to mock, will always remain inscrutable to him. Philip's imitation of Christ exemplifies the "unifying mimesis" because he does not treat Schriften as his rival. Young Vanderdecken is surprised when he discovers that the Pilot and himself are not united by the same goal. While Philip desires to save his father's soul, Schriften wants to annihilate the young man, whom he sees as an antagonist, and to appropriate Captain Vanderdecken's soul. In Marryat's novel, Schriften represents the "antagonistic mimesis."

Continuing his analysis of various aspects of the triangular nature of desire, Girard maintains that metaphysical desire is strictly associated with internal mediation, as in the case of external mediation the desired object, being purely physical, has hardly any metaphysical value. The researcher claims further that the transition from external to internal mediation entails the evolution from a concrete towards an abstract desire (Girard 87). In order to interpret the nature of Vanderdecken's desire, Girard's theses need to be modified. Although the Captain is the subject of external mediation, the metaphysical aspect of his desire is crucial for the interpretation of the novel. Girard ventures a statement that resorting to another mediator inevitably entails a metamorphosis of the hero (91). William Vanderdecken may serve as a good illustration of this thesis, as he definitely does not remain an unbroken unity throughout the novel. When the Captain is transformed into the Flying Dutchman, it is not only his name and ontological status that are changed, but also, and most importantly, his personality, character and his outlook on the nature of God. The "atomization of the personality" (92), to quote Girard, is the final stage of Vanderdecken's external mediation. The moment in which he loses his unity coincides with the breakdown of the external mediation and marks the beginning of a new stage of his desire – he chooses a different mediator. Interestingly enough, in the Captain's case the transition from one to yet another external mediation does not happen successively, but is preceded by the seventeen-year-long seafaring.

1.3. The Flying Dutchman's Progress: A Christian Metaphor

To illustrate the purifying journey of the Captain's soul, leading to the port of eternal salvation, Marryat alludes to a Christian version of the *peregrinatio vitae* metaphor, applied, among others, by John Bunyan. In his novel the doomed sailor represents a Christian *homo viator*, whose pilgrimage, fraught with danger and suffering, has an expiatory character. The sailor's symbolic journey towards eternal peace is evocative of Coleridge's lyrical ballad, already mentioned in this chapter, which

1.3. The Flying Dutchman's Progress: A Christian Metaphor 63

may be interpreted as Marryat's response to Coleridge's romantic vision. It is indeed very striking how similar the two authors are in their fictional visions of the redemptive aspect of wandering. Both the Mariner and the Captain start their cruises in union with nature and then rebel against it at a certain point. Moreover, the ontological status of the two sea-farers is not clearly stated. Although the Mariner claims that he is alive, the Wedding Guest has the impression that the old sailor is either a ghost coming back from the dead or a demonic spirit. The Flying Dutchman of *The Phantom Ship* defines his state as death-in-life. Furthermore, both works operate on an interpenetration of two spheres: the visible and the invisible one. Finally, a parallel should be made between the physical voyage and the spiritual experience of both the Mariner and the Captain.

In the *Biographia Literaria* of 1817, Coleridge emphasizes the fact that *The Rime of the Ancient Mariner* should not be regarded as a mere Gothic tale, as it belongs to symbolist and idealistic poetry. Coleridge felt disappointed that *The Rime of the Ancient Mariner* was misunderstood and neglected in its symbolic aspect. In his introduction to *Twentieth Century Interpretations of* The Rime of the Ancient Mariner, James D. Boulger, stressing the religious character of the Mariner's journey, claims that the meaning of the poem is strictly associated with the theme of guilt, punishment and salvation (Boulger 7). He regards the Mariner as a Christian skeptic and the poem as an illustration of the problem of knowing and truth-seeking (8–9). According to Boulger, the main body of the poem is a product of pure imagination and has the logic of a dream (10). He argues that the reader may be identified with the Wedding Guest, who appears in the central section of the poem, and tries in vain to explain rationally the phantasmagoric world presented in Coleridge's ballad. Only when the reader accepts the fact that the poem should be understood by the means of imagination, will he/she be able to perceive *The Rime of the Ancient Mariner* as a romantic vision with a religious dimension.

At the very beginning of the poem, the difference between the logical world of the land and the imaginative world of the sea is emphasized. The Wedding Guest, a reasonable man, will never fully participate in the Mariner's dreamlike reality of the voyage at sea, unless he distances himself from the world of logic on land. Similarly, the Flying Dutchman's voyage, which also takes place at phantasmagoric sea, should be understood as a romantic vision with a Christian aspect. Both in the poem and in Marryat's novel, noise and gaiety of the land are replaced by the world of pure imagination, reflected in the white and undisturbed mirror of the sea. *The Rime of the Ancient Mariner* operates on unusual combinations of colours and sounds, unacceptable in the world of waking consciousness, but perfectly preparing the reader to discover the religious dimension of the poem (Boulger 13). The essence of the Mariner's journey into the unknown is the acceptance of the unknowable as such. Moreover, while describing the Flying Dutchman's wandering into the unknown, Marryat does not present weight or size of the portrayed objects, especially the phantom ship, but rather utilizes colour and light imagery. It is particularly the appearance of the sea and its phantasmagoric quality that are the most significant not only for Coleridge, but also for Marryat. As the sea is hardly ever described as deep or vast, both authors, operating on colour and light, do not concentrate on realistic descriptions, but on phantasmagoric images.

In his introduction, Boulger also maintains that in the poem the return to the destined harbour symbolizes "a return to the ordinary world of sense realism and conventional order, and requires an adjustment of Imagination to Reason again" (18). However, in *The Phantom Ship* imagination does not adjust to reason, as in Marryat's novel the wanderer never reaches the harbour. The Mariner committed a sin and was punished at sea; thus, his redemption took place in the world of imagination, connected with limitless freedom, and has therefore no status on land, often associated with stability of home and logical thinking. The Mariner's request for Christian absolution on land may be interpreted as the necessity of his adjustment to the world of common sense. In Marryat's novel, Captain Vanderdecken similarly sins and does penance at sea. Unlike the Mariner, however, Vanderdecken does not have to seek absolution on land, because he finds aspersion in oceanic waters. Boulger regards the Mariner as "the living proof of a more serious and deeper moral order than ours" (19), and his voyage into "the seas of the Imagination" (19) as much more significant than the waking reality of the world of reason.

The Rime of the Ancient Mariner and *The Phantom Ship* differ in yet another respect. The Mariner regards his staying on land as a death-in-life state; the Flying Dutchman, by contrast, remains suspended between life and death while wandering at sea. Boulger points out that due to his being alienated from deepest dreamlike reality and forced to come back to the death-in-life world of reason, the Mariner suffers enormously (18–19). If it were not for presenting his haunting vision and spinning his nautical yarn, he would not be able to exist on land. The moment he says "There was a ship," the Mariner enters the world of imagination and finds relief from his suffering. Unlike Coleridge's character, neither Vanderdecken nor Ahab can soothe the unbearable pain by recounting their stories to the audience. The former's adventures are narrated by a third-person omniscient narrator, whereas the latter's by Ishmael, the central consciousness of *Moby Dick*, who witnessed both Ahab's and the *Pequod*'s tragedy.

In his essay entitled "A Poem of Pure Imagination: An Experiment in Reading," Robert Penn Warren interprets Coleridge's poem as "a story of crime, punishment and reconciliation" (21). Warren also considers the nature of the Mariner's transgression and regards the act of killing the Albatross as symbolic. He argues that in Coleridge's poem the individual becomes a responsible agent, fully aware of his actions (Warren 25) and claims that the unmotivated killing of the bird, which can be perceived as a Christian emblem, is a result of the Mariner's "Satanic pride and rebellious self-idolatry" (26). It is staggering *hubris* that makes the Mariner, Captain Vanderdecken and Captain Ahab so remarkably similar to each other. Warren interprets the Mariner's act as a crime not only against nature, but also against

God, stressing the religious significance of this deed. In the poem the cross, an ennobling religious symbol, is removed from the Mariner's neck to be replaced by the dead Albatross, a physical object rather than a symbol, connected with a defilement of beauty. There is a difference, however, in the nature of the crimes committed by the Mariner and Captain Vanderdecken. According to Warren, the Mariner's transgression is above all against the imagination. Therefore, he is punished with the penance of solitude, regarded as a "denial" of imagination, and horror, regarded as a "perversion" of imagination (36). Although the Captain is also punished with solitude and horror, his transgression seems to be much more severe, as it has moral rather than aesthetic dimensions. Defiling the creature associated with bringing peace and harmony, the Mariner sins indirectly against the Creator. By contrast, nature is not involved in Vanderdecken's blasphemy – it is aimed directly at God.

In the fourth part of his article, Warren underlines a *lux-tenebrae* dichotomy in the poem. He maintains that a contrast between moonlight and sunlight is significant in the poem. In *The Rime of the Ancient Mariner* the moonlight changes waking reality into a phantasmagoric vision and is associated with the friendly bird, the Albatross. All stages of the Mariner's redeeming process take place in the moonlight: there, he recognizes love and beauty, blesses the water snakes and frees himself from the curse. The sunlight, by contrast, has negative connotations in Coleridge's poem: it is the Mariner's killing the Albatross that brings the sun (29–31). In *The Phantom Ship* the order is reversed, as Marryat equals the positive and the certain with the day and the uncertain with the night. In Marryat's novel, which adheres to the Gothic convention, horror always comes in the moonlight.

In *The Phantom Ship*, the sea appears as the symbol of purification. Although the imagery associated with the ocean seems to be one of a powerful and cruel enemy, the monotony of the spiritual isolation at sea has a positive influence on the Flying Dutchman. It is within sea space that Vanderdecken commits his sin, does his penance and becomes redeemed. The ambivalence of the sea is an important aspect of Marryat's sea novel. It is the vastness of the sea that makes the Captain feel uncomfortable and that forces him to confront his loneliness. There is a correspondence between the image of the sea in Marryat's novel and that of the land of ice in Coleridge's poem. Although both appear to be awe-inspiring manifestations of nature, indifferent or even hostile to man, their positive influence on the Captain and the Mariner is undeniable. It is from the land of ice that comes the friendly bird, helping the seamen to endure their loneliness, and it is oceanic water that purifies the Flying Dutchman. Unfortunately, he fails to comprehend the healing nature of the sea.

Vanderdecken's obsessive desire to go round the Cape of Good Hope at any cost may be interpreted as a sadistic act towards the sea. It seems that at the beginning the Flying Dutchman regards his eternal voyage on the phantom ship as the revenge of the sea. He is, however, mistaken. In the chapter of *Deceit, Desire and the Novel* entitled "Masochism and Sadism," Girard defines the masochist as a person who "perceives the necessary relation between unhappiness and metaphysical desire, but […] nevertheless does not renounce his desire" (Girard 177). The researcher maintains that instead of abandoning misdirected transcendence, the masochist "tries paradoxically to satisfy his desire by rushing toward the obstacle, thus making his destiny one of misery and failure" (179). A closer examination of Captain Vanderdecken reveals then that he is a person tormented by masochism. Although he is aware of the connection between his desire and its disastrous results, he does not want to give it up. By contrast, he even desires for an obstacle. In his case it is the incomprehensible and all-powerful sea which he wants to master. Girard stresses that "[t]he impassioned person is seeking the divine through this insuperable obstacle" (182) which cannot be crossed by definition. In order to gain God's omnipotence and omniscience, Vanderdecken is ready to accept not only shame and humiliation, but also self-destruction. The Captain's desire to be God's equal thus tends towards masochism. As Vanderdecken is aware that he is too powerless to master the sea, he starts to hate himself for his weakness.

In his analysis, Girard emphasizes also the masochistic-sadistic structure of metaphysical desire. He claims that sadism is always preceded by masochism and "is the 'dialectical' reverse of masochism. Tired of playing the part of the martyr, the desiring subject chooses to become the tormentor" (184). The Captain begins to be cruel towards the sea, as "the sadist's violence is yet another effort to attain divinity" (185). Vanderdecken persecutes the sea because he knows that it is infinitely superior to him. In his staggering *hubris*, the Captain is unable to tolerate any superiority and is completely unaware of the redeeming role of the sea. It is the ocean that, using Percival's words, changes a demonic sufferer into an essentially religious person (110). Reconciling himself with the sea, the Captain is then able to beg for the reconciliation with the divine creator. Indeed, oceanic water not only purifies the Flying Dutchman from his sin, but also changes his nature, as during his eternal seafaring he shares the destiny of water. In his book entitled *Water and Dreams*, Gaston Bachelard emphasizes the fact that "[a] being dedicated to water is a being in flux. He dies every minute; something of his substance is constantly falling away" (6). Bachelard's statement seems to perfectly describe the Flying Dutchman, "a being dedicated to water."

It is the shapelessness of water that makes it multifaceted and unpredictable. Since time immemorial it has symbolized all that is not fully shaped and has been also associated with myths of the genesis. In the archetypal image of the sea, its waters represent primordial chaos, and are often presented as an enormous pre-ocean (Górnicki 18). Perceived as an incarnation of evil forces, the pre-ocean was immersed in silence and darkness, which connoted the gloom of the night prevailing before the creation of the world. In the Old Testament, the mysterious sea created by God, at first as rebellious and insubordinate, and then defeated and mastered by the Almighty, represents His power and strength. Moreover, in the New Testament God, by calming down the infuriated waves and walking on the surface

1.3. The Flying Dutchman's Progress: A Christian Metaphor 67

of the water, symbolically manifests His domination over evil. Interestingly, in the Bible each storm may be interpreted as the sea's act of rebellion against the order and the harmony established by God (27). The rebellious nature of the ocean is highlighted in Zdzisław Górnicki's book entitled *Woda w duchowych przeżyciach człowieka* [*Water in the Spiritual Life of Humans*]. Górnicki emphasizes that the sea belongs to the so-called "lower waters" which, because of their demonic nature, are commonly associated with evil, danger and fear. Jean Delumeau also defines the sea as "a privileged *itinerarium* of demons" (Delumeau 43). Illustrating a practice of performing exorcisms over the infuriated sea, Delumeau gives an example of Portuguese sailors who during a storm recited the Prologue to the Gospel of St. John, or Spanish seamen plunging relics of the saints into the waves. Only after such rituals were they able to overcome their fear and to continue the voyage at sea, an incarnation of evil and sin.

It is significant, however, that the demonic waters may acquire a sacred significance in the hands of God. Blessed by the Lord and at the same time devoid of its negative connotations, water can represent a transition from the sphere of *profanum* to the sphere of *sacrum*. The purgatorial nature of aspersion is stressed by Bachelard: "It is because water has an inner power that it can purify the inner being, that it can give back to the sinful soul the whiteness of snow. He who has been sprinkled physically is cleansed morally" (142). Similarly, Górnicki stresses the significance of ablution, a practice that washes away not only the dirt of the body, but, more importantly, the dirt of the soul. He gives an example of exorcized baptismal water which, having the power to nullify all sins, becomes a symbol of innocence, sanctity and divinity. In his analysis, Górnicki also maintains that because of its purifying and renewing nature, blessed water gives the possibility of leaving behind one's sinful past and opens the perspective of a new beginning. It is blessed water that brings spiritual rebirth and becomes a visible sign of God's invisible grace during baptism. Interestingly, Górnicki underlines that the Greek word *baptizein* and the Latin word *baptismus* denote immersion (a destruction of the past) and purification (a creation of a new life). Therefore, the liturgy of baptism emphasizes three main aspects of water: its power to destroy, to redeem and to create (Górnicki 115). The researcher also observes that sometimes salt is added to blessed water in order to strengthen its purifying quality. Symbolizing a new beginning and immortality, salt is believed to frighten evil forces and to remind a baptized person of a covenant with God. It is also worth noting that while blessed water represents the Lord's blessing, salt stands for bitterness of penance leading to redemption (117).

The sea portrayed in *The Phantom Ship* combines the symbolism of water and salt, representing bitterness of purifying penance leading to redemption. Beyond the veil of the material sea, there seems to exist some kind of superior, seemingly demonic, reality. Oceanic waters presented in the novel resemble the Biblical shapeless and rebellious chaos mastered by Yahweh. Immersed in impenetrable darkness and mysteriously silent, the ocean in Marryat's novel meets Burkean requirements of the sublime, already defined in the introductory chapter. Fascinating and frightening, the sea presented by Marryat, like the mythological pre-ocean, seems to be a domain of evil forces. It induces not only terror, but also astonishment and its lower degrees: admiration, reverence, and respect (Burke 53). In my opinion, however, the Captain's experience extends beyond the domain of the Burkean sublime. It seems to me that in Marryat's novel sublimity results not only in psychological reactions, but also in what I would like to call "a post-epiphanic reflection," revealing both a philosophical and a spiritual dimension of existence. Hence, in Marryat's novel sublimity operates as a source not only of moral elevation, but also of religious awakening.

A correspondence between sublimity and Christianity is stressed by Coleridge in his letter to Josiah Wedgwood from 1799. The English poet declares there that Christianity, operating upon "Hopes and Fears purely individual" and encouraging its believers to seek "an obscure and indefinite Vastness" is much more sublime than the religions of Greece and Rome (quoted in Wilczyński 176). Indeed, for Vanderdecken the sublime enhanced by the sea is the evidence of divinity. Suspended between life and death, that is being in an appropriate distance from a threatening phenomenon and at the same time observing the principal safety condition of the Burkean sublime, the Flying Dutchman seems to be more astonished than terrified. "Vacuity, Darkness, Solitude, and Silence" (Burke 65) of the sea turn out to be a revelation of the divine, elevating the Captain to a higher level of understanding. Stressing religious associations evoked in the novel, Błaszak calls Marryat's treatment of the sea "mythical-religious or Christian" (Błaszak 228). Indeed, associated with demonic forces and regarded as a means of punishment, Marryat's sea seems to resemble Styx, "whose heavy waters are burdened with evil" (Bachelard 140). Thus, examining the nature of evil waters, Bachelard writes:

> The barks loaded with souls are always on the point of sinking. It is an astonishing image, in which Death is afraid of dying, in which a drowned man is still afraid of shipwreck. Death is a journey which never ends, an infinite perspective filled with dangers. If the weight overloading the boat is so great, it is because the souls are heavy with sin. Charon's bark always goes to Hades. (79)

It should be noted, however, that unlike Charon's bark, the Flying Dutchman's vessel does not go to Hades. Although referred to as Devil's Ship, heavy with sin and accompanied by atmospheric phenomena such as immensely dark clouds, obscuring visibility, or flashes of lightning, illuminating the impenetrable gloom around, the doomed captain's ghost ship, paradoxical as it may seem, sails to Celestial Jerusalem. The Flying Dutchman's peregrination by water, which contributes to the Captain's religious awakening, is evocative of John Bunyan's *The Pilgrim's Progress* (1678). Despite some obvious differences, for instance that Bunyan's work illustrates the explicit Protestant theology, while Marryat is faithful to the Catholic doctrine, both authors are similar in that they allegorize the journey of life leading to the final bliss. Indeed, everlasting wandering stimulates the Flying Dutchman's progress and brings him salvation. Doomed to roam the seas forever, Vanderdecken, once blinded by his enthusiasm, optimism and apparent greatness, no longer refuses to believe in his littleness and insignificance. Perfectly illustrating the ruined Captain's condition, Marian Stala writes:

> To perceive oneself in this way, as a dead man, [...] means above all to reject, to cross out, to annul the whole life or its significant part. It means also to accept the suffering strictly associated with such an annulment and to cope with the abyss which replaces all that used to exist and now is no more. It means further to look at oneself not only from the inside, but also from an infinite distance which appears as a result of living in emptiness, in suffering, in the vicinity of death. It means, finally, to realize that the life which has been rejected (lost? marked by failure?) is not the only way of existing. (Stala 72 – my translation)

Rejecting his former existence and repudiating his desire for power, the Captain is able to look at himself from what Stala calls "the perspective of a dead man" [*perspektywa trupa*]. As he is now a man whose great past is lying in ruins, the Flying Dutchman may be regarded as an incarnation of humiliated pride. Significantly, in Christian symbolism ruins stand not only for fall and destruction, but, representing chances of revival, they are not devoid of a consolatory aspect. A man whose life has been ruined is given a possibility of freeing himself from certain forms, which used to enslave him, towards a new dimension of existence (Królikiewicz 17). Such a possibility is given to the Flying Dutchman at sea.

The sea in Marryat's novel, black and silent, is apparently a manifestation of the darkness of the underworld or a domain of the Greek goddess Nemesis, perceived as the spirit of divine retribution against those who succumb to *hubris*: insolence, arrogance and pride. Remorseless Nemesis personifies vengeful fate, and is zealous in re-establishing order and proportion through the punishment of excess in pride and undeserved happiness. Interestingly, the sea, one of the most common *loci communes* of sublimity, does not operate in Marryat's narrative as a source of destruction. In *The Phantom Ship*, the ocean is therefore much more than just a means of punishment. The sea, once defied by Vanderdecken, now becomes for him a manifestation of infinity and eternity, causing the doomed captain to feel God's presence. Indifferent, insensitive and even openly hostile as the sea seems to be, its vast expanses make the lives of seafaring men appear transient, insignificant and of little value. In Marryat's novel, it is oceanic water that enhances reflection and forces the Captain to define himself in confrontation with two infinities represented by the sea, that is time and space. Unchanging and imperishable as the sea is, this powerful force is contrasted with human beings characterized by instability and brevity. Unlike short-lived humans and ships, the sea is not only as malicious and cruel as death, but it resembles this phenomenon in yet another respect: the ocean has existed since time immemorial and will last eternally. Therefore, in *The*

Phantom Ship the sea is presented as an antivanitative element triumphing over *vanitas*.

Although in Marryat's novel the sea functions apparently both as a place and as a symbol, I would argue that it is realized almost exclusively as symbol. The sea serves as a condition of purification, just as purgatory, which, according to the Roman Catholic religion, is not a place, but a condition in which the souls of dead people expiate their sins and are made pure by suffering in preparation for Heaven. I fully agree with Błaszak's claims that in Marryat's novel the sea "bear[s] distinct relation to Christian symbolism" (Błaszak 223), being portrayed "as a purgatory for a sinful soul" (226). Although the darkness of the nocturnal sea seems to symbolize evil, pessimism, a lack of hope, and approaching death, Marryat focuses on a positive aspect of the nocturnal time, stressing its epistemological function. Reminding "the proud and greedy man of his own insignificance and transitoriness" (Błaszak 239), the apparently demonic sea makes the Flying Dutchman wiser, stifles his pride and leads to his profound *metanoia*.

Apart from the sea's blackness also its silence deserves attention. Exploring the silence that purifies and speaks, Górnicki draws a parallel between the sea and the desert. He claims that both at sea and in the desert God causes human beings to particularly experience His presence (Górnicki 144). Directing solitary wanderers towards religious contemplation leading to purification, the sea and the desert stimulate spiritual growth. Additionally, a solitary contemplative voyage resembles the so-called "experience of the desert" in that its silence speaks with three imperatives: *intra totus* (enter entirely), *mane solus* (remain alone), *exi alius* (exit changed). Not only does the deadly silent mirror-like sea symbolize the suspension of the Captain's spiritual state, but it may also reflect the Captain's acceptance of his apparently undeserved fate. Serving as an epiphanic instrument which reveals the truth concerning fragility of existence, the placid mirror of the sea encourages reflection and self-examination. Looking at the undisturbed surface of the ocean, the doomed captain, no longer an agent of events, but a passive participant, becomes an incarnation of reflection. After the seventeen-year-long sea voyage, the *vita activa* of Captain Vanderdecken, "rebel and outcast, champion of mankind and sinner, one who knows no compromise, [and] who strives for the forbidden" (Błaszak 160) is transformed into the *vita contemplativa* of the Flying Dutchman, a repentant Christian propagating ideals of hope, humility and forgiveness (156). The Captain's solitary pilgrimage at sea changes him so considerably that after seventeen years he is able to definitely reject the slavery of Satan's external mediation. No longer a victim of triangular desire, he becomes an incarnation of spontaneity. Due to the fact that in Biblical symbolism number seven stands for "perfection," "peace," "wisdom," "fulfillment," and "victory," it can be said that during his seventeen-year-long wandering the Captain gains wisdom, achieves perfection and finds fulfillment in the peace of death, marking his victory over mimetic desire.

1.3. The Flying Dutchman's Progress: A Christian Metaphor

In conclusion to his *Deceit, Desire, and the Novel,* Girard states that "[t]he ultimate meaning of desire is death but death is not the novel's ultimate meaning" (290). Underlying an optimistic aspect of some of Dostoyevsky's conclusions, Girard states that they may be regarded as "fresh beginnings; a new life commences, either among men or in eternity" (291). He also claims that the conclusions of Dostoyevsky's novels portray the conversion of solitary heroes, as, renouncing their false conviction of being divinely autonomous, they consciously resort to others. Girard concludes that it is the ability to look one's "nothingness in the face" (294) that leads to "the death of pride" (294), at the same time bringing an end both to mimetic desire and mimetic rivalry. He optimistically finishes his account by providing a set of binary oppositions marking the hero's liberation from the deception of mimetic desire. Faithful to the rhetoric of enslavement used throughout his book, Girard concludes:

> In renouncing divinity the hero renounces slavery. Every level of his existence is inverted, all the effects of metaphysical desire are replaced by contrary effects. Deception gives way to truth, anguish to remembrance, agitation to repose, hatred to love, humiliation to humility, mediated desire to autonomy, deviated transcendence to vertical transcendence. (294)

This is exactly what happens at the end of Marryat's novel as well. Presenting a character who triumphs over metaphysical desire in a seemingly Apocalyptic conclusion, the ending of *The Phantom Ship* is not deprived of a redemptive aspect. The image of an albatross peacefully falling asleep, standing for atonement for sin and restoration of natural order, may be regarded as the exact opposite of the dead white bird hanging over the Mariner's neck in Coleridge's poem, connoting sin and violation of natural order. Highly significant, the final scene is also saturated with Biblical symbolism of renewal, suggesting that a catastrophe is not an inevitable conclusion of mimetic desire. In the Captain's case, "the absurd project of self-divinization" (Girard 286) does not lead to self-destruction. His final gesture of self-denial, as well as Philip's self-sacrifice, nullify the blasphemy and save the doomed captain from everlasting perdition. It should also be noted that Philip, a traveler-pilgrim "of evangelical proportions" (Błaszak 249), releases not only his father, but also Schriften, who turns out to be the ghost of the mutinous pilot who was struck by Vanderdecken, fell overboard and drowned. Willing to lead Philip to destruction and to prevent his taking the Holy Cross to his father, Schriften is saved by the Christ-like magnanimity of the young sailor. No longer seeking revenge, the Pilot finally finds the peace of death. Moreover, Schriften's eye is significant in the final scene. Unlike the Mariner's fellow seamen, who all die cursing him with their eyes, the Pilot, before falling into dust, blesses Philip not only with words, but also with his one eye.

Repudiating his self-centeredness, in the concluding scene the Captain, like his son, becomes a figure "of evangelical proportions," as he not only finds his way back to God, but also embraces others, both in the literal and metaphorical sense.

The image of the father tightly holding the son aboard his phantom ship is evocative of Christian reconciliation of opposites, symbolized by the cross (Cirlot 209). Likewise, the wooden mast of the Captain's vessel with the yard lying crosswise, submerging in the purifying oceanic water, suggest the symbolism of the token of suffering and triumph (Forstner 339). The mast, resembling the vertical part of the cross, seems to connect heaven and earth, whereas the yard, representing the horizontal part, stands for unity between the self and the other. Interestingly, yet another cross appears in this highly symbolic scene. When the phantom ship sinks slowly under the sparkling water, the sky is suddenly illuminated by a lighting cross which may symbolically cross out the Captain's mimetic desire. Indeed, like Dostoyevsky's characters examined by Girard, the Flying Dutchman "is hurled from the summit of pride into the abyss of shame" (Girard 277). Strikingly, Wilczyński observes that it is the abyss that may be regarded as "an emblem of transcendence" (Wilczyński 47) and holds that the fathomless perspective of the oceanic water, being a manifestation of the sublime, may appear as "absolute becoming which defies any mimetic paradigm" (49). In the concluding scene, the Captain finally frees himself from the slavery of mimetic desire. No longer a human marionette and a victim of metaphysical desire, he replaces his craving for limitlessness with an acceptance of his finiteness. His almost mystic experience of God's presence at sea leads to his reaching a stage of non-desire.

CHAPTER TWO
Mimetic Form Versus Spontaneous Life: J. F. Cooper's *The Red Rover* (1828)

Looking at *The Red Rover* through the lens of Girard's rhetoric, one can argue that the protagonist of Cooper's novel, like Captain Vanderdecken of *The Phantom Ship*, is enslaved by desire. In their pride and avoidance of self-examination, both protagonists are deceived by illusory autonomy and remain completely unaware of the mimetic nature of their lives. Both may also be regarded as victims: while the Faustian William Vanderdecken is a slave of mimetic desire, the quixotic Red Rover seems to be a prisoner of form, as defined by Luigi Pirandello in his remarkable essay entitled *L'umorismo* (1908). In *L'umorismo* Pirandello, a famous Italian playwright, novelist and literary critic, investigates the antagonism between life, which is changeable and fluid, and form, which is a set of stable norms. According to Pirandello, a continual, spontaneous flow of life is forced to enter determined and stable forms, finally becoming imprisoned in them. Nevertheless, the flow continues as an internal life, powerful enough to destroy all fictitious forms imposed upon it. In his essay, Pirandello presents also a humoristic attitude towards reality, consisting in an ability to penetrate the ridiculous surface of form in order to detect the stifled flow of life. It is not accidental, according to Donato Santeramo, that having outlined the concept of *l'umorismo*, Pirandello explores Cervantes as one of pre-eminent humorists, as this author managed to combine perfectly the comic and the tragic. Santeramo claims that although the adventures of Don Quixote seem to be ridiculous, the reader is unable to laugh. Apparently comic, Cervantes' story may also arouse compassion and melancholy, and is thus not devoid of a tragic aspect (Santeramo 23).

Remarkably, apart from Pirandello, much later Girard and Auerbach investigated the figure of Don Quixote as well. Unlike Girard, who refers to the example of *Don Quixote* to outline the theory of the triangular nature of mimetic desire, Auerbach explores the representation of reality in Cervantes' masterpiece and the protagonist's distorted perception thereof. In the chapter entitled "The Enchanted Dulcinea," Auerbach examines the striking contrast between Don Quixote's illusion and ordinary reality. According to the author of *Mimesis*, Cervantes' work, even though it seems to be overwhelmingly comic, is in fact "sad, bitter, and almost tragic" (Auerbach 339). Auerbach, like Pirandello, insists that *Don Quixote* is not fully tragic, as "both tragedy and cure are circumvented" (340) in the explored text. Auerbach stresses further the importance of a momentary illumination, a shock, that leads to gaining awareness of one's condition and to becoming disillusioned with reality. It is awareness that may cause either utter despair or immediate liberation from illusions. Auerbach claims, however, that Don Quixote finds a solution which prevents him from becoming aware of the sharp contrast between his fictitious world and reality: he consciously avoids any self-examination, and is therefore completely ignorant of the mimetic nature of his existence. As the lack of self-awareness excludes any possible shift into the tragic, the mad knight is but a ridiculous puppet on the stage of the theatre of the world. Overwhelmed by his desire for chivalry and by imitation of the model of Amadis, not only is Don Quixote ridiculous, but he also arouses sympathy. Transforming the real world into a performance and, at the same, time remaining unaware of his own role-playing, the protagonist is an outcast from the well-ordered theatrical reality. In the reality that "willingly cooperates with a play which dresses it up differently every moment" (Auerbach 351), Don Quixote seems to be the only one to reject such a cooperation.

Interestingly, the Red Rover, the protagonist of Cooper's novel, may be interpreted as a quixotic figure, described by Pirandello as "out of tune" [*fuori di chiave*]. Indeed, his obsessive desire to free America from the British supremacy may be regarded as the folly to which he remains faithful, resembling Don Quixote's fixed idea of knight-errantry. The Rover seems to be the only one who rejects the cooperation with the well-ordered theatrical reality, and who stands in conflict with accepted conventions. The aim of this chapter is therefore to analyze the theatricality of the Red Rover's life. Although he is a prisoner of form, wearing a collection of masks, and unconsciously accepting role-playing as his identity, he dreams of autonomy. I seek to present Cooper's protagonist as a Byronic figure imprisoned in his role of a pirate who, during a masquerade aboard his ship – which may be evocative of the Bakhtinian carnival – experiences epiphany of life. The aim of this chapter is also to examine Cooper's novel, in which the narrator describes the narrative in terms of a theatrical performance, applying Pirandello's theory of form/life opposition. His statements on the superficiality of existence, the artificiality of role-playing, and man's strenuous efforts to gain freedom from all masks may be seen to bear directly upon Cooper's novel. The Red Rover, struggling with a variety of fabricated images, through which he seeks authenticity, is indeed similar to Pirandello's theatrical characters, who, immersed in the fictitious world of their own ideas, experience a disintegration of personality in confrontation with reality. Since the Italian dramatist and critic formulated his theory after Cooper's death and was not familiar with Cooper's novel, the affinity between them cannot be viewed in terms of a direct influence. Still, Pirandello's dichotomy of form and life may be quite illuminating in an analysis of *The Red Rover*, as he proposes his own version of *theatrum mundi*, showing critical potential of this topos. However, it is worth noting that the metaphor of the theatre of the world had already had a long history before Pirandello created his substantially modified variation on this topos and incorporated its notion in *L'umorismo*.

2.1. The History of the Topos of *Theatrum Mundi*

In the introduction to her book *Theatrum Mundi: The History of an Idea*, Lynda Christian states that "[t]he comparison of the world to a stage and of life to a play is one of the most enduring of all the commonplaces of European literature" (VII). The basis for this metaphor is the assumption of a fundamental opposition existing between two spheres: the divine and the earthly. Although the director of the play of life varies from one modification of the topos to another, one aspect is common to all variations: an all-powerful being much greater than man seems to direct the performance of life, cast the roles, and control whether human actors fulfill the foreordained parts. This powerful force, be it Fortune, God, or fate, thwarts all futile attempts of the human actors, who try to reject the *profanum* of the lower sphere, to usurp the role of the director of the play of life, and to enter the *sacrum* of the higher sphere.

The *theatrum mundi* metaphor has its origins in antiquity, together with theatres and acting. Greek writers of the time in which drama became a popular genre, started to notice a relationship between life and a theatrical performance. The idea was frequently used in the writings of classical philosophers as well. Although Heraclitus did not leave any specific statement regarding *theatrum mundi*, his formulation of *logos* has close connections with the idea of a human actor who plays in a performance directed by a kind of Necessity. Heraclitus calls *logos* the director of the play acted out by men on the stage of the world. As *logos* is Necessity, people must play the roles assigned to them by the creator of the performance. Apart from acting, it is also possible for people – the actors – to contemplate the parts which they are bound to play and to serve as models to follow for human spectators (3).

According to Jadwiga Kotarska, it is Plato who should be given the first place in the history of the topos (Kotarska 5). Similarly, Lynda Christian underlines the fact that Plato's "contribution to the history and development of the topos" cannot be denied (Chistian 6). In *Timaeus,* Plato calls the creator of the world the *Demiourgos* or artisan, making a comparison between God's creative work and artistic creativity. In the later uses of the topos, the Platonic idea of God the demiurge evolves, and the name *demiourgos* is replaced by that of *poetes*, usually translated as "the playwright." Christian observes, however, that the Greek word combines the idea of "maker" and that of "artistic creator." Therefore, the concept of *demiourgos* is implicit in that of *poetes* (7). In his other works, such as *Laws* or *Philebus*, Plato formulates a conception of man as a plaything of the gods. Human actors are compared to puppets, whose strings are pulled by Olympian gods, and whose actions are dependent on the caprices of the deities. The roles are assigned to human puppets, and capricious gods toy with people-actors just for fun. In the theological variety of the metaphor, Plato presents the Puppet Master as *Deus ridens* – a deity taking pleasure in watching human puppets performing their roles on the stage of the world, laughing both at their futile actions and their unawareness of playing the assigned roles (Kotarska 6). However, instead of viewing the role of the puppet as an example of human degradation, Plato sees it as a manifestation of divine sparks within all human beings (Świontek 54).

Apart from Plato, Aristotle also had an enormous influence on the development of the *theatrum mundi* metaphor. In *Nichomachean Ethics* Aristotle discusses in what way man as an actor is "ethically dependent" on man as a spectator "to delineate for him the moral basis for right action" (Christian 7). For Aristotle man is above all an actor, as he mainly explores the relationship between moral choice and moral acts. It is crucial for the philosopher to distinguish between man as an actor and man as a spectator, as he believes that the ideals of contemplative life and of active life cannot coexist in one person. One is either a man of thought, an actor, or a man of action, a spectator. It is worth mentioning that Christian describes Aristotle's thought as ambivalent. On the one hand, the philosopher claims that he mainly explores man as an actor, contemplating on a morally good life. On the other hand, he stresses that men do not become good by the contemplation of the abstract idea of goodness, but rather by acting in a good way. Therefore, he seems to give primacy to the man of action, the spectator, rather than to the man of thought (8–9).

As far as classical Greek theatre is concerned, Christian observes that the playwrights rarely underlined that life equals acting on the stage. A few plays of Aristophanes, however, may be regarded as exceptions. A case in point is his play produced in 405 B. C. entitled *The Frogs*. Christian claims that this play "exhibits a great deal of theatrical self-consciousness" (9), and cites the opinion of Cedric Whitman, who suggests that *The Frogs* may be regarded as one of the first examples of the play-within-the-play (10). Christian claims further that the unity of life and art, as well as the confusion between illusion and reality, is striking from the very beginning of the play. She notices that Dionysus pays two obols to cross the Styx, not the usual single obol. The price he pays thus equals the price of admission to the theatre (9). Hence, in his play Aristophanes seems to suggest that reality and acting on the stage constantly intertwine, and that the boundary between life and art may become blurred very easily.

In the Hellenistic era the *theatrum mundi* metaphor is very often associated with the figure of Tyche or the fickle and cruel Fortune, who is the director of the performance of life. This capricious goddess "may either punish the transgressor as he deserves, or reward the unjust and meddle in the life of man merely for her own delight" (Christian 11). In the Hellenistic times, Epicurus and the Cynics also employed the metaphor of the world as a stage. The former gives primacy to the spectator. For him, unlike for Aristotle, the actor's withdrawn contemplation does not lead to any action whatsoever and, therefore, is not regarded as a way of helping the spectator to achieve a moral life. According to Epicurus, God does not invite man to enjoy a wonderful performance and to treat it as an inspiration for a moral life. What he does is encourage the spectator to watch the hard work of the actors in

2.1. The History of the Topos of *Theatrum Mundi* 77

order to take more pleasure in his passivity. The Cynics, contrarily to Epicurus, value the actor more. Bion of Borysthenes, a Cynic who lived in the third century B. C., states in his work entitled *On Temperance*:

> Just as the good actor, who performs well whatever role the playwright assigns him, so the good man must perform well whatever role Tyche assigns him. Just like the producer of a play, she assigns each role, be it that of protagonist, deuteragonist, king or beggar. Do not then, being the deuteragonist, wish to assume the role of the protagonist. (quoted in Christian 12)

Bion claims that each man should play his role well, without any desire for being assigned a different, better one.

Stoicism, which stems from cynicism, incorporated the "World as a Stage" simile in its concern for the nature of human life directed by a divine power greater than human. The Stoics preached "no feeling" as the only proper response to all misfortunes that happen in the lives of all people. They stressed the importance of not only acting well, but also quitting the scene properly (Christian 13). Katarzyna Mroczkowska-Brand claims that the *theatrum mundi* metaphor was used by the Stoics to emphasize "the emptiness and brevity of worldly pomp and luster" (136–137). Likewise, Christian notices that it was stoicism that created the first literary work of *ars moriendi*. The Stoics strongly believed that it was much braver to finish the performance of life with the act of suicide than to await a disgraceful end (Christian 15). In *De Finibus* I, XV, 49, Cicero defines suicide as a way to "leave the theatre when the play no longer pleases" (quoted in Christian 16). He is convinced that such an ending is the climax of the play of life. In *De Senectute* XIX, 70, Cicero uses Cato the Elder to serve as his *porte parole* and to express his opinion on death, the last act of the play: "The actor, for instance, to please his audience need not appear in every act to the very end; it is enough if he is approved in the parts which he plays: and so it is not necessary for the wise man to stay on this mortal stage to the last fall of the curtain" (quoted in Christian 16). The Stoics were not perturbed by the ephemeral nature of life and treated it in an ironic and dispassionate way. Kotarska claims that the Stoics enriched the *theatrum mundi* metaphor with a new element: the awareness of being an actor on the stage of the world. According to the Stoics, man-actor can add his own element to the foreordained role, for instance by distancing himself from meaningless suffering or by fulfilling the assigned role against all odds (6).

The Stoic thought had a great influence on one of the Fathers of the Church, Saint John Chrysostom. However, one obvious difference between the Stoic doctrine and a Christian view on the metaphor of life as a play lies in the fact that the former approached death as a part of the performance and stressed its illusory nature. By contrast, the Fathers of the Church, St. John Chrysostom or St. Augustine, for instance, believed that although life is an illusion, death is the only reality, making all men equal and unmasking human actors (Christian 23). St. John Chrysostom strongly believed that even the illusory life is not worthless. As human life will inevitably be judged by God, it should not be regarded as of no value. He was also convinced that the life of a virtuous man, the actor in God's play who accepts suffering, may delight God the Spectator (35–36). Kotarska observes that in his *Ennarrationes in Psalmos mysticos*, St. Augustine encourages human actors to perform their roles in accordance with God's scenario and warns against the temptation of self-dependent acting (Kotarska 7).

The aesthetic aspect of the *theatrum mundi* metaphor was emphasized by Plotinus. He claimed that the human actor has relative autonomy as far as fulfilling the role is concerned. According to Plotinus, it is a divine power that casts the roles and directs the play of life. However, it depends on the human actor whether he will play his role well and contribute to the creation of universal Beauty and Harmony. Plotinus' comparison of life to a divine performance stresses the multiplicity of roles played by each human being. As actors are cast both in comic and tragic roles, life should be regarded as a constant overlapping of happiness and suffering (Kotarska 7).

Lynda Christian observes that from the times of Saint Augustine until the twelfth century the *theatrum mundi* metaphor seemed to be forgotten. She posits that "[t]his symbol of life appears to have died a quite unexpected death" (Christian 63). Although the metaphor was not used for seven hundred years, it was resurrected in the twelfth century by John of Salisbury, who compared the world to a stage in the *Policraticus* (1159) (63). According to him, the stage-director of the performance is Fortune, whose dealings with men are cruel and capricious. John of Salisbury claims that life resembles a tragedy rather than a comedy, as Fortune not only casts and directs the play of life, but also acts as "divine nemesis" (65). Therefore, John strongly encourages the human actor to hold this ephemeral and transient life in contempt, and to think of eternal happiness in heaven. He also stresses the importance of death, that is leaving the stage of the world. John of Salisbury is convinced that the moment when a personified Death takes all people away from the scene of the world is the only realistic moment in the life full of illusion. He speaks of the *theatrum mundi* metaphor *expressis verbis* at the end of Chapter Nine of *Policraticus*: "These are perhaps those who from the lofty pinnacle of virtue look down upon the stage of the world [*de alto uirtutum culmine theatrum mundi despiciunt*] and scorning the drama of fortune are not in any way allured to take part in acts of vanity and madness" (quoted in Christian 67). It was John of Salisbury who first used the phrase *theatrum mundi* in European literature. Christian claims that he utilized the metaphor of life as a play because he wanted to demonstrate his classical learning (70). After John of Salisbury employed the topos of *theatrum mundi*, it lay dormant until the late fifteenth century. There are definitely some reasons behind this three-hundred-year-long gap.

Christian assumes that the educated men of the Middle Ages were familiar with the works of Cicero, Seneca, or Saint Augustine, and were aware of the existence of the "World as a Stage" simile. Nevertheless, they hardly ever employed the met-

2.1. The History of the Topos of *Theatrum Mundi*

aphor in their own writings for the simple reason that they had never been in a theatre and had never seen a play performed there (Christian 70–71). What they might have seen were "dumb shows," street plays, *corpus Christi* processions or liturgical dramas performed in churches and in churchyards. According to Kotarska, in the Middle Ages the topos of *theatrum mundi* was regarded as a modification of the *vanitas vanitatum* theme (Kotarska 8). Świontek observes that in the Middle Ages the theatricality was manifested in *dances macabres*, in which a personified Death was presented as the director of the play of life. Świontek claims further that the theatrical distinction between actors and spectators could be regarded as a metaphor for two worlds: the earthly and sinful, on the one hand, and the divine and ideal, on the other. It was God who watched the performance and who allowed human actors to play in a way they wished. The directors of the play of life, in the Middle Ages presented as personified allegorical characters such as Sin, Evil, or Death, were to remind the audience that on the Day of Doom each actor will be judged by the divine spectator. Salvation may only be attained by the human actor through the proper performance of his or her role (Świontek 66). Of the same opinion is Mroczkowska-Brand, who claims that in the Middle Ages the metaphor was used for moral purposes – to demonstrate the vanity of life and earthly goods:

> The attractive, glittering, and yet transient qualities of theater decorations and costumes were an excellently obvious simile for the *vanitas vanitatum* of worldly honours and delights. The comparison reminded people that their only true and lasting role was as children of God, and not such mundane social ephemera as king, judge, or courtier. (137)

Danuta Künstler-Langner believes that the idea of *vanitas* is much broader than the *theatrum mundi* metaphor. The "Life as a Play" simile may be regarded as one of the topoi incorporating the *vanitas vanitatum* theme (Künstler-Langner 59). The term *vanitas* comes from the Latin word *vanus*, which means "vain," "futile," "idle," or "worthless." This word appears also in the famous verse from the Bible: *Vanitas vanitatum et omnia vanitas* (Ecclesiastes 1:2), corresponding to the meaninglessness of earthly life, as well as to the ephemeral and fleeting nature of pomp and luster. Künstler-Langner claims that *vanitas* may be related to the deceptive nature of life and the world, meaning "emptiness," "want of reality," "senselessness," or "illusion" (10–11). She claims further that the idea of *vanitas*, like the *theatrum mundi* metaphor, is rooted in ancient philosophy, and that both ideas signify the helplessness of a human being in confrontation with a force greater than himself, be it God, Providence, fate, or nature (19).

In the Middle Ages the emphasis was put on the vanitative aspect of the *theatrum mundi* metaphor. In the Renaissance, by contrast, the ludic and aesthetic aspects of the "World as a Stage" simile were stressed. The Renaissance humanism proclaimed the idea of man as *quasi-Deus*. According to this anthropocentric vision of reality, the human actor is created in the image of God; however, the Creator does not interfere in the performance of life taking place on the stage of the world. The human actor is not assigned a particular part to play. On the contrary, he or she is given the possibility of assuming an unlimited number of roles. As human beings are able to play whatever parts they wish, acting may be regarded as a way of realizing their dreams of freedom and independence (Świontek 66).

A famous comparison of the world to a stage appears in Shakespeare's play entitled *As You Like It*. In Act Two Duke Senior shows his compassion for human actors, whose lives have the play-like quality:

> Thou seest we are not all alone unhappy:
> This wide and universal theatre
> Presents more woeful pageants than the scene
> Wherein we play. (Shakespeare 1967: 95)

The old Duke's comparison of the world to the universal theatre and of his own life to the scenes in a performance, elicits self-dramatizing Jaques' world-famous monologue, in which he expresses his melancholy disillusionment with life:

> All the world's a stage
> And all the men and women, merely players;
> They have their exits and their entrances,
> And one man in his time plays many parts,
> His acts being seven ages. (Shakespeare 1967: 95)

Jaques is also convinced that all men act out their lives like actors in a performance, each of them playing at least seven roles: "the infant," "the whining schoolboy," "the lover," "a soldier," "the justice," "the lean and slipper'd pantaloon," and finally the role of the "second childishness" (95–97). Having performed all seven parts, each man-actor is removed by death from the stage of the world. Once the cycle is completed and an old and senile man has left the stage, his exit is immediately followed by the entrance of a new actor, a newborn child, and the seven-staged cycle begins again. This circular process will take place as long as the universal theatre exists.

In the later tragedies Shakespeare's protagonists employ the *theatrum mundi* metaphor at the climactic moments of the plays in order to express deep insights into the deceptive nature of life (Christian 157). When the prophecy of the three witches comes true and Birnam wood comes to Dunsinane, Macbeth realizes that due to his being just a performer playing the assigned role, he has no influence whatsoever on the play of life in which he takes part. Expressing his disillusionment with life, he admits sadly:

> Life's but a walking shadow; a poor player,
> That struts and frets his hour upon the stage,
> And then is heard no more; it is a tale
> Told by an idiot, full of sound and fury,
> Signifying nothing. (Shakespeare 1984: 154)

At the end of the play, it is Macduff, regarded as death's ally, who forever removes Macbeth from the stage of the world. Macbeth was believed to act out an unforgettable and outstanding role. As, contrary to what was expected, his performance turned out to be a complete failure, he vanished from the stage of the *theatrum mundi* like a shadow.

Christian claims that it is the death of kings, making them equal with the lowest classes, that arouses much pity and fear, as all-powerful death can humiliate even the monarchs of the world (Christian 158). A good illustration of this idea may be Shakespeare's play entitled *Richard II*. Having lost the crown, Richard is disillusioned with his role and nostalgic for the past. He is convinced that it is death that casts the parts and makes monarchs believe that their privileged role will last eternally. Death takes pleasure in sudden depriving the kings of all their privileges, reducing their position to that of an average man-actor, and eventually removing them from the stage of the world:

> [...] for within the hollow crown
> That rounds the mortal temples of a king
> Keeps Death his court, and there the antic sits,
> Scoffing his state and grinning at his pomp,
> Allowing him a breath, a little scene,
> To monarchize [...] (Shakespeare 1991: 102–103)

Richard confesses that there is a discrepancy between his role as king and that of an average man-actor. He proves to be a vulnerable and fallible creature, an ordinary human actor, who was for a while cast in the role of the king:

> For you have but mistook me all this while.
> I live with bread like you, feel want,
> Taste grief, need friends – subjected thus,
> How can you say to me, I am a king? (Shakespeare 1991: 103)

Also examining himself, "bankrupt of majesty" (140), reflected in a mirror, Richard realizes that there is no special grandeur in his pallid and tired face. At the end of the play he is humiliated by the citizens during his march through the town while accompanying his successor, Henry Bolingbroke. Duke of York describes Richard in the following way:

> As in a theatre the eyes of men,
> After a well-grac'd actor leaves the stage,
> Are idly bent on him that enters next,
> Thinking his prattle to be tedious;
> Even so, or with much more contempt, men's eyes
> Did scowl on Richard [...] (Shakespeare 1991: 154)

Richard, then, turns out to be an actor who augured well at the beginning of the play of life, but who finished the performance in a very humble way.

Hamlet is another play in which Shakespeare used the "World as a Stage" simile. Christian even believes that "the topos of *theatrum mundi* shapes the play" (167), and Kotarska calls *Hamlet* a play on acting (Kotarska 12). In this tragedy life, and, above all, life at Elsinore, is presented as a theatrical performance in which each human actor plays a particular role. However, in *Hamlet* there can be also found the play-within-the-play, whose staging is preceded by Hamlet's meeting with the players reciting some verses from the performance, his providing directions to the actors, and his remarking on the art of good acting. Hamlet strongly believes that

> [...] the purpose of playing, whose end both at the first and now, was and is, to hold 'twere the mirror up to nature; to show virtue her own feature, scorn her own image, and the very age and body of the time his form and pressure. (Shakespeare 1985: 153)

According to Hamlet, the theatrical art may be regarded as a kind of mirror, imitating life in meticulous detail and revealing things not as they seem, but as they really are. By staging the *Mousetrap* Hamlet wants to catch the king's attention. However, the effect turns out to be contrary to the expectations. Instead of pleasing the king, Hamlet reveals that he knows the secret of the old king's death and transforms the play into an accusation against his mother. Remarkably, he finds it much easier to direct a performance in a theatre than to control his passionate reactions in real life.

In staging the *Mousetrap* at Elsinore, Hamlet tries to be as powerful as Fortune and to play the roles which were not assigned to him. He believes that Fortune cast him in the role of Avenger, and that he must take revenge for his father's death. However, dissatisfied with the foreordained role, Hamlet attempts to usurp the part of Fortune and to direct the play of life in accordance with his own scenario. As Fortune does not approve of human attempts to dominate her production, Hamlet has to sacrifice his life for usurping Fortune's role. He is aware of his impending death when he prepares for the fatal duel with Laertes. Before death, Hamlet has no longer any aspiration for Fortune's power and accepts the role of a mere puppet in her hands. The Danish prince has realized that he is an actor whose part is to be determined by the Playwright not by himself (Christian 167–168).

In Shakespeare's late play, *The Tempest*, the "World is a Stage" topos is intertwined with that of the "Life is a Dream" (Mroczkowska-Brand 116). Mroczkowska-Brand claims that there are some aspects shared by the comparisons of life to a dream and to a theatrical performance. First of all, both emphasize the brevity of life and the illusory character of perception. What is more, the use of imagination is paramount when it comes to creating the world of a dream, or that of a play. The powers of perception are not always capable of making a clear-cut distinction between illusion and waking reality. Mroczkowska-Brand is convinced that

> [...] only in dreams or when taking part in a theater performance can man (playwright, actor, spectator, dreamer) satisfy his yearnings for a multiplicity of roles, for being something different [...], for being here and there at the same time, for touching the world on the other side of the mirror. Both the theater and the dream have this same magic. (Mroczkowska-Brand 131)

Prospero, the source of whose power is the magic art, directs the fate of others in accordance with his own magic vision. Having God's attributes, he may be regarded as the creator of the internal theatrical world. For him, unlike for Hamlet, the theatrical art does not mean imitating reality, but creating a new one by using the power of imagination. However, his God-like omnipotence is a mere illusion. When he rejects his magical abilities, thanks to which he could direct the internal play, he turns out to be an average man-actor who was for a while, like Richard or Macbeth, cast in a privileged role. The nature of this role was as ephemeral as that of a dream, and it passed by as quickly as a shadow:

> Our revels now are ended. These our actors,
> As I foretold you, were all spirits, and
> Are melted into air, into thin air,
> And, like the baseless fabric of this vision,
> The cloud-capped towers, the gorgeous palaces,
> The solemn temples, the great globe itself,
> Yea, all which it inherit, shall dissolve,
> And, like this insubstantial pageant faded,
> Leave not a rack behind. We are such stuff
> As dreams are made on, and our little life
> Is rounded with a sleep. (Shakespeare 1987: 180–181)

The turn of the sixteenth and seventeenth centuries is characterized by the presence of theatricality and the *theatrum mundi* metaphor not only in literature, but also in public life, and, above all, in court life. As court figures were constantly in the public eye, they were aware of being observed. Therefore, they often resorted to putting on a mask, hiding their true feelings and emotions and to conscious playing of a particular role. At the beginning of the seventeenth century the emphasis was put on extrovert gestures, mimics, and pompously theatrical character of expressing oneself. A strict code of language, dress, and behaviour reinforced the feeling that living equals playing a particular role (Kotarska 11). Self-dramatization was a crucial aspect of court life and included very spectacular ceremonies such as coronations, weddings of the royalty, or funerals of respected public figures. Even everyday activities of the monarch resembled performances, as they were almost always watched by others. Through constant role-playing and acting as a stage-director, the monarch tried to exercise power over and manipulate others. What is more, court theatre performances made real life overlap with a play. Particularly interesting were those performances in which the monarch and his courtiers played the roles of mythical gods, and at some point in a play quitted the stage and took part in the performance no longer as actors, but as spectators. Such theatrical performances gave splendour to the royal authority and served as allegories of monarchs' roles in real life (Mroczkowska-Brand 22–23).

The fact that human beings have a tendency to put on masks in order to hide their true selves from the eyes of others is stressed by Erasmus of Rotterdam in his remarkable work *Praise of Folly*. Erasmus popularized the secular and satiric aspect of the *theatrum mundi* metaphor. In his work, divine comedy is replaced by human comedy, the essence of which is worshipping unimportant ideas. Folly, the main protagonist of Erasmus' work, announces that human actors play the roles of fools on the stage of the world. According to Erasmus, the course of the world is determined by the follies of men, which are laughed at by the gods:

> [...] but once the nectar is flowing freely they [gods] want a change from serious business, and that is when they settle down on some promontory of heaven and lean over to watch the goings-on of mankind, a show they enjoy more than anything. Heavens, what a farce it is, what a motley crowd of fools. (Erasmus 22)

The performance directed by fools sooner or later will change into chaos, in which human actors are completely helpless and unaware of the impending catastrophe. A play in which a foolish human is not only an actor, but also a stage-director and a powerful being who casts and interprets the roles is beyond any doubt a tragicomedy reflecting the vanity of the world and all human efforts (Świontek 68–69).

Christian focuses on investigating the sixteenth and seventeenth centuries, as they were the heyday of the *theatrum mundi* metaphor. In the eighteenth and nineteenth centuries the "World as a Stage" simile was still in usage; however, it was not employed that frequently. The *theatrum mundi* metaphor appears for instance in one of Frederick Marryat's novels, entitled *The King's Own* (1830). At one point in the novel the narrator announces: "Our novel may, to a certain degree, be compared to one of the pantomimes which rival theatres annually bring forth [...]. We open with dark and solemn scenes, [...] till the illusion disappears, at the fall of the green curtain, which [...] tells us that all is over" (quoted in Błaszak 105). Marryat regards his novel as a performance and its protagonists as actors playing their roles. The director of this play is the author himself: an all-powerful God-like figure who casts the roles and makes decisions regarding the fates of the performers. In his being a creator directing the lives of others and removing some of the actors from the stage of the world whenever he wants, Marryat bears much resemblance to Conrad. The performances directed by them reflect the universal theatre, while their intellects, as well as their creative imagination, make the status of an author akin to that of God the Playwright.

The "World as a Stage" simile is employed also by William M. Thackeray in his *Vanity Fair* (1848), named thusly after one of the stages of the Pilgrim's progress. In the introduction to the novel, entitled "Before the Curtain," Thackeray presents himself as "the Manager of the Performance" (5), a puppet master inviting his readers to watch the Show which he, as the author, directed and produced himself. He refers to the world as "Vanity Fair," a place in which an eternal performance takes place, and to its inhabitants as Puppets, the essence of whose existence is playing. Thackeray, like Marryat and Conrad, also encourages his readers to watch and evaluate the show directed by him. However, the main difference between acting in Marryat's narrative and in *Vanity Fair* lies in the fact that the characters in Thackeray's novel play their roles consciously. "The famous little Becky Puppet" (6), that is Becky Sharp, is a mercenary and a highly hypocritical social climber, determined to achieve her personal goals at any cost, constantly pretending to be a sensitive and vulnerable young woman. Therefore, Thackeray refers to her

2.1. The History of the Topos of *Theatrum Mundi* 85

as "a perfect performer" (72). Acting lies also in the natures of George Osborne and Rawdon Crawley. These egoistic dandies, for whom fame, wealth, and success are the most important, do their best to be regarded as gentlemen by Victorian society. Surprising as it may seem, also Amelia Sedley and William Dobbin are referred to as "the Amelia Doll" and "the Dobbin Figure" (6). Although they are not corrupt and hypocritical, they consciously hide their true feelings and emotions behind a mask. There is a discrepancy between the persons they pretend to be and those they really are. Hence, Thackeray strongly believes that "[...] the truth may surely be borne in mind, that the bustle, and triumph, and laughter, and gaiety which Vanity Fair exhibits in public, do not always pursue the performer into private life [...]" (211). Although in public Amelia and Dobbin pretend to be sociable and self-confident, deep inside both of them are shy and lonely.

Thackeray finishes his Show with a pessimistic reflection: "Ah! *Vanitas vanitatum*! Which of us is happy in this world? Which of us has his desire? or, having it, is satisfied?" (809). According to Thackeray, playing a certain role, more or less consciously, is in fact futile, as it does not lead to happiness and satisfaction with life. Death puts off the masks and reveals the true natures of the actors; at the end of the show it turns out that happiness is as illusory and transient as the nature of life. The last sentence of the novel, "Come children, let us shut up the box and the puppets, for our play is played out" (809), seems to suggest that the author has already performed his task: he created the play and presented it to the audience. The rest, that is the evaluation of the show and the reflection on it, is assigned to the spectator.

Apart from *The King's Own* and *Vanity Fair*, *Moby Dick* (1851) may also be interpreted through the *theatrum mundi* metaphor. However, unlike Marryat and Thackeray, Herman Melville does not present himself as a powerful creator, who in his book directs the lives of his fictional characters. His status is in between that of a playwright and that of a spectator. In using his creative imagination and presenting "the show" to the audience, he resembles a playwright. However, unlike Marryat, Thackeray and Conrad, he does not consider himself to be a creator. He bears resemblance rather to a spectator who watches the play and reflects on what is being performed. In Melville's fiction, like in Conrad's, it is the sea that is the arena of the drama. Captain Ahab, the protagonist of *Moby Dick*, who fights with a force much greater than him and who does his best to take his fate into his own hands, is similar to Conrad's young Marlow and Jim. The white whale, Moby Dick, which for Ahab represents the evil of the world, is as cruel and malevolent as fate. Moby Dick, which once defeated Ahab and made taking revenge his obsession, toys with the Captain and tortures him psychologically, just to win a resounding victory over him at the end of the book. Ahab, however, is a greater loser than Marlow and Jim. Their destruction is the price they had to pay for gaining the knowledge that in confrontation with an omnipotent force that assigns roles to human puppets and pulls the strings, man is completely powerless and insignificant. Ahab, by contrast, never manages to either get to know himself or realize his insignificance within the system of the universe. Not only is he soundly defeated, but he also dies in a remarkable ignorance of both the theatrical quality of the universe and his role-playing in the performance of life.

It is, however, Joseph Conrad's vision of the theatrical quality of human existence that seems to run parallel with Pirandello's. Although Pirandello and Conrad never met, they lived in the same historical period and both perceived modern life as chaotic and multifaceted. In his collection of reminiscences entitled *A Personal Record*, Conrad observes:

> The ethical view of the universe involves us at last in so many cruel and absurd contradictions, where the last vestiges of faith, hope, charity, and even of reason itself, seem ready to perish, that I have come to suspect that the aim of creation cannot be ethical at all. I would fondly believe that its object is purely spectacular [...]. (*Personal Record* 92)

Conrad claims further that both the values associated with religion, such as faith, hope, or charity, and those connected with philosophy, such as the power of human intellect, are on the verge of extinction. Hence, he believes that the universe should not be judged in terms of good and evil, but, rather, by the quality of the play of life taking place on the stage of the world. He is also convinced that the reader of his fiction, who is at the same time the viewer of the play, is to judge the performance taking place in front of his eyes. The spectator's "appointed task on this earth" (92) is to pay "the unwearied self-forgetful attention to every phase of the living universe [...]" (92). The evaluation of the play is, therefore, a task assigned to the viewer.

The moment of gaining awareness is explored by both Conrad and Pirandello. In his pessimism, fatalism, and nihilism, the source of which is the conviction of the absurdity of the world and the tragedy of human existence, Conrad stresses that acquiring self-knowledge inevitably leads to self-destruction; conversely, Pirandello celebrates his protagonists' liberation thanks to self-awareness. In Conrad's short story *Youth* (1898), young Marlow refuses to accept his insignificance. Thanks to the sparks of tremendous optimism, great zeal, and boundless enthusiasm, he feels strong enough to challenge destiny, defeat the sea, and master his own fate. Commenting on the character of Singleton, one of the protagonists of his novel *The Nigger of the "Narcissius"* (1897), Conrad wrote to R. B. Cunninghame Graham (14. 12. 1897): "Would you seriously wish to tell such a man: 'Know thyself.' Understand that thou art nothing, less than a shadow, more insignificant than a drop of water in the ocean, more fleeting than the illusion of a dream. Would you?" (quoted in Karl 423). Conrad's words may be also applied to young Marlow. Blinded by his enthusiasm and optimism, and displaying a kind of naivety, he refuses to believe in his littleness and insignificance, but is convinced that his apparent triumph over the sea only proves his greatness. Unfortunately, Marlow's victory over fate is only temporal and illusive. Although he manages to take his life in his own hands, act freely and independently on the stage of the world, outwit fortune, and withstand the malice of its ally, the sea, he achieves an incomplete triumph. As his youth succumbs to time, brutal in its merciless succession, forty-two-year-old Marlow looks back with painful nostalgia and regret on his lost certitude in the possibility of man mastering his fate. Marlow's unconscious youth has been replaced by disillusioned maturity, as he learned in life that it is impossible to defeat one's own fate. Therefore, as a middle-aged man he does not even try to fight destiny, and remains overwhelmingly passive. Experience has taught Marlow that on the stage of the world man plays the role ascribed to him and that all independent attempts are bound to failure. Man is only a toy in the hands of almighty fortune and has to accept the fact that in the face of the innate cruelty of this powerful force, nothing is possible. It is no use fighting with the enemy who is incomparably stronger and more powerful, and in confrontation with whom a human being resembles a speck of dust trying to change the course of the universe. The mature Marlow fully accepts his being a mere puppet, the strings of which are pulled by the Puppet Master. The youthful fire burning in the twenty-two-year-old Marlow, which was for him the source of inner strength pushing him into action and enabling him to take his own fate into his hands, vanished forever after twenty years. The first, romantic part of Marlow's motto, "do or die," encourages human actors to be dynamic and show initiative in their roles performed in the theatre of the world. By contrast, its second, deeply pessimistic part connotes passivity and blind acceptance of the role.

The protagonist of *Lord Jim* is similarly unaware of his utter insignificance within the system of the universe and of the fact that, sooner or later, all men have to submit to the dictates of fate. Blinded by his youthful ardour, he is unaware that he is playing the role of a powerless puppet whose strings are pulled by the Puppet Master, that his actions are deranged, and that his free will is just an illusion. Jim, like Marlow of *Youth*, constantly oscillates between dream and waking reality, and his experiences in Patusan, which have the "detailed and amazing impression of a dream" (*Lord Jim* 278), are of phantasmagoric quality. For him the people of Patusan are like characters in a book, who "exist as if under an enchanter's wand" (287). In that remote land he acts as if he were a brave knight conquering his enemies, adored by his people, and eventually winning the hand of a beautiful maiden. However, this dream will remain unfulfilled for Jim, the quixotic protagonist, who is himself almost like an ephemeral and transient figure from the land of mist. In his letter to E. Garnett, Conrad wrote: "[...] one's own personality is only a ridiculous and aimless masquerade of something hopelessly unknown" (quoted in Karl 267). The aforementioned statement can be also applied to Jim, who remains inscrutable even to himself. It is due to his downfalls that Jim manages to gain self-knowledge in the final part of the book. Exploring "the tragic course of knowing [oneself]" (Heilman 108), Conrad writes to Małgorzata Poradowska:

But you are afraid of yourself; of the inseparable being always at your side – master and slave, victim and tormentor – who suffers and causes suffering. That's how it is! Man must drag the ball and chain of his individuality to the very end. It is the price one pays for the infernal and divine privilege of thought; consequently, it is only the elect who are convicts in this life – the glorious company of those who understand and who lament, but who tread the earth amid a multitude of ghosts with maniacal gestures, with idiotic grimaces. Which do you prefer – idiot or convict? (quoted in Karl 162–163)

No longer a self-loving, self-forgiving, and overwhelmingly passive figure, deeply convinced of his strength and ability to outwit fate, at the end of the book Jim is a "convict" who gained bitter awareness of his inability to change his condition and to find a new role, a more challenging and independent one. As Jim's image of himself as a powerful actor having his life in his own hands is shattered to pieces after the fatal decision, Jim becomes thoroughly disillusioned with his life. In a sense his existence bears resemblance to the life of Marlow of *Youth*; however, his disillusionment with the role he plays came much earlier than Marlow's. What is more, Jim's life can also be regarded as a progress from innocence to bitter experience, and from ignorance and self-delusion to self-awareness. However, there is an obvious difference between those characters in the effects the disillusionment has on their lives. In his youth Marlow is active and powerful enough to win the tussle with the sea, and to defeat destiny for some time. The disillusionment with life, which comes together with his maturity, brings him weakness and passivity. By contrast, Jim's dissatisfaction with life pushes him into action. While at the beginning of the novel he is extremely weak and passive, at the moment of his death the protagonist is characterized by unflagging persistence and determination. Young Marlow's optimism and enthusiasm have been stifled by time and replaced by pessimism and passivity. Thus, his impressive victory over fate has turned out to be temporal and illusory. The knowledge and awareness which he gained as a mature man led to his inability to perform any decisive action, and to his disillusionment with life. By contrast, Jim acquires knowledge of the human inability to overcome *fatum* and to master fate after his fatal error of judgement when he is still in his youth. Moreover, the price he has to pay is much greater than disillusionment, and his victory is much more spectacular than Marlow's. Destined to fail, Jim rebels against fate's scenario, chooses self-sacrificial death, and for one moment manages to master his own life and to become triumphant. Although he is eventually defeated, he wins a moral victory. Paradoxical as it may seem, Joseph Conrad, much as Pirandello, tends to prefer such self-destructive and defiant individuals to puppets unable to show their own initiative, and he glorifies victories-in-defeats. In his treatment of the topos of *theatrum mundi,* Conrad strongly resembles the Pirandellian concept of the humorostic theatre of the world.

2.2. The Red Rover: A Prisoner of Form

Exploring the dichotomy of form and life in his essay *L'umorismo*, Pirandello stresses the illusory quality of perception and the impossibility of objectivity. Lost in a deceptive world of numerous masks and, at the same time, too vain to reflect on his or her condition, a given individual is no longer able to distinguish between form and life. Therefore, it is the humorist who, being aware of the tragicomic aspect of human nature, unmasks all the weaknesses and miseries so scrupulously hidden under the masks of appearances. According to the Italian writer, all the phenomena are either illusory or their real nature appears to be ungraspable, as human knowledge of man and the world only seems to be objective. In fact, it is a continuous deceptive construction (*L'umorismo* 154). Due to the fact that the cognitive process is limited to appearances, a person is susceptible to becoming an unaware victim not only of social hypocrisies, but also of individual illusions. Pirandello claims that this artificial existence is based both on psychological and social lies, resulting in a conscious or unconscious self-deception. The Italian author, applying the notion of the topos of *theatrum mundi*, presents artificial existence as a theatre on the stage of which all his characters are involuntarily projected. A given individual constitutes a part of a false and dehumanized society, "an immense theatre of forms, in which every creature recites the assigned role" (Manotta 107)[2]. Each actor on the stage of the huge theatre of the world is reduced to the automatic movements of a puppet, whose existence is fixed in forms. "Forms," Pirandello writes, "are all the ideas, all the ideals to which we want to remain faithful, all the fictions that we create, all the conditions in which we want to establish ourselves" (*L'umorismo* 159). There is, therefore, cogency in Marco Manotta's definition of form as "the conventionality that rules over life" or, in other words, "the reality stiffened in schemes, formulas and concepts" (Manotta 106). Manotta also emphasizes the fact that the formalized existence is but "a mask put on the consciousness and hence worn with astonishing naturalness" (192). In a world devoid of spontaneity and authenticity of action, the fixed expression of the mask becomes a powerful symbol of an existence imprisoned in a statuesque form of a puppet. "Masks, masks…," Pirandello underlines, "a puff and they vanish only to give place to others. […] Everybody does their best to fix the mask – the exterior mask. Because inside there is another mask, which usually does not harmonize with the outer one. And nothing is true" (*L'umorismo* 161). Pirandello concludes by observing that the individual is always masked and although he or she neither wants nor is aware of being so, he or she cannot do without acting. It is also significant that the human marionette, assuming his or her role in the surrounding society, finds in him- or herself nothing but a reflection of the others' blindness and ignorance. It seems to me that Pirandello's statement on the unconscious mimesis of someone else's be-

---

2   All quotations from Italian sources in the present chapter are provided in my translation.

haviour is worth noting. The Italian author emphasizes that each individual constitutes a part of the race or the collectivity to which he or she belongs, and that he or she unconsciously imitates opinions, feelings, and actions of others (*L'umorismo* 157).

One of the crucial aspects of Pirandello's analysis is, in my opinion, his observation on human vanity which can be perceived as the main cause of a lack of self-reflection on the part of an individual. Pirandello observes:

> We experience over and over again the vanity of pretending to be different from what we are, which is an indispensable form of our social life. At the same time, we avoid the self-analysis which, unveiling the vanity and stimulating the pricks of conscience, would humiliate ourselves in our own eyes. (*L'umorismo* 157)

According to Pirandello, it is vanity that forces an individual to hide him- or herself under the mask of form. This opinion is shared by Vincenzo Faenza, a psychiatrist, who, exploring Pirandellian works from a psychological point of view, observes that "the masks from under which rises an unpleasant odour of inauthenticity" (Faenza 73) offer "the stability of a support" (89). Faenza also notices that, on the one hand, the individual is too vain, and, on the other, too fearful to finish his or her continuous role-playing. In the society represented as an unreflective *vanity fair*, it is the humorist who performs an analysis and whose task consists in unmasking all the vanities. Mario Aste observes that Pirandello, having a broad and profound knowledge of his characters, is able to identify himself with them (Aste 16). As a result, the Pirandellian *sentimento del contrario*, "feeling of the contrary," is generated by "the *pathos* of the identification with the subject which produces the ridicule" (39). When the humorist unmasks the characters, deconstructs their habitual fictions and provokes a sense of perplexity, he always performs his task not with contempt, but with compassion.

In a famous excerpt from *L'umorismo*, Pirandello illustrates humoristic attitude towards reality, presenting a hypothetical case of an elderly lady, dressed in youthful clothes and wearing heavy make-up. Undoubtedly, that character may provoke laughter. However, having reflected on her condition and having penetrated under the mask of appearances, the humorist finds himself in a state of perplexity. Highlighting the importance of reflection in a humoristic approach, Pirandello claims that its crucial role is that of "breaking the spontaneous movement which organizes all ideas and images in a harmonious form" (*L'umorismo* 140). The Italian author claims further that the main function of humorism is to create the *sentimento del contrario*, that is a movement from the initial laughter to its opposite, pity. Pirandello also stresses a fundamental difference between the comic, on the one hand, and the humoristic, on the other: while the former consists only of the "awareness of the opposite" [*avvertimento del contrario*], the latter goes deeper into that superficial perception of the contrary and reaches the "feeling of the opposite" [*sentimento del contrario*]. Becoming aware that the old lady's ridiculous physical aspect is in fact a desperate attempt to hide her age and to attract the attention of her much younger husband, the humorist is no longer capable of a comic reaction. The discovery that each image evokes a contrary image and that there is a huge discrepancy between appearances and reality makes the initial laughter bitter.

The Red Rover is also a character who arouses both laughter and compassion. As a *pars pro toto* figure put in chains of form, he may represent the imprisonment of humanity to this concept. Cooper's novel seems to be a dialogue with the reader, in which the author tries to transform the adventures of a particular character into a universal experience. Although Cooper underlines the difficulty of leaving the limiting form, he, like Pirandello, does not negate the possibility of liberation from the prison of mimesis in the direction of authentic life. On the contrary, both Pirandello and Cooper appear to glorify the individual trying to transcend the limitations of form. Assigning the role of the spectator to the reader, Cooper asks his audience to evaluate the performance and to interpret the presented events. Participating in a play of the formalized existence, the reader is in/voluntarily projected upon the huge stage of the world portrayed in the novel. Although the Rover's adventures are apparently comic, the fact that Cooper attributes a universal dimension to them and narrates them with a humoristic approach evokes in the reader-spectator a feeling of disturbing perplexity. As the narrator's attitude provokes the "feeling of the opposite," the reader does not laugh, but rather treats the protagonist with compassion.

Gazing into the unattainable, the Rover is characterized by immense pride and faith in himself. Convinced of his greatness, uniqueness, and exceptionality, in his own eyes Cooper's protagonist is above the rest, especially those living on land, and treats others with disdain. It is his youthful enthusiasm and mastery in seamanship that push him into action. Indeed, the Rover is presented as an incarnation of *actio*. Too vain and proud to penetrate through masks, the Rover avoids all sorts of self-analysis. Although he seems to be perfectly satisfied with his being imprisoned in form, in fact his life is nothing but anxiety, disharmony and torment. Numerous roles, which the Rover assumes and colourful costumes, which he constantly changes, perfectly illustrate the inauthenticity of his existence. Additionally, the protagonist does not speak but recites, oscillating between being and pretending on the stage of the *theatrum mundi*. The Rover, whose masked life resembles that of a marionette, lives in a phantasmagoric world, perfectly performing his role of a bloodthirsty pirate. Although he is admired by sailors, the character is also unpredictable in his hatred, and can be cruel when it comes to keeping discipline on his ship. Therefore, his fellow-seamen perceive him both as fascinating and frightening. Thomas Philbrick claims that "Cooper dwells on the superstitious fears" (Philbrick 60) in order to present the Rover as larger than life. In the eyes of people living on land, the Rover is the Devil's ally and, therefore, possesses supernatural abilities. They regard him as an incarnation of the Flying Dutchman, a bold and daring seaman who was eventually punished by God for his pride and sentenced to everlasting wandering at sea.

However, Cooper is far from portraying the Rover as intrinsically evil. On the contrary, he wants to present his protagonist as a victim of thwarted ambitions: the Rover becomes a pirate who takes enormous pleasure in attacking English ships because his merits remain unnoticed by his British superiors (62). In the creation of the Rover Cooper fuses Byronic romanticism with heroic maritime nationalism, as the essence of the pirate's existence is conducting "a private war of independence" (56). As the condemned visionary, the Rover may represent the awakening of the American national consciousness and a yearning for political liberty. However, as this means that he constructs himself in accordance with the society's expectations, the Rover unconsciously accepts the mask imposed by others as his second nature. The fact that the protagonist is forced to recite in a gigantic puppet theatre of the world condemns him to a suffocating rigidity of form, which stifles any spontaneity.

Apart from being imprisoned in the form of a cruel rover, the protagonist is also forced to play the part of an ideal male. In *The Red Rover* Cooper constructs an image of the perfect sailor as bold, daring, demonstrating mastery and effortlessly confident. For him masculinity means proving victorious when being subjected to a series of tests challenging one's masculine identity. Cooper stresses the significance of the sea not only to national existence, but also to the construction of masculinity. The sea is presented as the perfect proving-ground of human character, providing an opportunity to test the seamen's strength and skills. The ability to meet the challenge of the ocean and to steer a vessel through the open sea may be regarded as a manifestation of power, traditionally reserved for men. In Cooper's fiction women hardly ever appear at sea, as they are believed to be unable to tolerate the harsh conditions of ship life. As far as the presence of women on ship is concerned, *The Red Rover* is an exception. Gertrude Grayson, the romantic heroine of the novel, is kidnapped by the Rover aboard his ship and treated by him almost like a goddess. Gertrude's fragile and angelic femininity is strongly contrasted with the Rover's masculinity. The pirate secures his masculine identity by differentiation from the "Other," that is Gertrude. He identifies himself with the female character in a negative way – the Rover is what Gertrude is not. Moreover, the fact that Gertrude's captor never reveals his true identity to her, but perfectly plays the role of an amorous captain, may be interpreted as Cooper's attempt to stress that masculinity is also regarded by the protagonist as a role performance. By emphasizing that the Rover is masculine in all the roles that he adopts, be it that of a lawyer, Captain Heidegger or Captain Howard, Cooper seems to suggest that the character wears various kinds of masks with astonishing naturalness. Although it is not explicitly mentioned, the protagonist's ship, a tiny stage of the huge theatre of the world, may symbolize the Rover's existential prison. Referred to as the devil's ship, with red sails resembling the Flying Dutchman in its evoking the colour of blood, the character's vessel acquires some aspects of infernal space, while the Rover is compared to Satan. Therefore, the Red Rover's identity "seems to be a limitation of the subject and a construction imposed by others [...] who have formed this identity and have imprisoned a potentially free subjectivity in a cage" (Ricciardi 30).

The protagonist is also presented as a victim of political and historical situation. Obsessed with the idea of America's independence, he strongly believes that the victory of American seamen over the British supremacy is possible. Never discouraged by misfortunes and determined to fight until the very end, the protagonist treats the tussle with the ocean and the ships belonging to the British Royal Navy as an unforgettable adventure and a trial of life. The theme of heroic maritime nationalism is also visible in the Rover's quest for a flag. Throughout the novel, the Rover searches for his national identity and tries to liberate himself from the sense of non-belonging. In the final scene of the book, taking place in the 1780s, the dying Rover finds the flag and the nation of which he has dreamt: the American (Philbrick 57).

The Rover, a character crushed by circumstances, may be considered similar to the mythological Orestes, who in Greek mythology is the son of Agamemnon and Clytemnestra. Interestingly, Pirandello makes of that character a famous metaphor for the existence imprisoned in form. When Agamemnon is assassinated by Aegisthus, the lover of Clytemnestra, the Delphic oracle imposes on Orestes the role of his father's avenger. Although the young hero is forced not only to homicide, but also to matricide, he does not rebel against his fate. Orestes avenges the death of his father, killing both Clytemnestra and Aegisthus. Like Orestes, the Red Rover accepts the chains of the blind determination of marionettes, constructing himself in accordance with the forms imposed from the outside. Not at all used to reflecting, the protagonist easily accepts falsity and futility of role-playing as his identity and seems to feel fulfilled. However, the Red Rover differs considerably from Orestes in one respect: he is not a tragic figure. As, according to Pirandello, tragedy is strictly associated with the consciousness of one's condition, the Rover's artificial and inauthentic existence may be regarded as squalid and contemptible, but not tragic. It is the discovery of the paper sky of the puppet theatre, up to this point wrongly perceived as the real world, that makes the life of the marionette tragic and the puppet perpetually incoherent [*perennemente farneticante*] (*L'umorismo* 20). It is this awareness that transforms the blind determination of mythological Orestes into the existential insecurity of a modern Hamlet.

2.3. The Rover Becomes Hamlet: Epiphany of Life

In Chapter XII of Pirandello's novel *Il fu Mattia Pascal* [*The Late Mattia Pascal*], regarded by critics as a masterpiece, Anselmo Paleari informs Adriano Meis that one of Sophocles' tragedies is going to be performed in a Roman puppet theatre. Paleari continues:

> Supposing that, just at the climax, when the marionette representing Orestes is about to avenge his father's death on Aegisthos and his mother, someone should suddenly tear a hole in the paper ceiling over the stage [...], Orestes [...] would become Hamlet. The whole difference between the ancient theatre and the modern comes down to a rent in the paper sky. (*Il fu Mattia Pascal* 136)

It seems that by dedicating the first edition of his essay *L'umorismo* to Mattia Pascal, Pirandello wanted to draw a parallel between the two works. Salvatore Guglielmino observes that the excerpt devoted to "the demystifying hole of the blue sky of conventional values" aims at stressing "the conflict, the collapse, the dissonance which constitute existential characteristics of a 'modern' character: who from the hole in the paper sky of the puppet theatre gets the consciousness of his own condition" (Guglielmino 8). In other words, the mythological Orestes becomes a modern Hamlet.

Unlike the active Orestes, Hamlet, the protagonist of one of the most famous Shakespearean plays, may be perceived as an incarnation of reflection. Living in a dimension of continuous perplexity, Hamlet is not able to establish a confident relation with reality. Aware of his condition of a marionette on the stage of the *theatrum mundi*, the Danish prince wants to escape through the hole in the paper sky and to reject the role that he plays. It is the awareness of his condition that makes Hamlet incoherent, that is totally different from other marionettes "above whose wooden heads the artificial sky is preserved without any tears" [*su le cui teste di legno il finto cielo si conserva senza strappi*] (*Il fu* 137). The prince's monologue, "to be or not to be," constitutes the most famous fragment of the tragedy. The doubts concerning being (living) and non-being (dying) reflect Hamlet's indecision which paralyzes his ability to act. Arnaldo di Benedetto observes that the mysterious hole, the appearance of which flabbergasts Orestes, transforms his blind determination of a marionette into existential insecurity (di Benedetto 116). Marco Manotta stresses the discovery of the tear as well, calling that particular moment "the most beautiful of Pirandellian epiphanies" (Manotta 242). In *L'umorismo*, the Italian writer defines this experience, which he calls "interior silence," in the following way:

> At certain moments of interior silence, in which our soul gets undressed of all habitual fictions and our eyes become more acute and penetrating, we see ourselves in life, in nothing but life, almost in disturbing nudity; we feel attacked by a strange impression, as if, in a flash, it became clear that there exists a different reality from the one that we normally perceive, a reality existing beyond human sight, outside all norms imposed by human reason. (160)

According to Pirandello, epiphany is a momentary illumination during which the character sees a collapse of all the fictitious forms that imprison life. In other words, it is a moment in which the individual learns to look beyond the masks, which suddenly become naked. Having experienced the destruction of the world of the masks, a given individual discovers a flux of life, still flowing despite the ri-

2.3. The Rover Becomes Hamlet: Epiphany of Life

gidity of form imposed upon it. Pirandello underlines that "there is life in us, the flow continues, indistinct, under embankments, beyond the limits that we impose" (159). Concluding his discourse, the author observes that the flow of life exists in all humans.

Pirandello was definitely not the only one to apply epiphany as a literary technique in the twentieth century. It was frequently used in James Joyce's works, for example in *Dubliners* (1914), *A Portrait of the Artist as a Young Man* (1916) or *Ulysses* (1922). When this technique is employed, an object, an insignificant gesture or even a trivial situation may cause a spiritual illumination of the character, thanks to which he or she is able to understand him- or herself and the surrounding reality. Epiphany may therefore be perceived as a "revealer" of profound existential meaning. In Joyce's works, some apparently unimportant episodes are in fact deeply symbolic and become crucial in the protagonist's life (Cuddon 277). Manotta defines Pirandellian epiphany, which has much in common with that applied by Joyce, as "a suspension of the usual existence which opens a human being to a renewed contact with things, outside any practical relation, discovered in their gratuitousness and hence in their total otherness" (Manotta 243).

In Pirandello's works there appears to be a connection between what I have called "the post-epiphanic reflection" and the act of looking in a mirror. Faenza observes that Pirandello stresses "an insoluble paradox: there is no possibility of living and, at the same time, of seeing oneself living. It is possible only to see oneself arranged, devoid of naturalness and spontaneity: living naturally means ceasing to observe oneself" (Faenza 91). As the mirror represents disappearance of beauty and the inevitability of death, according to Künstler-Langner that object constitutes one of the symbols of *vanitas vanitatum* (29). Pirandello seems to apply that instrument both to evoke the atmosphere of suspension between reality and fiction, and to project the reader into a symbolic dimension of death-in-life. After the epiphany of life, the collapsed world of form is but an ephemeral and fleeting phantasmagoria created by mirror reflections. Having discovered the fictitious world of form, a given individual becomes aware of being surrounded by mirages and phantasms, vainly looking for stable identity. It is but numerous personas that appear as a result of the disintegration of personality. The Italian writer also observes that due to the Hamlet-like self-awareness, a given individual is no longer able to identify him- or herself with all the masked personas which used to function as his or her identity. The individual who has been violently deprived of all the masks feels estranged not only from others, but above all from himself.

The Red Rover is also faced with a crisis of identity. Chapter XX seems to be crucial, as the moment of carnival may be regarded as epiphany revealing the truth concerning his formalized existence to the protagonist. Unlike in *The Phantom Ship*, in Cooper's novel epiphany no longer means the experience of the sacred. Devoid of theophany, in *The Red Rover* it remains a literary device, which suspends the meaninglessness of mimetic form and, revealing meaningful, spontaneous life, introduces an existential dimension into the text. Perceived as a manifestation of meaning in the insignificant everyday existence, epiphany elevates the individual from ignorance to awareness, contributing to the epiphanee's profound metamorphosis. The epiphanic moment presented in Chapter XX of *The Red Rover* deserves particular attention, as, surprisingly enough, it is stimulated by the carnival taking place aboard the Rover's ship. As the experience of carnival is evocative of Mikhail Bakhtin's theory, a brief reference to his concept seems important for the further interpretation of Cooper's text. According to Bakhtin, carnival is characterized by the world being turned topsy-turvy, as well as by the interpenetration of high and low, virtuous and vicious, beautiful and ugly, daily routine and festive extraordinariness. Bakhtin also claims that during the carnival time, a given individual feels he or she is a part of the collectivity and that hierarchy is inverted. Revealing the deceptive nature of hypocritical human society, the masquerade, paradoxically, unmasks all kinds of inauthenticity. Offering anti-images of "established 'fixities' of every sort" (Castle 904), a carnivalesque episode destabilizes the orderly theatrical world and encourages topsy-turviness. As the chaos of the carnival world challenges all fixed forms, this "discontinuous, estranging, sometimes even hallucinatory event" carries with it "a powerfully cathartic and disruptive éclat" (Castle 913).

Although the Pirandellian theory of form/life opposition seems hardly comparable to the Bakhtinian concept of carnival, the Italian critic and the Russian scholar resemble each other in that both are celebrators of liberation from all that is fixed and complete. In *Rablais and His World* Bakhtin, like Pirandello in *L'umorismo*, explores "the interface between a statis imposed from above and a desire for change from below" (Clark and Holquist 298). Additionally, both the humoristic and the carnivalesque attitudes seem to seek all that is not mentioned *expressis verbis* in the text, concentrating on what is left implicit. Surprising as it may seem, Bakhtin identifies carnival, a social phenomenon, with grotesque realism, a literary device. Similarly, in Pirandello's concept the social, that is the institution of theatre, and the literary, that is *l'umorismo*, seem to interact. According to Bakhtin, carnival, which may be regarded as a theatre without any border between stage and gallery, celebrates mutability, incompleteness, and relativity of all forms of non-carnivalized life. Strikingly enough, Bakhtin's statement that carnival is "life itself, shaped according to a certain pattern of play" (quoted in Clark and Holquist 300) seems to suggest that this phenomenon, regarded as a manifestation of the dynamic, has much in common with Pirandello's concept of spontaneous life as opposed to static form. However, despite those similarities between the Pirandellian theatrical existence and the Bakhtinian carnivalized reality, there are also some differences between the two. While in the latter's theory the mask symbolizes the joy of liberation from stable forms, according to the former it stands for hiding a terrifying emptiness of existence. A fundamental divergence between the two, however, lies in the nature of revealing moments central to both experiences. As a joyful celebra-

2.3. The Rover Becomes Hamlet: Epiphany of Life

tion of metamorphoses, carnival may be regarded as "a victory over fear" (Clark and Holquist 311). By contrast, the bitter awareness of living a masked life, underlined by Pirandello, instills fear of any changes.

In *The Red Rover,* like in Pirandello's concept, carnival seems to be inscribed with a code of danger rather than with that of pleasure, as the masquerade episode introduces a disturbing instability into the theatrical reality presented in Cooper's novel. A provocative event, "it intimates an alternative view of the 'nature of things' and embodies a liberating escape from the status quo" (Castle 904). Frequently, such an episode is "the prerequisite [...] to a general collapse of decorum in the fictional world" (904). Indeed, in *The Red Rover* carnival may be regarded as the prerequisite to a collapse of form. Introducing an imbalance and topsy-turviness, the masquerade episode deranges fixed distinctions, presenting the Rover, a leading actor on the stage of the world, in the role of a spectator. Having the luxury of becoming a passive spectator in the theatre of the world, the Rover watches others enacting the drama with a humoristic attitude. Although the scene should arouse laughter, the Rover does not laugh; on the contrary, he reflects:

> While most of those who were not actors in the noisy and humorous achievements of the crew steadily regarded the same, some with wonder, others with distrust, and all with more or less of the humour of the hour, the Rover, to all appearance, was quite unconscious of all that was going on before his face. (Cooper 199)

As a result of his "post-epiphanic reflection," the Rover experiences the *sentimento del contrario* – he asks the orchestra to play a melancholy piece of music and starts to cry:

> The strains which now rose upon the night, and which spread themselves soft and melodiously abroad upon the water, would in truth have done credit to far more regular artists. The air was wild and melancholy and perhaps it was the more in accordance with the present humour of the man for whose ear it was created. Then, losing the former character the whole power of the music was concentrated in softer and still gentler sounds, as if the genius who had given birth to the melody had been pouring out the feelings of his soul in pathos. The temper of the Rover's mind answered to the changing expression of the music; and, when the strains were sweetest and most touching, he even bowed his head like one who wept. (233)

The Rover, no longer an incarnation of *actio,* but rather that of *contemplatio,* resembles the passive Flying Dutchman, reflecting on his adventurous past. The Rover suddenly realizes that "a blood-seeking, remorseless pirate" (282) is but a role imposed upon him and, to stay within the Pirandellian metaphor, becomes aware of the rent in the paper sky. Revealing his sensitive and mysterious nature, he rejects the mask of the cruel rover and reveals his true nature: the Byronic one.

Influenced greatly by Byron, in the creation of the Rover Cooper combined the essence of masculinity with supernaturalism, Satanism, and exoticism (Philbrick 53). It is worth noticing that when the American author was writing his nautical romances, Byron was at the height of his popularity. The Rover is neither presented as the amorous captain of classical romance nor as a cruel pirate, but, rather, he is portrayed as a noble outcast, a passionate rebel who is mysterious and guilt-ridden (61). In his loneliness, the burden of guilt for which he wants to make up, as well as the truth of his past which remains a dark secret hidden at the bottom of his heart, he strongly resembles Giaour, a typical Byronic hero.

According to Irena Dobrzycka, the heroes of Byron's poetic tales fight with fate and the world, are melancholy and rebellious, and perceive the world in a very pessimistic way (51). Dobrzycka claims further that their pessimism is a consequence of their outlook on the fatalistic nature of the world (62), as a mysterious crime committed by a hero in the past has a disastrous influence on his further life. It becomes a kind of *fatum* haunting the protagonist's mind. Giaour defines the state of his mind in the following way: "Alas! The breast that inly bleeds / Hath nought to dread from outward blow: / Who falls from all he knows of bliss, / Cares little into what abyss" (Byron 1948: 180). As far as Giaour is concerned, he has not managed to arrive on time to prevent his beloved Leila from being killed. The awareness that he has failed when his mistress needed his help constantly haunts his mind. Similarly, the Rover has failed the British Royal Navy and chose the life of a pirate. Both of them are punished by life incommensurably to their blame, as they are rejected by the society and treated with disdain. "For infinite as boundless space / The thought that conscience must embrace, / Which in itself can comprehend / Woe without name, or hope, or end" (157). Another similarity between the two protagonists lies in the fact that neither of them seeks consolation in religion, but rather in confessing the state of their minds and their mental sufferings to another human being: in Giaour's case to a monk, in the Rover's to his friend, Wilder. As the fragmented action in Byron's poetic tales emphasizes the inability of one human being to understand the other, the protagonist's confession of his secrets from the past, as well as the expression of his deepest thoughts and feelings, is for him a way of self-consolation. The dying Giaour confesses to his listener: "Such is my name, / and such my tale. / Confessor! To thy secret ear / I breathe the sorrows I bewail [...]" (184). The Rover resembles Giaour also in his being rejected by the whole world. He remains mysterious and inscrutable even to his fellow seamen, to whom he cannot reveal the truth about his troubled past, carefully hidden under the mask of appearances, as they would not understand him. Because of his emotional and intellectual capacities, which are superior to those of an average man, the Rover is as arrogant, confident, and conscious of himself as all Byronic heroes. Byron describes Giaour in the following way: "Though bent on earth thine evil eye, / As meteor – like thou glidest by, / Right well I view and deem thee one / Whom Othman's sons should slay or shun" (155).

In his analysis of Cooper's sea novels, Philbrick also points out that the Rover is similar to Conrad, the protagonist of Byron's poetic tale entitled *The Corsair*. According to Philbrick, "both men combine great vigour with rather slight statures; the originally fair complexions of both have been dyed red by exposure; both have

2.3. The Rover Becomes Hamlet: Epiphany of Life

luxuriant curls, and each reveals his scornful arrogance in the shape of his mouth" (61). Furthermore, not only Conrad, but also the Rover are serene heroes of few words, who ponder in loneliness before giving a certain order: "And oft perforce his rising lip reveals / the haughtier thought it curbs, but scarce conceals" (*The Corsair* 310). Yet another similarity between Conrad and the Rover lies in the fact that both sailors are great leaders, whose orders are obeyed and who are worshipped by their fellow seamen:

> That man of loneliness and mystery,
> Scarce seen to smile, and seldom heard to sigh;
> Whose name appals the fiercest of his crew,
> And tints each swarthy cheek with sallower hue;
> still sways their souls with that commanding art
> That dazzles, leads, yet chills the vulgar heart. (309)

The masquerade aboard his ship unmasks the Byronic protagonist and stimulates self-examination, which the Rover has avoided out of vanity. "The post-epiphanic reflection" reveals to the protagonist that his apparently satisfying existence in the role of a rover is but death-in-life or, in other words, a flow of life caught in a trap of form. Having become aware of the authentic life which infiltrates through the hole in the paper sky, the Rover is unable to forget about the existence of this disturbing tear. No longer looking in the mirror, the Rover rejects mimetic form and desires spontaneous life. The looking glass is a recurring symbol in Cooper's novel, as the protagonist's cabin is full of mirrors. In *The Red Rover* it becomes a "revealer" of the true human condition, imprisoned under the mask of form. The object is used not only to reveal numerous fabricated images of the Rover, but also to underline the illusoriness of form which appears to be reality. It is the mirror that suggests the multiplicity of the protagonist's identities, his infinite *Doppelgänger*, with whom he is no longer able to identify himself. As his self-perception and the way he is perceived by others do not coincide, the Rover can be described as Robert Musil's "man without qualities." After the illuminating carnivalesque moment, the Rover perceives himself as no one, a mere shadow deprived of personality. The condition of a phantom without quality, unable to pretend to be an authoritarian rover, makes the protagonist utterly estranged from the crew, still acting on the stage of the world. No longer a marionette of himself devoid of any spontaneity of action, the Rover-Orestes is transformed into Hamlet.

The protagonist's overwhelming separation provokes a feeling of disturbing perplexity. I agree with Mario Ricciardi, who observes in his article that "it is not possible to find any sort of reconciliation after the tear" (Ricciardi 29). Aware of his condition of a stranger and feeling instinctively the flow of the not yet extinguished life, the Rover rejects the futility of form in order to follow the unknown authenticity. Interestingly, Vitilio Masiello emphasizes that the rejection of the mask and the limiting role on the stage of the world is strictly associated with becoming "a victim of much more radical estrangement and seclusion, 'a stranger to life'" (Masiello 76). As an emblem of an individual who is aware of his or her condition and consciously condemns himself to inevitable loneliness, the Rover acquires the symbolic dimension of a stranger. The protagonist's alienation is perfectly described in the words of Federico Italia, who emphasizes that "the loneliness intended here is not a superficial one but that inherent in human existence, existential loneliness, which always accompanies human beings [...], even when they are pressed by a crowd" (Italia 38). The Rover, who no longer participates in the universal performance and rebels against the role assigned to him, becomes an utter outcast.

His condition resembles that of Mersault, the protagonist of Albert Camus' novel entitled *The Stranger* (1942). In an interview Camus declared:

> I summarized *The Stranger,* a long time ago, in a sentence which still seems to me very paradoxical: "In our society, any man who does not cry during a funeral of his mother risks to be sentenced to death". I just wanted to say that the protagonist of the book is condemned because he avoids any kind of role-playing. Hence, he is estranged from the society among which he lives, roams, always marginalized in the suburbs of his private, isolated life. Mersault does not play. The response is simple: he refuses to lie. (http://lafrusta.homestead.com/rec_camus.html, consulted 05.08.2011 – my translation)

The Rover, like Mersault, no longer participates in the play of masks and refuses to lie that there are no holes in the paper sky. The protagonist's estrangement from people and his fear of authenticity are similar to Mersault's senseless existence. In both cases the epiphanic moment makes the automatic lives of the protagonists tragic. The carnival aboard the Rover's ship and the murder of the Arab drastically change the formalized existences of the respective characters, condemning them to the condition of strangers. However, despite some similarities between the two novels, their endings differ considerably. Mersault's spectacular death acquires a symbolic dimension of liberation from the restrictive social conventions. In a gesture of protest, the protagonist of Camus' novel rejects social hypocrisy and chooses disturbing authenticity. Having achieved self-awareness, Mersault perceives death as liberation from the absurdity of inauthentic existence. Unlike Mersault, the Rover is not sentenced to death. Desiring a radical transformation of his existence, the protagonist of Cooper's novel chooses the unknown authenticity, at the same time accepting the condition of a stranger.

However, liberation from form in the direction of authentic life is extremely difficult. In *L'umorismo* Pirandello stresses that a person has no idea about life, as, imprisoned in form, a given individual treats all his or her misconceptions concerning life as if they were real. Giving the example of Prometheus, Pirandello underlines that a person knows of life, which resembles the sun, only a small part, which can be compared to the Promethean spark. Stolen from Zeus' fire, the spark emits very faint light, which seems to be surrounded by immense darkness. The author emphasizes, however, that the dense shadow perceived as deep mystery is but "an insubstantial phantom, a miserable deceit" (*L'umorismo* 164). As life overwhelmed

2.3. The Rover Becomes Hamlet: Epiphany of Life 101

by form is imprisoned in the weak light which each individual produces around him or her, all that belongs to universal life, comparable to Zeus' fire, gives the impression of being "the eternal night after the obscure day of our illusion" (163). Concluding, Pirandello stresses that the shadow remains frightening for those who are not aware of the disastrous deceit. For each individual imprisoned in the inauthentic form, the nudity of authentic life is disturbing. Underlying the difficulty of rejecting form, the author presents the individual who wants to free him- or herself towards life as suspended between nothingness and emptiness: everyday existence "seems to be senseless, aimless; and that different reality appears horrible in its mysterious and imperturbable crudeness" (160). Similarly, Masiello claims in his article that the rejection of form inevitably leads, on the one hand, to "the disturbing experience of nothingness" and, on the other hand, to "a paradoxical fear of 'being a prisoner outside'" (Masiello 76). Applying the famous Pirandellian metaphor, Masiello observes that "the empty cosmic immensity shines and penetrates" (77) through the tear in the paper sky, making Orestes feel perplexed and paralyzed.

Gaston Bachelard's *The Poetics of Space* illustrates how difficult it is to reject form and to escape through the hole in the paper sky. In the chapter entitled "The Dialectics of Outside and Inside," Bachelard juxtaposes claustrophobia and agoraphobia, defining man as a "half-open being" (222). Like Giovanni Macchia, who compares the imprisonment in form to "a torture chamber" (Macchia 59), Bachelard perceives the narrow intimate space as hostile. Interestingly enough, both Macchia and Bachelard celebrate liberation into open space, seemingly abyssal and frightening. According to Bachelard, human is susceptible to be suspended half-opened between the claustrophobia of form and the agoraphobia of life. Applying Bachelard's statement to the condition of the Pirandellian protagonists, it can be observed that after the epiphanic experience the "[i]ntimate space loses its clarity, while exterior space loses its void, void being the raw material of possibility of being" (Bachelard 218). Strikingly enough, Bachelard, like Pirandello, stresses the fact that having rejected the prison of form, the individual is condemned to loneliness: "And then, onto what, toward what, do doors open? Do they open for the world of men, or for the world of solitude?" (224). Therefore, Pirandello observes that frequently a given individual lacks courage to throw him- or herself into the abyss of life. He or she stands on the threshold of the abyss, glances at the insoluble mystery and stops. The return to the astonishing naturalness of wearing a mask as one's second nature is, however, impossible. Never again will the individual be able to accept role-playing as his or her identity.

Indeed, the protagonist of Cooper's novel is no longer able to put on any mask. However, he does not stop on the threshold of the abyss, but rather goes a step further. As the Rover, unlike the Pirandellian protagonists, is not characterized by an agoraphobic attitude towards life, he does not fit Bachelard's definition of a "half-opened being." After the epiphanic experience the Rover definitely rejects the claustrophobia of form, as he is not afraid of throwing himself into the abyss of life. No longer looking at himself in the mirror in order to control each gesture, the protagonist starts to live spontaneously and manages to reach authenticity. Although, to stay within Conrad's metaphor presented at the beginning of this chapter, having experienced epiphany, the Red Rover is a "convict" among idiots unaware of their being insignificant specks of dust within the system of the universe, the ending of Cooper's novel is not pessimistic. On the contrary, it celebrates a triumph of spontaneous life over mimetic form, symbolized in the novel by America's liberation from the restrictive British supremacy. It is worth noting that the Rover's victory over mimesis resembles the Flying Dutchman's liberation from the slavery of desire. In both cases the return to the *status quo ante* is not possible.

CHAPTER THREE
"Mimetic Mirror": R. H. Dana's *Two Years Before the Mast* (1840)

The pleonastic expression "the mimetic mirror" was used by M. H. Abrams as a metaphor for art perceived as a reflector of the external world. As in the preface to *Two Years Before the Mast* Dana complains that "[a] voice from the forecastle has hardly yet been heard" (Dana 7), the aim of his reportorial account is to present real life at sea according to the basic concept of mimesis as a mirror held up to reality. Dismissing Cooper's romantic and theatrical attitude towards maritime life presented in his early nautical romances, especially *The Red Rover*, Dana states: "My design is, and it is this which has induced me to publish the book, to present the life of a common sailor at sea as it really is – the light and the dark together" (7). In an attempt to overcome the enslaving mimetic desire to replicate the romantic attitude towards the sea and to free himself from the imprisonment of the established conventions of sea narratives, Dana creates "a real-life narrative of actual experiences" (Gale 108), "a log-like account" (109), "a book of facts" (111), giving the reader the impression of participating in the author's adventures. Using the metaphor of a mirror and shifting towards realism, he seeks to show life at sea as it really is. The concept of the sea as a polished mirror employed in Dana's novel is also masterfully explored in Conrad's collection *The Mirror of the Sea*, written between the years 1904 and 1906, with an "Author's Note" added to it in 1919, five years before the author's death. In Conrad's collection of essays the young Dana's youthful enthusiasm and optimism, as well as his determination to take fate into his own hands and to act independently on the stage of the theatre of the world, are replaced by the first-person narrator's reflection on human helplessness against the changing form of the world. Using the symbolism of *vanitas*, in *The Mirror of the Sea* Conrad emphasizes man's insignificance and vulnerability in confrontation with the all-powerful death. In other words, *The Mirror of the Sea* highlights the vanitative aspect both of the mirror and of the *theatrum mundi*. The leitmotif of this collection is a fleeting mirror reflection. It is worth noting that theatre may be compared to a mirror because one of its main functions is to imitate and mirror the real world. As a sheet of water may serve as a plate-glass, it may be perceived as a mirror both in the literal and the metaphorical sense. First of all, like all looking glasses, the sea can mirror the outside world: the sky, stars, ships, and mysterious lands rising above the horizon. Secondly, it may be regarded as a magic mirror, becoming a means of communication between the past and the present. The stimulus for writing down distant reminiscences was Conrad's desire to examine himself in a mirror. Watching his image in a looking glass, Conrad seems to be reflecting on his seafaring past, observing in his wrinkled face the chart of all his remarkable journeys. In contrast to Dana's regeneration as an effect of his two years spent before the mast, it is the *vanitas vanitatum* theme that is omnipresent in the reflection of the sixty-two-year-old Conrad, who seems bitterly aware of the approaching death.

As a comparative analysis of *Two Years Before the Mast* and *The Mirror of the Sea* may be illuminating to the interpretation of both texts in terms of mimetic aspects, the present chapter examines Dana's and Conrad's use of the mirror symbolism. It is argued that Dana, operating in his narrative only on the reflective properties of the mirror-like sea, produces exact pictures of reality, as opposed to Conrad, who presents photographs containing spots of indeterminacy, combining reflective and projective capacities of the surface of the sea. This analysis of *Two Years Before the Mast* and *The Mirror of the Sea* focuses also on binary oppositions based on the symbolism of the mirror: Dana versus Conrad, reality versus fiction, or outer space versus inner space, which contribute to a *mise-en-abyme* effect.

3.1. Sea Narrative: A Mirror of Maritime Life

As far as the genre of *Two Years Before the Mast* is concerned, Dana's narrative has some features of a novel, as defined by Mikhail Bakhtin in his "Epic and Novel – Toward a Methodology for the Study of the Novel." According to Bakhtin, one of the basic subjects of the novel is "the theme of the hero's inadequacy to his fate or his situation" (Bakhtin 37). A given individual does not accept his or her fate; hence, he or she feels that in his or her situation, the realization of his or her seemingly limitless potential and the fulfilment of his or her dreams is impossible. The hero's conviction of his or her being larger-than-life is only an illusion. In fact, he or she cannot cope with his/her fate, which overpowers him or her. Middle-aged Dana, disillusioned with his life, feels melancholy and nostalgic for the past. He wishes he had now the enthusiasm, strength, and optimism he used to possess in his twenties. For him, now a respected lawyer, both his youth and the sea were ultimate joys, his political career and mature life being but a failure. Unfortunately, his dreams were never fulfilled and his potential, having vanished too quickly together with his youth, was never fully realized.

Bakhtin claims further that the novel is the only "genre-in-the-making" which "squeezes out some genres and incorporates others into its own peculiar structure" (5). As the expansion of the novel has been so remarkable and its influence on other genres so great, Bakhtin calls the process "the phenomenon of novelization" (7). Dana's narrative may be regarded as a novel, as is suits Bakhtin's definition. In *Two Years*, like in novels, the past is in the sphere of direct contact with the present-day reality. This connection with the past involves constant re-thinking and re-evaluating. Looking from the perspective of more than twenty years, Dana would perceive his first voyage, California, and himself in a completely different, less enthusiastic and less optimistic way. What is more, Dana, like heroes of novels, combines in himself both negative and positive features. On the one hand, he lives in the world of illusion, reciting poetry aboard his ship, and takes pride in his youth, but, on the other hand, he manages to prove that he is responsible, reasonable, and trustworthy. Moreover, in the aforementioned essay Bakhtin claims that while reading a novel, the reader experiences "the impulse to continue (what will happen next?)" and "the impulse to end (how will it end?)" (32). While reading *Two Years*, the reader is curious about the subsequent episodes and wants to find out how they will end. The final similarity between *Two Years* and the novel, as defined by Bakhtin, lies in the fact that it was written about and for Dana's contemporaries.

To a certain extent *Two Years* is also a Bildungsroman. Robert L. Gale observes that when Dana begins his "poor boy's grand tour," he is "greener than Walt Whitman's grass" (Gale 28); therefore, his twenty-five-month-long experience as a sailor may be perceived as a symbol of his transition from immaturity to maturity, and from ignorance to experience. The young Dana is portrayed in the process of becoming, as an inexperienced sailor who learns from life. He continues to develop alongside the progression of the voyage and achieves maturity through experiencing various ups and downs of life. As Gale puts it, "Dana had sailed from Boston on the *Pilgrim*, a pilgrim lad in search of freedom and new lands; he returned on the *Alert*, a man alert in mind and body" (31).

The genre of *The Mirror of the Sea* is far more difficult to determine. This work bears hardly any resemblance either to a novel or to a Bildungsroman. Probably the most autobiographical of Conrad's books, in its existential depth and close attention to detail *The Mirror* is similar to a philosophical treatise, "a formal work containing a systematic examination of a subject and its principles" (Cuddon 944). In a number of ways *The Mirror of the Sea* resembles Aristotle's *Poetics*. In his work Conrad examines and guides the ignorant reader through the intricacies of one particular subject, seamanship. He uses numerous naval terms, such as rigging, anchoring, or landfall, in order to acquaint the reader with at least the basic ones. Like Conrad, Aristotle also thoroughly explores one subject matter, that is the dramatic art, using a plethora of literary terms, such as tragedy, action, or mimesis. What is more, *The Mirror*, like *Poetics*, is divided into many short titled sections, each dealing with a different aspect of the given subject. *The Mirror* is a collection of numbered passages divided under fifteen heads, and subdivided into forty-nine chapters. However, apart from many similarities between *The Mirror* and *Poetics*, there is one considerable difference between the two. In his book Conrad treats landfalls, departures, and anchoring as emblems and allegories of mortal life. In other words, Conrad's book encourages both a literal and a metaphorical reading, whereas Aristotle's *Poetics* is devoid of puns and symbols.

Apart from having the features of a treatise, *The Mirror* is, beyond any doubt, autobiographical. In his article entitled "*The Mirror of the Sea*: Fragments of a Great Confession," Avrom Fleishman posits that the only requirement of autobiography is "that an author write of himself by name, verbally projecting his images from their source in memory" (Fleishman 663). Fleishman asserts further that there always remain doubts regarding the accuracy and historical referentiality of Conrad's self-portrait, as all narrative is by its nature fictive. Therefore, the scholar speaks of *The Mirror* as a "self-referential" narrative.

Dana's book is also a "self-referential" narrative. His narrative may be regarded as a mirror reflection of his life before the mast and in California between 1834 and 1836, as in *Two Years* he presents "the truth exactly as he saw and felt it" (Gale 114). At the same time Gale stresses how difficult it must have been for Dana to distinguish between what he really felt and what he was romantically expected to feel (115). D.H. Lawrence, aware of what Gale calls "Dana's schizophrenia" (131), also describes the writer as torn between feeling and knowing. According to Lawrence, Dana tells his story faithfully when he describes what he feels (sees, hears and senses), using the technique of accurate reporting. However, when he seeks to know the sea and the life spent before the mast, "it [is] a step in his own undoing. It [is] a new phase of dissolution of his own being. Afterwards, he would be a knower: but more near to mechanism than before" (Lawrence 196). As Dana describes what he feels, his writing, to apply Meyer Abrams' famous metaphor, may be regarded as a mimetic mirror.

If Dana's realistic *Two Years* is a mirror, then Conrad's symbolic work is a combination of the mirror with a lamp, as Conrad "reflects a world already bathed in an emotional light that he has himself projected" (Abrams 52). Indeed, in Conrad's book bare truth and narrative fiction are interwoven. On the one hand, *The Mirror* contains events drawn from Conrad's maritime service between the years 1875 and 1895, such as his shore duty while serving on the *Duke of Sutherland* (Chapters XXXI, XXXIV), his adventures aboard the *Loch Etive* (Chapters XI, XII, XXXVI), finding a fatherly friend in Captain B. of the *Tilkhurst* (Chapter III), his stay in frozen Amsterdam with the *Highland Forest* (Chapters XIV, XV), and commanding his own ship, the *Otago* (Chapters V, XXIII, XXXIV). On the other hand, however, there are some discrepancies to the historical record. A case in point is the highly imaginative story of Dominic Cervoni's murder of his nephew, Cesar, for the theft of Conrad's money. The historical Cesar Cervoni lived to a ripe old age. According to Fleishman, there is a parallel between this fictive event and young Conrad's attempted suicide. Fleishman is convinced that Conrad's act of violence "was one of self-punishment for youthful follies that include his squandering of his uncle's money, designated for his nautical career" (Flieshman 670). Young Cesar Cervoni steals money and is punished by death. Similarly, Conrad, also a young mariner, wastes money and becomes an inflictor of self-punishment.

The Mirror is, however, much more than just a personal narrative. Fleishman calls this book "one of the finest examples of the peculiarly modern version of autobiographical art" (Fleishman 664). Conrad himself claims that in his writing he tries to present truth and fidelity to personal impressions:

> My little *voli* of autobiography of course is absolutely genuine. The rest is a more or less close approximation to facts and suggestions. What I claim as true are my mental and

emotional reactions to life, to men, to their affairs and their passions as I have seen them. I have in that sense kept always true to myself. (quoted in Sherry 284)

The snatches of his reminiscences are therefore like a record of glimpses caught in the past. As memory is unreliable, the images are discontinuous, distorted, and blurred, much like mirror reflections. *The Mirror* may also be compared to a mosaic. From a distance it seems to be created out of unrelated small pieces; however, a closer look reveals that the fragments are not gathered at random, but form a unified sequence, a complete, meaningful, and highly symbolic whole.

Unlike in Conrad's fragmented mosaic-like narrative, the principles of balance operate throughout Dana's narrative. Gale claims that *Two Years* has a sonata form, as it consists of three parts. The first section of the book describes Dana's experiences aboard the *Pilgrim* and the protagonist's tests during his journey to California. The middle part concerns the author's stay in California, where he is tested anew but this time ashore. The third section of the book is devoted to Dana's adventures aboard the *Alert* and describes situations which challenge the protagonist on his way back home. Tests of Dana's strength, obedience, and alertness on the *Alert* are an exact reflection of those on the *Pilgrim*, with the episode of rounding Cape Horn in mid-winter constituting a variation on the repeated theme. According to Gale, the book's three-part structure resembles the exposition, development, and recapitulation of a sonata (112).

Gale uses not only music, but also architecture as a point of reference in his discussion of Dana's book. He claims that the chapter structure of *Two Years* has the shape of a Gothic façade, which consists of three parts: two peripheral, one being a mirror reflection of the other, and a central part, which differs considerably from the two. By analogy, eight chapters devoted to the voyage on the *Pilgrim* reflect eight chapters depicting adventures on the *Alert*, whereas twenty chapters portraying the narrator's stay in California represent the middle part of the façade, significantly different from the other two. Strikingly enough, several events presented in early chapters are mirrored in the corresponding later chapters. In Chapter I the *Pilgrim* leaves Boston, and in Chapter XXXVI the *Alert* returns to Boston; in Chapter II Dana is seasick, and in Chapter XXXV he is the only one who does not suffer from seasickness. Chapters IV and XXXIII concern Captain Thompson and his arguments with officers, while in Chapters V and XXXII Dana rounds Cape Horn. In Chapter VI George Ballmer falls overboard and loses his life, and in Chapter XXXI Dana's life is endangered. Finally, in Chapter VIII the *Pilgrim* reaches California, whereas in Chapter XXIX the *Alert* leaves California (Gale 112).

Depicting reality, Dana occasionally shifts from pictures to music and architecture; therefore, he seems to oscillate between *mimesis* and *creatio*. In *The Mirror and the Lamp* M. H. Abrams observes that in the criticism of the romantic period, the "expressiveness" of poetry is hardly ever compared to painting. *Ut pictura poesis*, Horace's famous phrase, widespread in the eighteenth century, is no longer used to indicate analogies between painting and poetry in the romantic criticism, but rather to emphasize the similarity between the canvas reflecting the state of mind of the artist and the mirror. Abrams underlines that instead of painting, it is music that becomes the kind of art frequently pointed to as being strongly connected with poetry. The author of *The Mirror and the Lamp* announces: "For if a picture seems the nearest thing to a mirror-image of the external world, music, of all the arts, is the most remote" (Abrams 50). Music and architecture, as non-representational harmonious expressions of the artist's inner realm, are non-mimetic by nature. Hence, Dana's references not only to mirror-images, but also to the sonata form and to the Gothic façade perfectly illustrate his oscillation between imitation and creation. Although his aim is to present life at sea according to the concept of mimesis as a mirror, Dana frequently shifts from documentary realism towards Cooper's idealistic treatment of the maritime material.

In contrast to *Two Years*, *The Mirror* does not pretend to be an exact copy of reality, but, rather, it contains spots of indeterminacy. Here, the reader is in a privileged position, as an active role is demanded from him or her. Since the story is a fictive mirroring of the writer himself, it may be called "the mirror of Conrad" (Skutnik 20). It is the reader who is asked to create a whole out of the seemingly unrelated and dim fragments, and to decipher its allegorical meaning. A mirror reflection in Conrad's narrative is much more ambiguous than a one in Dana's. Conrad himself is both a spectator and an actor, a person who is looking and who is being looked at. He looks back at the experiences of his youth and middle age in the mirror of his memory. The reader, peering into Conrad's mirror, identifies with the author as an actor, a participant in those scenes recalled in fragmented reminiscences. In this case, the mirror functions almost as a magic object, a means of communication between the past and the present, thanks to which the reader's imagination travels back in time. The reader is asked to leave behind the *profanum* of the land, to plumb the mysteries of navigation and the *sacrum* of the sea. While referring to his book, Conrad compares *The Mirror* to "a last hour's confession" (*The Mirror* VII), at the same time admitting that he makes "a full confession not of [his] sins but of [his] emotions" (IX-X). As the veracity of Conrad's recollections has been questioned by critics, *The Mirror* may be defined as "autobiofiction" (Adamowicz-Pośpiech 160). The elderly Conrad, in all likelihood aware of the approaching death, confesses to the reader, revealing the most intimate and hidden details of his life, as if expecting to be listened to, understood, and to be given absolution.

Likewise, *Two Years* may be classified as an "autobiofictional" narrative. Dana confesses to the reader:

> In the following pages I design to give an accurate and authentic narrative of a little more than two years spent as a common sailor, before the mast, in the American merchant service. It is written out from a journal which I kept at the time, and from notes which I made of most of the events as they happened. (7)

The Polish translation of the title, *Pamiętnik żeglarza* [*A Sailor's Diary*], indicates that Dana's work belongs to the genre of log-like sea diaries. Samuel Shapiro stresses that the detailed sea-journal Dana had kept on the voyage was lost by his cousin in Boston. Therefore, the author of *Two Years* created the story from his notebook account that was twenty pages long (Shapiro 192). Gale also underlines that Dana had only a pocket notebook and his prodigious memory to rely on (109). Constructing his reminiscences along the idealist-realist opposition, Dana, like Conrad, gives romantic and nostalgic overtones to his maritime material. However, in producing images of the external world, Dana differs from Conrad, who in his "autobiofiction" focuses on the internal aspect of the depicted reality – the state of the perceiving mind.

3.2. The Self and Sea Space: Reciprocal Mirrors[3]

Relying on Gaston Bachelard's and Hanna Buczyńska-Garewicz's philosophical considerations, in this section of my study I seek to analyze the sea space presented in Dana's *Two Years Before the Mast* and Conrad's collection of reminiscences, *The Mirror of the Sea,* in order to show how this kind of space exists in the sailors' minds and how their imagination endows the sea with spirituality. I also focus on the different ways in which young and mature seamen perceive and interiorize the sea, and on a variety of features of their character they ascribe to the ocean.

In *The Poetics of Space*, Gaston Bachelard distinguishes between two major kinds of space: outer, that is the geometrical space visible and perceptible through the senses, and inner, that is the invisible space existing in thoughts, memories, and dreams. As Bachelard perceives space as a spiritual relation between a human being and his or her surrounding, in *The Poetics of Space* he investigates the impact of various spaces upon human inhabitants and vice versa. Bachelard stresses the fact that any outer space, if inhabited and experienced, may become an inner one. Once a space becomes intimate, "not open to just anybody" (Bachelard 78), it is then interiorized and begins to exist in a person. As a phenomenologist of space, Bachelard refutes the notion of absolute space. He is convinced that "[i]nhabited space transcends geometrical space" (47) and, rejecting Aristotelian idea of space, he supports that of Heidegger. Aristotle stressed the priority of a place to a thing. He claimed that the place is a condition for the thing to exist. The thing depends on the place; however, the place can exist independently of the thing, being empty or

---

3   For an extended version of the following section on sea space, see Joanna Mstowska, "Inner Sea Space in Joseph Conrad's *Youth* and *The Mirror of the Sea*" in PASE 2009 post-conference volume entitled *Exploring Space: Spatial Notions in Cultural, Literary and Language Studies*, vol. 1, *Space in Cultural and Literary Studies*. Ed. Andrzej Ciuk and Katarzyna Molek-Kozakowska. Newcastle: Cambridge Scholars Publishing, 2010, 58–65.

filled with the thing. Heidegger, by contrast, rejected Aristotelian idea of space and believed that the place is never empty but exists thanks to its physical or spiritual content.

Convinced that thanks to the human impact on each inhabited space, this space is no longer an object, but is elevated to the role of a subject and has a kind of a "psyche," in his book Bachelard explores what he calls "topoanalysis," that is "the systematic psychological study of the sites of our intimate lives" (8). What is more, Bachelard asserts that children view and interiorize intimate spaces in a completely different way than adults. As in childhood the boundary between the real and the imagined is disturbed and blurred, children perceive spaces not only through the senses, but also through the prism of their lively imagination. By contrast, adulthood is characterized by "dry" rationalism. In the chapter devoted to nests, Bachelard writes: "But the dreams of today do not go this far, and an abandoned nest no longer contains the herb of invisibility" (94). Once a child achieves maturity, his/her great imagination vanishes forever.

In her book on phenomenology of space, Buczyńska-Garewicz echoes Bachelard's philosophical considerations. She corroborates the view that a place is characterized by its spiritual content, not by its size or by its distance from other places. In her book, she goes beyond the physical sense of space and concentrates on its spiritual aspect. Like Bachelard, she is convinced that once a space is experienced and interiorized, it lives on in human consciousness and psyche. Buczyńska-Garewicz insists that space is by no means empty, but, rather, full of memories, wishes, dreams and desires. Interpreting space in terms of geometry means for her concentrating only on its physical aspect and reducing space to technological pragmatism and utilitarianism. Geometrical space is finite, limited and measurable, whereas inner one, existing in memories and dreams, is infinite, limitless and immeasurable.

Buczyńska-Garewicz deals specifically with the urban spaces of Venice and imagined cities, whereas Bachelard mainly explores significances of the house. Both, however, seem to ignore sea space. Still, their observations are applicable to my investigation of sea space, which appears to have been left unnoticed by philosophers investigating space. With its *genius loci*, sea space, full of spiritual content, is much more than just a travel channel for ships. Young and inexperienced seamen, like Dana or young Marlow of *Youth*, regard sea space as strikingly similar to the experienced space of ships. There is no place for women on the ship; therefore, personified and feminized ships become the loves of the young seamen's lives. In *Youth* the ship called the *Judea* is ancient, outmoded, dilapidated and unseaworthy. Nevertheless, in the men on board she inspires faith, a sense of security, hope, loyalty, and fidelity. Although dirty and rusty, in the eyes of Marlow the ship is beautiful and precious. He loves her unconditionally, and is fully aware that the ship will never be able to requite his feelings: "There was a touch of romance in it, something that made me love the old thing" (*Youth* 5). He idealizes the ship, speaking about the *Judea* in a highly elegiac tone and treating her as a beloved old wife. For Marlow the vessel is not only capable of human emotions but also, like all human beings, she has a soul. Although the *Judea* is not of breathtaking splendour, Marlow remains blind to her weaknesses and perceives her as precious and unique. Similarly, Dana extols both beauty and bravery of the *Alert* during the ship's fight with the icy ocean, stressing "the desolate character of her situation – alone, as she was, battling with storms, wind, and ice, at this extremity of the globe, and in almost constant night" (165). Dana is not only proud of the feminized vessel, but also full of compassion.

Similarly, for the narrator of *The Mirror of the Sea* ships are not just objects, but living creatures who have iron hearts and are able to feel. Here, the ships are also feminized figures who should be admired and adored. The narrator admits that he idealizes those ships which fascinate him; to his eyes they are attractive mistresses whose imperfections he simply overlooks. A ship is a figure that men "shall learn to know with an intimacy surpassing the intimacy of man with man, to love with a love nearly as great as that of man for woman, and often as blind in its infatuated disregard of defects" (*The Mirror* 58). In his unreasonable, inexplicable, and overwhelmingly strong love for ships, Conrad regards them as delicate creatures who "do want humouring" (51). Each ship, just as each woman, is not only unique and exceptional, but also mysterious: "You must treat with an understanding consideration the mysteries of her feminine nature" (56). The above-mentioned examples illustrate Bachelard's statement in which he claims that "[i]f we look at it intimately, the humblest dwelling has beauty" (Bachelard 4).

The sailors' relationships with the vessels they adore and admire are, beyond any doubt, intimate. Apart from perceiving the ships as women, young seamen regard the vessels as their natural homes, as "the non-I that protects the I" (5). Bachelard characterizes the space of the house as "intimate space" [*l'espace intime*], stressing the fact that in each house there are corners where the inhabitants can hide to find solitude, essential for meditations and reflections upon the world and human condition. Convinced that houses are to be experienced and interiorized, Bachelard gives primacy to the spiritual aspect of home over the physical one. Bachelard also claims that to inhabit a particular place means to interiorize it and to be in that place not only physically, but also spiritually. He even goes a step further in claiming that it is possible to inhabit places that do not exist in a physical sense; thus, he stresses the value of oneiric phenomena. Bachelard believes that the houses seen in dreams may never materialize and, as imagined and desired places, remain forever only in the sphere of human psyche. Nevertheless, in his account they always evoke reminiscences and dreams of safety, security, and happiness (38–61).

However, as "the space we love is unwilling to remain permanently enclosed" (Bachelard 53), in the eyes of young seamen intimate space extends beyond ships and encapsulates the sea as well. The young Dana loves, admires and respects the sea, which for him belongs to the sphere of *sacrum* and is contrasted with the *profanum* of the land. Displaying a kind of naivety, bold and energetic Dana refuses to believe in his insignificance and regards himself as powerful enough to domesticate the sea. The young Dana associates sea space with the feelings of safety and security, as the sea, like all "really inhabited space[s], bears the essence of the notion of home" (Bachelard 5). The vast majority of young seamen are, much as Dana, men of extremes; no limitations are placed upon their imagination. They are often subject to flights of imagination, live on the verge of reality and dream, and seem incapable of making a clear-cut distinction between illusion and waking reality. In perceiving the world through the prism of their imagination, they resemble children. Hence, the quality of their experience is phantasmagoric and dreamlike. It is their extreme sensitivity and their susceptibility to daydreaming that enable them to inhabit the sea oneirically. In their eyes, sea space becomes greater than reality, is inscribed in them and "engraved in [their] soul[s]" (Bachelard 11). Thanks to the unimaginable depths of their psyche and imagination, they feel enclosed and protected even while sailing.

In *The Poetics of Space* Gaston Bachelard gives an example of a hermit who feels safe and at home within the intimate space of his hut, despite the fact that the hut is situated in the middle of a wood and it is snowing heavily. The feeling of security given by the intimate space of the hut makes the hermit able to reduce the outside world to just one word – snow. To quote Bachelard, snow "reduces the exterior world to nothing. [...] It gives a single color to the entire universe which, with the one word, snow, is both expressed and nullified for those who have found shelter" (40). Bachelard's statement concerning the perception of vast spaces is also applicable to sea space. Young seamen who feel safe on their ships reduce the immensity of the sea and regard the inhospitable space as an intimate one. Sea space becomes for them what Bachelard calls "intimate immensity" [*l'immensite intime*]. Bachelard believes that there is "correspondence between the immensity of world space and the depth of 'inner space'" (205). He also states that "the impression of immensity is in us, and not necessarily related to an object" (XXXIX). If it were not for the immature sailors' "inner immensity," they would never be able to domesticate the sea and, in consequence, to become inhabitants of the world.

According to Hanna Buczyńska-Garewicz, only human beings are capable of inhabiting spaces. For her, much as for Gaston Bachelard, inhabiting a place means interiorizing it in one's consciousness and psyche and giving spiritual life to it. A place becomes a home when its spiritual content harmonizes with that of the inhabitant's soul. Without that harmony, she regards the given space as abstract and empty, and people therein as homeless. Buczyńska-Garewicz insists that inhabiting space should be perceived as a spiritual relation, as not only human beings live in space, but space also exists in them, in their memories and dreams. She claims further that by inhabiting numerous spaces, people broaden their horizons, as well as realize their freedom of wandering. According to Buczyńska-Garewicz, a wanderer is open to otherness and it is possible for him or her to transform strangeness into familiarity, as was the case with the young sailors domesticating the sea. A stimulus for every wandering is not emptiness, but rather a kind of fullness characterized by a tendency to exceed. The wanderer's openness to broaden his or her horizons does not signify that he or she inhabits empty space, but, on the contrary, that he or she has interiorized numerous spaces. Being a wanderer means extending one's home and becoming an inhabitant of the world, and, at the same time, enlarging the capacity of one's soul. Buczyńska-Garewicz seems to support Bachelard's thesis when she claims that the ability to domesticate vast spaces in a spiritual way reflects the immensity of a particular human being's inside.

By contrast, the sea space interiorized by mature and experienced sailors is by no means intimate, but rather hostile, cruel and malicious. As the seamen grow old, they begin to regard the sea as an opponent, fighting with which becomes the essence of their existence. When Dana's unconscious youth is replaced by disillusioned maturity, he realizes that the sea is not static and approachable, but monumental and awe-inspiring. It is, indeed, its overwhelming vastness and great ferocity that is both frightening and enchanting for the mature Dana. He regards the sea no longer as intimate space, but as hostile immensity, stressing that his idealistic approach towards the sea disappeared after the moment of initiation:

> The romantic interest which many take in the sea, and in those who live upon it, may be of use in exciting their attention to this subject, though I cannot but feel sure that all who have followed me in my narrative must be convinced that the sailor has no romance in his every-day life to sustain him, but that it is very much the same plain, matter-of-fact drudgery and hardship, which would be experienced on shore. (201)

The mature narrator of *The Mirror of the Sea*, in all likelihood Conrad's *porte parole*, also perceives sea space in a completely different way than the young Marlow of *Youth* or the inexperienced Dana. Having spent twenty years at sea, he has experienced various kinds of enchantments and bitterness associated with maritime life. Having achieved maturity through countless battles with the ocean, the narrator has acquired a considerable knowledge concerning the true nature of the sea. Enthusiasm and optimism, which characterized him when he was a youthful and inexperienced seaman, have vanished forever. Looking from the perspective of twenty-five years, in his "Author's Note" to *The Mirror of the Sea* Conrad confesses that his feeling towards the sea was neither "the lyric illusion of an old, romantic heart" nor "a foolish infatuation," but "it was great passion for the sea – something too great for words" (*The Mirror* VIII). In his youth, his attitude towards the sea used to be like that of a young inexperienced lover towards his mistress: "I surrendered my being to that passion which various and great like life itself had also its periods of wonderful serenity which even a fickle mistress can give sometimes on her soothed breast, full of wiles, full of fury, and yet capable of an enchanting sweetness" (VIII). The great love for the sea has quickly become the essence of his existence: "Beyond the line of the sea horizon the world for me did not exist" (VIII). As the young narrator is fascinated and enchanted by his beloved mistress, his attitude towards the sea is similar to that of the young Marlow of *Youth* and Dana. However, when the narrator has achieved maturity, he has learned to look beyond the surface, and realized that the ocean "is ready to beguile and betray, to smash and to drown the incorrigible optimism of men" (137), and that regarding the sea as a tempting mistress giving sweetness and delight was just the vision of his youth.

The older the narrator grows, the more ambiguous the way in which he perceives the sea becomes. He recollects a moment, calling it the moment of initiation, when he realized that the essence of a seaman's existence is not showing love and admiration for the sea, but constantly fighting with this malevolent force, while loving it at the same time. This is the moment when he adopts a new role, that of a real seaman: "I had looked coolly at the life of my choice. Its illusions were gone, but its fascination remained. I had become a seaman at last" (142). It is in his maturity that he has become fully aware of the inherent cruelty and malevolence of the sea, carefully hidden beyond its tempting and encouraging surface – the only layer visible to the eyes of an enthusiastic and naive youth. While spinning his reminiscences, the narrator once again recollects the moment of initiation and confesses to the reader:

> Already I looked with other eyes upon the sea. I knew it is capable of betraying the generous ardour of youth as implacably as, indifferent to evil or good, it would have betrayed the basest greed or the noblest heroism. [...] Open to all and faithful to none, it exercises its fascination for the undoing of the best. (148)

The mature narrator of *Two Years* regards the sea as a testing-ground of his strength and his character, as he is aware that "[t]here is a witchery in the sea, its songs and stories, and in the mere sight of a ship [...]" (Dana 201). He also recollects a young seaman whose attitude towards the sea was a typical romantic infatuation: "I have known a young man with such a passion for the sea, that the very creaking of a block stirred up his imagination so that he could hardly keep his feet on dry ground" (201). When the inexperienced sailor grew older, his perception of the ocean has drastically changed: "No sooner, however, has the young sailor begun his new life in earnest, than all this fine drapery falls off, and he learns that it is but work and hardship, after all. This is the true light in which a sailor's life is to be viewed" (201). The mature narrator describes the sea as a force that invites him to come out of himself and to extend beyond all limits. The ocean is brutal and hostile, but, at the same time, encouraging, and affording a chance of success. If it had not been for the sea, the narrator of *Two Years Before the Mast* would have never been tested and he would have never adopted the role of a respected and reasonable sailor. As it stimulates the longing for distant, unknown and limitless spaces, the immensity frees sailors from limitations and opens up new horizons. Experienced seamen become aware of the possible inspiring function of the immense sea space.

In *The Poetics of Space*, Bachelard underlines not only the impact of geometrical space upon human beings, but also their influence on space. Young and inexperienced seamen regard sea space as the extension of the intimate space of their ships, and love it as blindly and unconditionally as they adore the feminized and idealized ships. It is their strong attachment to the sea that elevates sea space to the role of a subject. In their eyes the sea takes on the form of a seductive mistress who should be admired, but who will always remain an inscrutable mystery. By contrast, mature and experienced seamen do not live in a phantasmagoric world, but, rather, the way they perceive the sea is deeply rooted in reality. They no longer regard the ocean as a mysterious woman, but conceptualize sea space as a fierce enemy, fighting with whom becomes the essence of their existence. Having spent years at sea, they are aware of the changeable and malevolent nature of the ocean. However, the sea still tempts them, as struggling with this element allows them to go beyond all limits, to test their characters and to rediscover their latent strength. Despite numerous disillusionments, disenchantments, and tussles with the malicious sea, the mature narrator of *The Mirror of the Sea* can neither resist his great passion for the sea nor is able to hate it. His love towards the impenetrable and inherently cruel ocean turns out to be unimaginably strong and eternally lasting. As Conrad confesses in his "Author's Note" to *The Mirror of the Sea*: "My relation with the sea [...] went on unreasoning and invincible, surviving the test of disillusion, defying the disenchantment that lurks in every day of a strenuous life; went on [...] without bitterness and without repining, from the first hour to the last" (VII-VIII). If it were not for both young and mature seamen's attachment to the ocean, sea space would never gain its spirituality and would exist only in a physical sense. Having interiorized the sea, the seamen have given to its either intimate or immense space a part of themselves.

Gaston Bachelard's transcendental geometry is applicable also in the interpretation of sea fiction. Beyond any doubt, his concept of interiorized space reshapes the way of perceiving sea space and endows it with new significance. I have presented various ways in which the protagonists of Dana's and Conrad's fiction approach sea space, as well as different features of character they ascribe to the ocean. On the one hand, young and inexperienced seamen, who live on the verge of dream and waking reality, regard the sea as the extension of the intimate space of the house. Displaying a kind of naivety, they feel powerful enough to domesticate sea space and to reduce its immensity to intimacy. In their youthful dreams sea space exists as a tempting lover who, much like ships, is to be blindly admired and adored. On the other hand, mature sailors are aware of the hostile and ferocious immensity of sea space. Thus, they perceive and interiorize the sea as a malevolent opponent, fighting with whom enables them to rediscover their latent strength and to make sense of their lives. In his book Bachelard concentrates on spirituality of various spaces, stating at one point that "the desert is reflected in the wanderer" (204). Dana's *Two Years* and Conrad's *The Mirror of the Sea* may well exemplify the claim that the sea is not only reflected in sailors' memories and dreams, but also, being personified either as a seductive woman or as a malicious opponent, the sea reflects human feelings and emotions.

3.3. Sea Voyage: A Reflection of the Journey of Life

In his analysis of *Two Years Before the Mast*, Gale underlines that Dana's work failed to excite critics because they read it as "a juvenile untouchable" (119), completely ignoring the book's archetypal elements. According to Gale, Dana's journey to strange places and back home, his "twenty-five-month Odyssey" (113), should be perceived as a neglected masterpiece with numerous mythological overtones, while its narrator should be interpreted as a typical mythic hero (131). In an attempt to cure his eye weakness and to experience an adventure, the author of *Two Years* voluntarily leaves his home and begins a self-imposed wandering. As a well-born Bostonian and Harvard undergraduate, Dana, "snobbishly and seriously aristocratic," (Gale 139) is isolated by pride from the rest of the crew. It seems, however, that the protagonist's wandering at sea should be treated not only as a mythological voyage, but also as an existential state. In his loneliness, which, unlike that of mythic heroes, has mainly a philosophical dimension, Dana resembles the Conradian protagonists. Considering the plausibility of an existential approach to Conrad's fiction, Wiesław Krajka points to loneliness as a theme regarded by the vast majority of scholars as predominant in Conrad (Krajka 1999: 133). Interestingly, Conradian characters, as well as the narrator of *Two Years*, are similar to tragic mythological heroes. Furthermore, Krajka underlines that ancient tragedy provides another framework for the interpretation of Conrad's fiction. One of the themes of this writer's works, with their numerous features of a Greek tragedy, seems to be the strenuous human effort to overcome fate, and to orchestrate his or her life in accordance with his or her own scenario. Therefore, I want to explore both Dana, a young novice with whom the inexperienced reader can easily identify, and Conrad's narrator, who embodies a movement from ignorance to experience, as *pars pro toto* figures representing existential loneliness of every human being. However, the aim of my analysis is not to examine human loneliness from a psychological perspective, but rather from a philosophical, or, to be more precise, from a "monoseological" one.

"Monoseology" [*monoseologia*] is a term coined by Piotr Domeracki to describe the philosophy of loneliness (Domeracki 16). Domeracki claims that loneliness is a complex phenomenon, arguing, at the same time, that it is not post-relational, that is emerging as a result of broken relationships, but pre-relational, that is independent of any relationships. In other words, the scholar stresses the fact that this phenomenon constitutes a part of human existence: for him being human means being lonely. According to Domeracki, "monoseology" has been described throughout the centuries according to two major meta-narratives: the individualistic [*metanarracja indywidualistyczna*] and the communitarian one [*metanarracja komunitarystyczna*]. The main difference between the two lies in the fact that while the former extols a lonely individual and emphasizes positive aspects of loneliness, the latter glorifies communitarian life and is characterized by a critical attitude towards being lonely. Domeracki is convinced that philosophy of loneliness *par excellence* is represented by the individualistic meta-narrative, which can be studied from two completely different perspectives. On the one side of the spectrum there is the approach which investigates loneliness from the surface, on the other side there is the existential attitude, which explores loneliness from the very depth of existence. As it was José Ortega y Gasset who first defined human being as lonely by nature, I want to examine *Two Years* and *The Mirror* applying his theses concerning the existential dimension of loneliness presented in the book entitled *Man and People*. However, the present discussion of various aspects of loneliness has been limited to those linked in an obvious way to the themes explored in this study. It is worth noting that both Dana's and Conrad's works seem to belong to individualistic meta-narratives and that the two protagonists, functioning as "central consciousness" in the analyzed works, are entirely isolated in the world of values, as their passion for literature is ungraspable to other seamen. Representing communitarian meta-narratives, their fellow sailors, strongly devoted to hardships of maritime life and the bonds of seamanship, do not exist as individuals, but have collective identity. Similarly to the mutually exclusive individualistic and communitarian meta-narratives, Dana's and Conrad's central characters, due to their being sensitive and imaginative, have absolutely nothing in common with the rest of the crew. Their condition is perfectly described by Ortega: "[S]ince human life in the strict sense is untransferable, it is essentially *solitude, radical solitude*" (Ortega 46). It is indeed Dana's and Conrad's praising their individual sensitivity to values ungraspable to others that creates a sense of utter desolation and makes their loneliness even more profound.

Dana and Conrad, representing the individualistic meta-narrative, and their fellow seamen, being a part of the communitarian one, will never be able to exchange their solitudes. Analyzing the appearance of "the other," the author of *Man and People* observes:

> We shall see that the Other Man also has his *here* – but this here of the Other is not mine. Our "heres" are mutually exclusive, they are not interpenetrable, they are different; with the result that the perspective in which the world appears to him is always different from mine. Hence our worlds do not adequately coincide. For the present, I am in mine and he in his. And this is a fresh reason for radical solitude. Not only am I outside of the other man, but my world is outside of his: we are, mutually, two "outsides" [*fueras*], and hence radically strangers [*forasteros*]. (75)

Although Dana quickly makes friendships with Ben Stimson, Tom Harris, or George Marsh, the sense of loneliness accompanies him throughout the journey. This is perfectly illustrated by the protagonist's "deliberate system of time-killing"

(177) – during his watches Dana recites not only passages from the Bible, but also his favourite verses from Cowper, Horace and Goethe.

In the existential aspect of loneliness Dana differs considerably from the mythic heroes. Still, his journey of self-discovery may be regarded as archetypal. Like Odysseus, Aeneas, or Stephen Dedalus, he must be tempted and tested in order to discover his limitless potential and prove victorious. Gale interprets Dana's experience before the mast as a typical ritual of rebirth consisting of three stages: separation, initiation, and return (131). Following the cycles of nature, the author of *Two Years* stresses the regenerative aspect of his journey, from which he returns substantially changed and greatly enriched. As he manages to resist temptations and remains ethical according to his own standards, the perseverance at sea contributes to his higher self-esteem. Gale also observes that during the journey of self-discovery, Dana creates his own substitute religion in order to strengthen his belief in himself among the members of the crew who do not fully accept a college man (131). Standing on a bare rock, the solitary Dana feels united with the immensity of the sea and the sky. Using his imagination and intelligence to unite with the atmospheric seascape, he behaves as if he were an actor who manages to free himself from the puppet theatre of his ship and play an independent role:

> Everything was in accordance with my state of feeling, and I experienced a glow of pleasure at finding that what of poetry and romance I ever had in me, had not been entirely deadened by the laborious and frittering life I had led. Nearly an hour did I sit, almost lost in the luxury of this entire new scene of the play in which I had been so long acting. (77–78)

Gale further observes that the protagonist is tested not only at sea, but also on land. He carries animal skins and cargo purposelessly up a hill, like Sisyphus. Like Odysseus and his fellow seamen, Dana takes part in feasts abundant with wine, but manages to resist the temptations of "the local Calypsos" (132). Gale even ventures a statement that, like Hamlet, the protagonists remains pure, at least in his own eyes (132). Extremely self-controlled and intelligent, the protagonist also manages to deal with the villainy of "the Cyclopean [officer] Russell," due to whose intrigues the crew runs out of food in California (Gale 132). What is more, Dana's social position and his education constitute both an Achillean armour, which protects him, and the thread of Ariadne, which leads him out of the Californian inferno to Boston (133). Although bound to stay in California for a long time, the protagonist manages to rebel against the gods' scenario and to outwit forces much greater than human. Like Prometheus, he dares to take his fate into his hands and to act against the gods' will. Dana's return aboard the *Alert* is marked by "an archetypal deluge" of ice, snow and hail off Cape Horn (133). Gale underlines the fact that because of a violent toothache, the hero is forced to abandon the deck and to descend to his cabin, where he is as frightened as Jonah "in the belly of the whale-like ship" (133). Apart from Gale's mythological reading of Dana's bestseller, the situation described in the novel may also be interpreted as *nemesis* for the protagonist's staggering *hubris* and Ahab-like self-divinization. Finally, Gale observes that just before his return home again, the protagonist experiences mysterious melancholy and the sense of time lost (133). "As for myself, by one of those anomalous changes of feeling of which we are all the subjects, I found that I was in a state of indifference, for which I could by no means account" (199), the protagonist comments on his malady.

Although Gale's interpretation seems to be too far-fetched, he is right in claiming that Dana's narrative is "partly mythic" (108). In my view, *Two Years* has some features of the ancient epic, as in Dana's book contemporaneity is shown as a darkened reality of a lower order, the past being idealized and of greater importance. In the final chapter, entitled "Twenty-Four Years After," the tone of which is similar to Conrad's melancholy "Author's Note," Dana describes his nostalgic return to California in 1859, contrasting the present situation with the past, which is inaccessible to him. Although his voyage still exists in his memory, he would be able neither to experience it once again nor to perceive it now exactly in the same way as twenty-four years before. Moreover, in *Two Years* past and present are separated by epic distance. In the past everything was good, as it was the time when all the unforgettable experiences took place. Now, looking from afar, the protagonist feels melancholy and nostalgic about his journey of self-discovery, presenting the past as a world of "firsts" and "bests." Having spent two years before the mast, the protagonist, resembling a larger-than-life epic hero, portrays himself as one of the best seamen aboard his ship and refuses to accept his own insignificance. It is worth to refer here to Conrad's aforementioned question "Would you seriously wish to tell such a man: 'Know thyself' (quoted in Karl 423). This ancient Greek maxim, "Know thyself," inscribed in the forecourt of the Temple of Apollo at Delphi, is also quoted by Lawrence in his analysis of Dana's novel and may therefore be applied to the protagonist of *Two Years*. Blinded by his enthusiasm and optimism, and displaying a kind of naivety, he refuses to believe in his littleness and insignificance, but is convinced that his triumph over the sea only proves his greatness.

Surprising as it may seem, *Two Years* describes an event that could be likened to an epic battle. In the ancient epics the main conflict is between man and the cosmic forces that govern his voyage of life. This voyage, as in the *Odyssey*, is fraught with seemingly endless and insurmountable series of hazards. Ancient Greeks felt themselves in the grip of the capricious, irrational, and merciless powers, hostile and sarcastic with regard to the most strenuous human endeavours. Similarly, the men of the *Alert* find themselves pitted against cosmic powers, as their efforts to round Cape Horn in mid-winter are thwarted by the implacable and cruel obstinacy of the universe. The struggle of the crew of the *Alert* against the overpowering cosmos constitutes the epic battle in Dana's book. Indeed, it seems to the protagonist that it is a malevolent spirit, an anthropomorphized almighty power that orchestrates the battering icy storms and outrageous seas, making sport with the *Alert*:

It seemed as though the genius of the place had been roused at finding that we had nearly slipped through his fingers, and had come down upon us with tenfold fury. The sailors said that every blast, as it shook the shrouds, and whistled through the rigging, said to the old ship, "No, you don't!" – "No, you don't!." (Dana 176)

The extreme difficulty of going round Cape Horn is also masterfully described by Conrad in *A Personal Record*, where he writes on

> the everlasting somber stress of the westward winter passage round Cape Horn. For that too is the wrestling of men with the might of their Creator, in a great isolation from the world, without the amenities and consolations of life, a lonely struggle under a sense of over-matched littleness, for no reward that could be adequate, but for the mere winning of a longitude. (99)

Chapter XXXI of Dana's account, a meticulous description of passing round the Cape after two failures, is by far the most fascinating in the whole book. Putting emphasis on sensation rather than on reflection, Dana portrays the challenging ordeal using a sea diary approach. Praising Dana's realistic description, Melville observes in his *White-Jacket*: "But if you want the best idea of Cape Horn, get my friend Dana's unmatchable *Two Years Before the Mast*. But you can read, and so you must have read it. His chapters describing Cape Horn must have been written with an icicle" (Melville 452). Indeed, Dana's pictorial techniques turn his narrative into a mimetic reflection mirrored in polished surfaces of countless icebergs and ice fields. Dana's sublime description, delineating both the beauty and horror of the icy seascape, makes the reader see an "immense mountain-island, its cavities and valleys thrown into deep shade, and its points and pinnacles glittering in the sun" (*Two Years* 166), feel the coldness of frozen bare hands "cut with the hailstones, which fell thick and large" (168), and hear "the thundering sound of the cracking of the mass [of ice], and the breaking and tumbling down of huge pieces" (166). Fascinating and frightening, the frozen ocean presented by Dana, like the purgatorial sea portrayed by Marryat, seems to be a domain of mysterious forces. Its immensity and nearness induce not only terror, but also astonishment. However, Dana's experience does not extend beyond the domain of the Burkean sublime, already defined in the introductory chapter. In contrast to Marryat's novel, in Dana's book sublimity is reduced only to sensual reactions, as it stimulates neither an epiphanic experience nor results in what I have called "the post-epiphanic reflection." Hence, in *Two Years* sublimity does not contribute to the protagonist's moral elevation, but serves only as a background to the young sailor's voyage of self-discovery.

Although Dana's graphic presentation of the land of ice operates on light, it is devoid of any illumination, constituting only a mere mirror reflection of reality. Thomas Philbrick underlines the fact that all American writers of Cooper's day must have been aware of the existence of a literary convention which established the South Pole as "a place where events have more than their common significance, a place which, by its remoteness from everyday experience, sets man's existence in

3.3. Sea Voyage: A Reflection of the Journey of Life 121

a new and truer perspective" (Philbrick 229). A good illustration of this fact may be Coleridge's *The Rime of the Ancient Mariner* (1798), in which icy setting gives allegorical meaning to the Mariner's voyage, or E. A. Poe's *The Narrative of Arthur Gordon Pym* (1838), in which the icy seascape transforms the protagonist's voyage into symbolic fantasy. Cooper's descriptions of frightening winter in the vicinity of Cape Horn in his late novel entitled *The Sea Lions* (1849) may be yet another example of referring to the mysterious and desolate world of ice. Stressing human insignificance and futility of all efforts in confrontation with the all-powerful polar winter, Cooper presents the world of ice as an epiphanic setting revealing the truth concerning the weakness of human nature.

It is worth noting that for Dana both whiteness and lightness are deprived of any epiphanic potential, as he explores only the aesthetic aspect of the described objects, be it a solitary albatross or a sparkling ice-berg. In his description of the bird, Dana stresses the creature's beauty, especially its immaculate whiteness intensified by the brightness of the mirror-like sea:

> This day we saw the last of the albatrosses, which had been our companions a great part of the time off the Cape. I had been interested in the bird from descriptions which I had read of it, and was not at all disappointed. We caught one or two with a baited hook which we floated astern upon a shingle. Their long, flapping wings, long legs, and large, staring eyes, give them a very peculiar appearance. They look well on the wing; but one of the finest sights that I have ever seen, was an albatross asleep upon the water, during a calm, off Cape Horn, when a heavy sea was running. (23–24)

As the passage quoted above indicates, Dana does not progress from aesthetics to ethics, but he focuses entirely on the visual aspect of the depicted image by which he is impressed. By contrast, Melville, also impressed by the beauty of the bird, responds creatively to the perceived image, investigating the epiphany evoked by the sensory stimulus:

> I remember the first albatross I ever saw. It was during a prolonged gale, in waters hard upon the Antarctic seas. [...] Through [the bird's] inexpressible strange eyes methought I peeped to secrets not below the heavens – the white thing was so white, its wings so wide, and in those for ever exiled waters, I had lost the miserable warping memories of traditions and of towns. – I assert then, that in the wondrous bodily whiteness of the bird chiefly lurks the secret of the spell. (quoted in Lawrence 241)

D. H. Lawrence underlines in his analysis of Melville's masterpiece that although both Dana and Melville are impressed by the albatross, the author of *Moby Dick* goes beyond the beauty of the bird, concentrating on "the strange, supernatural spell which is cast by pure whiteness" (241). Appearing in a note to the chapter on the colour of Moby Dick, the description of the albatross emphasizes the creature's epiphanic properties, comparable to that of the white whale.

If in depicting the albatross Dana focuses on the beautiful, then in his impressionistic descriptions of an iceberg he concentrates on the sublime:

> Its great size – for it must have been from two to three miles in circumference, and several hundred feet in height – its slow motion, as its base rose and sank in the water, and its high points nodded against the clouds; the dashing of the waves upon it [...]; and the thundering sound of the cracking of the mass, and breaking and tumbling down of huge pieces; together with its nearness and approach, which added a slight element of fear, all combined to give to it the character of true sublimity. (166)

Indeed, the ice-berg depicted by Dana meets all Burkean requirements of the sublime. Unlike Marryat's Flying Dutchman, Dana's protagonist does not experience moral, let alone religious, elevation as a result of his confrontation with sublimity. Nor does Dana resemble Cooper's Red Rover, who experienced epiphany, having watched and reflected on the performance presented aboard his ship. Although some of Dana's descriptions of an icy phantasmagoria are highly spectacular, they do not evoke an immediate epiphany or stimulate any "post-epiphanic reflection," as examined in the previous chapters. What Dana investigates is visual stimuli, not the onlooker's creative reaction to them:

> It was a contrast to much that we had lately seen, and a spectacle not only of beauty, but of life; for it required but little fancy to imagine these islands to be animate masses which had broken loose from the "thrilling regions of thick-ribbed ice," and were working their way, by wind and current, some alone, and some in fleets, to milder climes. [...] This is the large iceberg; while the small and distant islands, floating on the smooth sea, in the light of clear day, look like little floating fairy isles of sapphire. (175)

As the passage quoted above indicates, Dana is not always a mere imitator of reality, but also a creator of impressionistic images. Although his poetic depiction of phantasmagoric ice-bergs definitely extends the scope of realism, the author ignores the potentially revelatory function of mirror-like sparkling surfaces. Still, a conclusion that Dana does not look into any mirror whatsoever would be erroneous. However, this aspect will be explored in the concluding section of this chapter.

An interesting use of an icy setting appears in Conrad's *The Mirror of the Sea*. Unlike Dana, who reduces reflection only to a mimetic process and produces an exact picture of terrifying winter in the region of Cape Horn, Conrad's description of frozen Amsterdam contains numerous spots of indeterminacy. Aware not only of the reflective qualities, but also of the luminosity both of the sea and icy, mirror-like surfaces, Conrad presents photographs rather than exact pictures, exacerbating the potential for countless concretizations and interpretations. As the sea not only mirrors, but also intensifies light, Conrad, combining reflective and projective properties of the ocean, is both an imitator of reality and a creator of epiphanies. His highly photographic narrative encourages the reader-viewer "to extend the mind's imagery and construct further meaning in the 'darkroom' of the mind" (Thwaites 218). In other words, he not only replicates reality, as Dana did, but also stimulates "post-epiphanic reflections."

In the artistic approach towards portrayed reality, there are similarities between Conrad and Louis-Jacques Daguerre (1789–1851), a French physicist, painter and inventor of the first practical photographic process. His daguerreotype, a photographic technique employing a iodine-sentitized silvered plate and mercury vapour, was presented to the French Academy of Sciences in 1839. Since its very origins the process was referred to as "magic mirror." Coined by the Parisian art critic, Jules Janin, the term perfectly illustrates the attitude of the nineteenth-century public towards the invention. Approached with fascination because of the astonishing clarity of the produced images, and with suspicion because of the captured presence creating illusion of necromancy, the daguerreotype redefined the relation between the artist and his or her art (Thwaites 209–210). As photographic approach demanded not only reception, but also projection, it may be regarded as a complex form of visual experience, combining *memesis* with *creatio*. Oriented both towards the object perceived and the perceiver, photography perfectly illustrates "an interaction, the joint effect of inner and outer, mind and object" (Abrams 51). Although seemingly mimetic, as the pictures produced on small silvery plates were so exact that the original was almost indistinguishable from the copy, in fact the daguerreotype process is creative. Described as the art of "writing with light," the technique gave a sense of wonder and utilized "creative" properties of light, the catalyst of the invention. As, operating on light, the daguerreotypist presents reality from his own subjective perspective, the produced images are, in a way, already interpreted. The seeming absence of light on the photographs is deceptive. In fact, as it is omnipresent, light serves as an interpretative element (Thwaites 212–213). Daguerre's method of polished mirrors combines, therefore, the reflective and the projective properties of light, constituting both a mirror and a lamp. As Sarah Thwaites puts it: "Reflection is proved problematic; mirrored light should according to mimesis produce a copy, or illusory imitation, but conversely, in the case of light it reproduces itself and sheds further light" (220). It is indeed paradoxical that a monochromatic plate and colourless light "[touch] all objects in colourful revelation" (221), stressing the possibility of numerous interpretative meanings.

I do not claim that Conrad's sea fiction was influenced by the enormous artistic potential of early photography. What I want to demonstrate is the photographic quality of his descriptions, as opposed to the picturesque property of Dana's images. In *The Mirror* the "photography" of the icy Amsterdam, embedded in Conrad's reflection on the brevity of existence, is presented as an anti-vanitative carnivalistic phantasmagoria, temporarily triumphing over *vanitas*. On the one hand, Conrad is probably afraid of death; on the other hand, he seems to be curious about that which is on the other side of the mirror. Hence, apart from mirror reflections, the *vanitas vanitatum* theme is another motif that keeps recurring throughout the book[4]. To begin with, for Conrad the voyage of the ship stands for the journey of life, and it is the *peregrinatio vitae* metaphor, one of the variants of the idea of *vanitas*, that

---

4   For an extended version of the discussion on *vanitas* in Conrad's narrative, see Joanna Mstowska, "The Idea of *Vanitas* in *The Mirror of the Sea*" in *Secret Sharers: Melville, Conrad and Narratives of the Real*. Ed. Paweł Jędrzejko, Milton M. Reigelman and Zuzanna Szatanik. Zabrze: M-Studio, 2011, 185–204.

he uses to emphasize the brevity of existence. "Landfall and Departure mark the rhythmical swing of a seaman's life and of a ship's career. From land to land is the most concise definition of a ship's earthly fate" (*The Mirror* 3). I would add that this is also a good definition of human fate. The moment of a ship's departure, of leaving the land behind, symbolizes the moment of birth. Then, the ship's voyage – fraught with danger and marked by constant fight with winds, storms, and, above all, with the infuriated sea – stands for achieving adolescence, maturity, growing old and leading life marked by toil and emotional and physical suffering. The essence of human life lies in the constant battle with inexorable fate and its misfortunes: "And yet sometimes one gets a hint of what the last scene may be like in the life of a ship and her crew, which resembles a drama in its struggle against a great force bearing it up, formless, ungraspable, chaotic and mysterious, as fate" (59–60).

Finally, the landfall, tying up to the bank and reaching the destined harbor, is an apt metaphor for the moment of death: mysterious, inexplicable, and frightening. The second motto of the book, taken from Chaucer's *The Frankeleyn's Tale*, was chosen to highlight that the voyage of the ship, and at the same time the journey of life, lasts for a very short time and that death comes upon humans much sooner than they would expect: "And shippes by the brinke comen and gon, / And in swich forme endure a day or two" (3). The route of each cruise is different, unique, and unforeseeable, much as is the course of the journey of life of each human being. No matter how much one tries, it is impossible to predict future vicissitudes: "To see! To see! – this is the craving of the sailor, as of the rest of blind humanity. To have his path made clear for him is the aspiration of every human being [...]" (87). Only one aspect of the journey is certain, that is death, which each human being meets in the destined harbour.

It is no wonder then that at the age of twenty-four the narrator avoids by all means staying in the harbour, a place characterized by the omnipresence of death. The young Marlow of *Youth* also could not stand the inactivity of waiting on the dock, preferring instead the drudgery of working aboard his ship for eight hours a day. The image of ships trapped in the harbour in Amsterdam due to frozen canals triggers associations with corpses for Conrad – "so silent, so lifeless, so soulless they seemed to be" (50). Conrad's ship is as cold as ice, and his berth is "like a chilly burial niche" (50). Not only all those ships, but also the narrator himself seems to be "in grim depression for want of the open water" (49). In order to run away from the motionlessness of the harbour that brings associations with death, he undertakes travels by tramcars, as if travelling were the necessary condition for continuing to live. The moment he leaves the harbour and enters the centre of Amsterdam is when he takes part in a kind of carnival. The reality is turned topsy-turvy and what was severe and silent is replaced by the joyful and boisterous atmosphere of the city centre. The narrator enters a sort of a wonderland, where everything seems to be extremely fragile and phantasmagoric:

From afar at the end of Tsar Peter Straat, issued in the frosty air the tinkle of bells of the horse tramcars, appearing and disappearing in the opening between the buildings, were like toy carriages harnessed with toy horses and played with by people that appeared no bigger than children. (48–49)

"The Arctic waste land" (49) over which he travels may represent the open space of the sea, whereas the glazed tramcar may be regarded as a mirror reflection of a ship. However, one mirror, the mirror of the sea, is replaced by numerous mirrors, as each flat surface in frozen Amsterdam seems to reflect the world. A glazed tramcar, the Arctic waste land, "houses bowed under snow-laden roofs" (48), "a landscape of ice" (50), all dazzling white and shining, resemble the sea whose flat sheet shimmering in the sunshine may function as a mirror. In the very heart of the city the whiteness and coldness no longer bring associations with death, but rather with a magic land reflecting the real world, producing blurred and hazy images of reality. Although after some time there comes a meltdown and the ephemeral and transient wonderland of snow and ice vanishes forever, the twenty-four-year-old narrator, naive as he is, strongly believes that he will neither let "that Dutch tenacious winter penetrate into [his] heart" (50) nor extinguish the "sacred fire for the exercise of [his] craft" (50). Still in his youth, he does not want to think about death, with which he associates the cruel winter of the harbour.

I would like to use the description of frozen Amsterdam not only as a way of bringing to light certain differences between Dana and Conrad, but also as a point of connection between the two writers. In the passage on "the Arctic wasteland" Conrad defamiliarizes the familiar urban space of Amsterdam. Similarly, in the final chapter entitled "Twenty-four Years After," Dana renders unfamiliar the intimate space of San Francisco. Modifying his habitual perceptions of the place, the author of *Two Years* draws the reader's attention to its strangeness. Viewed from a perspective of twenty-four years, San Francisco is no longer the hostile space which the young Dana managed to domesticate and interiorize:

> When I awoke in the morning, and looked from my windows over the city of San Francisco, with its storehouses, towers, and steeples; its court-houses, theatres, and hospitals; its daily journals; its well-filled learned professions; its fortresses and light houses; its wharves and harbor, with their thousand-ton clipper ships, more in number than London or Liverpool sheltered that day [...], when I saw all these things, and reflected on what I once was and saw here, and what now surrounded me, I could scarcely keep my hold on reality at all, or the genuineness of anything, and seemed to myself like one who had moved in "worlds not realized." (212)

As the passage quoted above shows, the protagonist is struck by the artificiality of the presented reality. Since the interiorized intimate portraits from the past do not coincide with the perceived images, the phantasmagoric snatches of recollections are much more real for Dana than the hostile and unfamiliar reality. He confesses to the reader: "The past was real. The present, all about me, was unreal, unnatural, repellant" (219). Although mastered by man and well-ordered, the urban space described by the author of *Two Years* turns out to be as immense and uncontrollable as sea space. Paradoxically, following a predetermined charted course in San Francisco, Dana feels much more estranged and insecure than during his self-imposed aimless wandering at sea. In his being suspended between the phantasmagoric past and the defamiliarized present, the protagonist resembles the Flying Dutchman, existing between life and death. Dana is similar to the damned captain in yet another respect; although he seems to follow a planned route, his wandering is, in fact, both purposeless and senseless. Wherever he goes, he feels displaced; hence, the suffering caused by the defamiliarization is evocative of the Flying Dutchman's unbearable monotonous movement in spaces whose ontological status is uncertain. Constituting the exact opposite of "intimate immensities" described by Bachelard, the urban space of San Francisco may be defined as "defamiliarized intimacy."

In its pessimism, nostalgia for the past, and reflections on death, Dana's final chapter is similar to the melancholy mood of both Conrad's "Author's Note" and his collection of reminiscences. Conrad recalls, for instance, Captain B., a person he much respected, and the last words he spoke to the author of *The Mirror* aboard his ship. Conrad adds immediately that "there is a pathos in that memory, for the poor fellow never went to sea again after all" (10). After some time Captain B. fell ill, and Conrad accepted an invitation and visited the Captain in his home. Apart from Captain B. and his wife, the house was inhabited by another woman, Mrs. B.'s sister, "in a plain black dress, quite grey-haired, sitting very erect on her chair with some sewing" (11). A dignified matron clad in black and holding a thread, she resembles one of the Parkas, Cloto, spinning the thread of life. Hence, she may be interpreted as the harbinger of Captain B.'s impending death. "Evidently he [the Captain] was reluctant to take his final cross-bearings of this earth for a Departure on the only voyage to an unknown destination a sailor ever undertakes" (10). It turned out that the Captain died soon after Conrad's visit. An elderly woman resembling Cloto appears also in *Heart of Darkness*. Marlow meets her in the waiting-room of the company before he goes to Africa. For him this mysterious figure spinning a black thread bears resemblance to the guardian of the door of Darkness, evoking associations with the underworld and death, which await the daredevils who decide to go to the heart of Africa.

3.4. The Sea: A Mirror Reflecting Images from the Past

At one point in *The Mirror of the Sea*, the narrator says with conviction: "Twenty-five years is a long time – a quarter of a century is a dim and distant past" (143). Beyond any doubt it is a period saturated with death – not only of some of the seamen Conrad used to know, but also of seamanship and ships. The narrator admits regretfully that both the sailing and racing of yachts are no longer what they used to be, as these vessels have lost their importance and have been replaced by steamships. "And the sailing of any vessel afloat is an art whose fine form seems already receding from us on its way to the overshadowed valley of Oblivion" (30). Similarly, Dana also expresses his contempt when he refers to the steamer as "an unromantic, sail-less, spar-less, engine-driven hulk" (*Two Years* 217). Both Conrad and Dana agree that the seamanship of yesterday was an art, as seamen used to devote themselves entirely to sailing, wanted to achieve perfection in their profession, and were able to forget about themselves and to surrender all personal feelings in the service of seamanship. By contrast, the essence of the seamanship of tomorrow, devoid of any feeling, is punctuality, speed, and the reduction of risk. Hence, it is no longer an art, but rather a craft. Contemporary seamanship is characterized by a lack of intimacy and companionship between the sailor and his ship: "The taking of a modern steamship about the world has not the same quality of intimacy with nature, which, after all, is an indispensable condition to the building up of an art" (*The Mirror* 30). Contemporary sailors treat seamanship as a way of making money and remain unaware of the fact that the essence of a true seaman's existence is the constant battle with the sea. Conrad observes: "The machinery, the steel, the fire, the steam have stepped in between the man and the sea" (72). In the section entitled "The Fine Art," Conrad seems to sum up his reflection on the decay of the art of sailing in the following sentences: "[...] the special call of an art which has passed away is never reproduced. It is as utterly gone out of the world as the song of a destroyed wild bird" (30). By comparing the vanishing art of sailing to the song of a bird, Conrad seems to emphasize that this art, as much as a song, was beautiful, unforgettable, irreplaceable, but also ephemeral and fragile. This supreme form of art disappeared forever much too soon, giving people who loved and admired it no time to fully appreciate its beauty and charm.

If seamanship, compared to the song of a destroyed wild bird, has vanished forever, then sailing-ships, bearing resemblance to a flock of swans, are also bound to become destroyed. In the concluding chapter of *Two Years,* Dana evokes memories from the past, nostalgically reflecting on all the ships that no longer exist: "I saw the big ships lying in the stream, the *Alert,* the *California*, the *Rosa* with her Italians; then the handsome *Ayacucho*, my favorite; the poor, dear old *Pilgrim.* [...] All, all were gone!" (219). Likewise, Conrad throughout the whole collection recalls numerous ships which no longer exist, but, nevertheless, still remain fresh in his mind. In his "Author's Note" Conrad confesses that this book "is the best tribute my piety can offer to the ultimate shapers of my character, convictions, and, in a sense, destiny – [...] to the ships that are no more" (X). He presents ships as mortal creatures; each of them has a soul, which at the moment of death leaves its body, lives eternally, and never deserves condemnation. Conrad is convinced that as both good and evil ships go "into the limbo of things that have served their time, there can be no harm in affirming that in these vanished generations of willing servants there never has been one utterly unredeemable soul" (120). Analogically, Dana describes the "deaths" of the *Pilgrim*, which was sold to a merchant in New

Hampshire and then burnt at sea in the region of North Carolina (226), and the *Alert*, "a victim in the cause of her country," (229) burnt by rebels.

As both in Dana's and Conrad's narratives men and ships are very fragile, transient, and short-lived creatures, they may be regarded as signs of the *vanitas vanitatum* theme. Conrad's observation that "[a]ll passes, all changes" (*The Mirror* 194) is strikingly similar to Dana's confession: "I wished to be alone, so I let the other passengers go up to the town, and was quietly pulled ashore in a boat, and left to myself. The recollections and the emotions all were sad, and only sad. *Fugit, interea fugit irreparabile tempus*" (Dana 219). As has already been mentioned, both Dana and Conrad present sailing as a pilgrimage, at the same time stressing that the voyage lasts only a moment in comparison with eternity. Conrad argues that life is a constant approach towards death, for "neither years nor voyages can go on forever" (*The Mirror* 22). Similarly, the names of Dana's ships, the *Pilgrim* and the *Alert*, seem to emphasize the brevity of the pilgrimage at sea, stressing the necessity for being alert and prepared for unexpected death. Presented as a phantasmagoric and evanescent creature, a ship appears to be suspended between reality and the world of illusion: "The sailing-ship [...] seemed to lead mysteriously a sort of unearthly existence, bordering upon the magic of the invisible forces" (64). A ship is also compared to symbols of *vanitas,* such as stalks, cobwebs, and gossamer. Conrad concludes his reflection on the changing nature of the world with a fundamental question: "For what is the array of the strongest ropes, the tallest spars, and the stoutest canvas against the mighty breath of the infinite, but thistle stalks, cobwebs, and gossamer?" (37). The answer given by the author himself is: "Indeed, it is less than nothing" (37).

Not only ships, but also humans exemplify the theme of *vanitas vanitatum*. When the narrator of *The Mirror* recalls the long gone seamen he used to know, he sighs: "Shadows! Shadows!" (123). Similarly, when he reflects on life, he calls it "beclouded existence" (87). He looks at humans and their lives as if through an opaque looking glass which produces blurred and fading images. The voyage of life has also an ephemeral and phantasmagoric quality, as if a ship and its crew had entered a wonderland in which there is no present, and each of the fleeting moments immediately blends into the sphere of the past. No sooner are the images created than they disappear like air-bubbles. According to Künstler-Langner, apart from shadows, bubbles, wind, cobweb, and a candle, a mirror, representing the passing of the beauty of the face and the inevitability of growing old, may be interpreted as a vanitative symbol as well (Künstler-Langner 29). Conrad claims that "nowhere else than upon the sea do the days, weeks, and months fall away quicker into the past. They seem to be left astern as easily as the light air-bubbles in the swirls of the ship's wake, and vanish into a great silence [...]" (*The Mirror* 7). Dana, recollecting the old times of the *Pilgrim* and the *Alert* that will never return, similarly admits: "I almost feel as if I were lamenting the passing away of something loved and dear" (Dana 217). What he also evokes are the snatches of reminiscences concerning the deaths of his fellow seamen: John the Swede, whose grave he was never able to find, Sam, who died during his sea voyage to Brazil, or Captain Thompson, who was buried at sea.

Not only stalks, cobwebs, gossamer, and bubbles, but also two human figures, Dominic Cervoni and his nephew Cesar, seem to symbolize the brevity of life and unavoidable death. The former, Dominic, with ebony hair, black moustache, and "remorseless eyes set off by the shadow of the deep hood, looked piratical and monkish and darkly initiated into the most awful mysteries of the sea" (*The Mirror* 164). Compared to a monk, he seems to call out *Memento mori*! and to preach that sooner or later all earthly vanities will disappear. However, Dominic Cervoni's blackness has positive connotations as well. Reminding people of the shortness of their time on Earth, he encourages them to reconsider their lives. By contrast, Cesar may be interpreted as the personification of death. Contrasted with Dominic, "black and cowled" (172), Cesar is white, transparent, and cold. His whiteness brings associations with evil, cruelty, ugliness, and monstrosity:

> To look at Cesar was not pleasant. His parchment skin, showing dead white on his cranium through the thin wisps of dirty brown hair, seemed to be glued directly and tightly upon his big bones. Without being in any way deformed, he was the nearest approach which I have ever seen or could imagine to what is commonly understood by the word "monster." (165)

I would claim that in his hatred, disgust, and unpredictability, Cesar is a mirror reflection of death.

The elderly Conrad, no longer able to be the seaman the essence of whose existence is constant fighting with the sea, is melancholy and nostalgic for the past. Convinced that if there is no powerful force to fight against, then there is nothing to live for, he feels useless and depressive. It is looking in the mirror of the sea that helps him to create images of bygone people and ships. He strongly believes that the sea is the only element to which he can resort in order to find consolation. Imperishable and everlasting, the ocean is able to encapsulate all reflected images. When Conrad recollects the *Tremolino*, a ship of phenomenal speed, he observes: "She took the secret of her speed with her, and, unsightly as she was, her image surely has its glorious place in the mirror of the old sea" (42). Looking in the mirror of the sea indeed consoles Conrad, but only temporarily. The images of men and ships are even more fleeting and short-lived than the men and ships themselves. Therefore, they fade away very quickly, and blend into the dark oceanic depths, "leaving no record upon the mysterious face of the sea" (135–136). Heartless and indifferent, the sea will never be merciful enough to comfort fully one of its enemies, even if he is a lonely and suffering retired seaman.

Although the transient and ephemeral images reflected in the mirror of the sea aggravate rather than soothe Conrad's emotional pain, he finds pleasure in looking at them. Conrad may therefore be compared to Narcissus, a beautiful youth who saw his image reflected in a fountain and became enamoured thereof. Although there are some obvious differences between the two, for instance the fact that Narcissus is in his youth, whereas Conrad is at the end of his days, or that the former fell in love with his own image, while the latter – with the scenes from his seamanship, there are also striking similarities between them. First of all, both Narcissus and Conrad adore a mirror image so much that they are no longer able to distinguish reality from its mirror reflection and so enter a world of phantasmagoria. In love with the fleeting, dim, and hazy images, they are not aware of the fact that all formless and ungraspable phantasms are bound to evaporate. What is more, for both of them looking at a sheet of water that serves as a looking glass is a sign of impending death. Finally, as both have acquired self-knowledge, they are indeed ready to die. When Narcissus was a child, his mother, Liriope, consulted the seer Tiresias, asking him whether her son would live to a ripe old age. His answer was: "Yes, if he will not have come to know himself." Unfortunately, the beautiful youth has finally gained knowledge of himself, and he has realized that it is impossible for him to enter the wonderful and desired mirror reflection. Unable to accept the fact that the reflected image is beyond his reach, he has grown desperate and killed himself. Beyond any doubt, Conrad, as much as the young Dana, has eventually come to know himself. Having spent twenty years at sea, he experienced various kinds of enchantments and bitterness associated with life at sea. Having achieved maturity after various ups and downs of life, he has acquired a considerable self-knowledge. The enthusiasm and optimism, which he used to be full of as a youthful and inexperienced seaman, vanished forever.

In her article entitled "Conrad's self-portraiture," Eloise Knapp Hay claims that in *The Mirror of the Sea* "[w]e see Conrad progressing from an active youth – fired by mysterious impulses and illusions – past a dividing line of shock, engagement, and disenchantment, to a last stance of disengagement and reflection" (Knapp Hay 58). Hay states further that elderly Conrad confronts "the spectacle of an inexplicable universe with troubled resignation" (58). Having written the last sentence of *The Mirror of the Sea,* Conrad probably stopped looking at his wrinkled face in a looking glass, finished rekindling his distant and fading memories, and started waiting peacefully and patiently for the death to come.

Unlike in *The Mirror of the Sea*, it is not only the vanitative aspect of a mirror reflection, but also its connotation with life that is stressed in *Two Years Before the Mast.* D. H. Lawrence offers a convincing interpretation of the significance of a mirror reflection in Dana's novel. I would argue that in his insightful study of *Two Years*, Lawrence compares the author's two-year-long experience at sea to a magic mirror revealing the truth concerning maritime life. "Dana's small book is a very great book: contains a great extreme of knowledge," writes Lawrence, "knowledge of the great element. And after all, we have to know all before we can know that knowing is nothing. Imaginatively, we have to know all: even the elemental waters. And know and know on, until knowledge suddenly shrivels and we know that forever we don't know" (Lawrence 214). The author of *Studies in Classic American*

Literature stresses the fact that it is impossible "to be" and "to know" at the same time, praising the idealistic "being" much higher than the realistic "knowing." Aware of the antagonistic relation between the two, Lawrence states:

> This is what Dana wanted: a naked fighting experience with the sea. KNOW THYSELF. That means, know the earth that is in your blood. Know the sea that is in your blood. The great elementals. But we must repeat: KNOWING and BEING are opposite, antagonistic states. The more you know, exactly, the less you *are*. The more you *are*, in being, the less you know. (196)

Striking as it may seem, Lawrence interprets the famous maxim, "know thyself," as "cease to know and commence to be." I would venture a statement that there is a correspondence between Lawrence's reading of the novel and Pirandello's form/life dichotomy. "Being," as defined by Lawrence, is evocative of the Pirandellian "life," a spontaneous and unstoppable flow, as opposed to "form," or Lawrence's "knowing," a set of norms and conventions which tend to imprison the flux of life. What Lawrence also investigates in his analysis is the Cape Horn episode, in his opinion, as in Gale's, a climactic moment of the book:

> The horrific struggle round Cape Horn, homewards, is the crisis of the Dana history. It is an entry into chaos, a heaven of sleet and black ice-rain, a sea of ice and iron-like water. Man fights the element in all its roused, mystic hostility to conscious life. This fight is the inward crisis and triumph of Dana's soul. He goes through it all consciously, enduring, *knowing*. It is not a mere overcoming of obstacles. It is a pitting of the deliberate consciousness against all the roused, hostile, anti-life waters of the Pole. After this fight, Dana has achieved his success. He knows. He knows what the sea is. He knows what the Cape Horn is. (208)

As the passage shows, Lawrence interprets Dana's struggle with the polar winter as an epiphanic experience. I would argue that there is a connection between fighting with the frozen ocean and becoming aware of the Pirandellian rent in the paper sky. Hamlet-like self-awareness makes the protagonist a tragic figure, as for Dana, like for Conrad, tragedy is not "a fact of nature," but, rather, resides in "a certain awareness of nature" (Gekoski 18). Indeed, Lawrence describes Dana's style not only as "great and hopeless," but also as that "of a perfect tragic recorder" (197). It is worth noting that Lawrence compares the young Dana to Hamlet, at the same time stressing that after the Cape Horn ordeal, the protagonist is no longer a mere puppet, but a "chief actor in the play of his own existence" (205).

The evolution of Dana's world views resembles that of the Melvillean characters, whose transformation, according to Paweł Jędrzejko, consists of three phases: idealistic "provisions" [*pro-wizje*], a traumatic event functioning as epiphany, and realistic "postvisions" [*post-wizje*]. Applying Paweł Jędrzejko's terminology, it is therefore possible to define Dana's battle with the icy ocean, during which he "strikes the polar death-mystery" (Lawrence 209) as "an intensive experience of being" [*intensywne doświadczenie bytu*] (Jędrzejko 199), which shatters the protagonist's visions of the domesticity of sea space and opens his eyes to its hostility.

Aware of the rent in the paper sky, Dana leaves the prison of form and "seems to pass into another world, another life, not of this earth" (Lawrence 206). Although Lawrence celebrates the possibility of liberation towards life, his conclusion, unlike Pirandello's, is pessimistic:

> He had been. He KNEW. He had even told us. It is a great achievement. And then what? – Why, nothing. The old vulgar hum-drum. That's the worst of knowledge. It leaves one only the more life-less. Dana lived his bit in two years, and knew, and drummed out the rest. Dreary lawyer's years, afterwards. (213)

As the passage demonstrates, Dana has enjoyed the freedom of real life only during his two-year-long experience before the mast. Afterwards, beginning his career as a lawyer, he has returned to the "life-less" prison of form, never being able to forget about the disturbing rent in the paper sky. Referring to the reader, Lawrence concludes that Dana did not present a mirror reflection of his epiphanic sea voyage in vain. Having read *Two Years*, the reader is in a privileged position, as, like Dana, he or she knows: "And from his book, we know too. He has lived this great experience for us, we owe him homage" (Lawrence 209). Dana's work is therefore presented as an epiphanic object revealing the truth concerning both the sea and maritime life. Lawrence claims that having experienced a revelation and having reflected on it "We know enough. We know too much. We know nothing" (213). Hence, in his epiphany and "the post-epiphanic reflection," the reader-spectator resembles the Red Rover who, having watched the performance of formalized existence, becomes aware of the rent in the paper sky and liberates himself towards the freedom of real life.

Conclusion

The analysis conducted in the study have revealed a variety of mimetic aspects embedded in Frederick Marryat's, James Fenimore Cooper's and Richard Henry Dana's fictional works. The discussion has started with *The Phantom Ship* examined in Chapter One. Informed by René Girard's theory of mimetic desire, I have investigated Marryat's protagonist as an incarnation of Faust, overwhelmed by his craving for God's omnipotence and omniscience. Viewed from the perspective of desire and suffering, Captain Vanderdecken's wandering at sea is not meaningless, as it purifies him of the staggering *hubris*, leading to the Captain's liberation from the slavery of desire for God's attributes. Hence, it can be concluded from the discussion that the sea portrayed in *The Phantom Ship* resembles purgatory. Chapter Two has explored mimesis as an imitation of established social conventions, which entails a more or less conscious role-playing on the stage of the *theatrum mundi*. Through the lens of Luigi Pirandello's form/life dichotomy, I have interpreted Cooper's *The Red Rover* as a novel marking a transition from mimetic form to spontaneous life. Initially a prisoner of form who lives in a masked world of illusion, the Rover finally rejects the role of a bloodthirsty pirate and chooses authenticity. The analysis has shown that in contrast to Marryat's purgatorial waters, Cooper's sea is depicted as a stage of human theatrical existence. In Chapter Three I have focused on the examination of a mirror reflection and its role in Dana's *Two Years Before the Mast*, treating Conrad's *The Mirror of the Sea* as an intertext. Informed by Meyer Abrams' famous metaphor of the mirror and the lamp, the examination of Dana's narrative has revealed that the explored novel is not a mere reportorial account regarded as a copy of authentic maritime life, but that it transcends the limitations of mimesis. It has been demonstrated that the author, concentrating on not only the mirror-like sea's capacity of reflecting nature, but, above all, on stimulating a lonely seaman's self-examination, is torn between *mimesis* and *creatio*.

The discussion of the selected nineteenth-century novels constitutes, therefore, an attempt at a penetration of various mimetic relations depicted in sea fiction. From the point of view of twentieth-century variations on the theories of *mimesis*, the analyzed outline of various aspects of imitation found in the three novels is interesting, as it involves religious, psychological, and philosophical perspectives. Girard's mimetic desire, Pirandello's mimetic form, and Abrams' "mimetic mirror" are similar to one another, as they focus on four elements typical of all critical theories: the work, the author, nature, understood as a subject of the work which imitates certain aspects of the universe, and the audience to whom the work is addressed (Abrams 6). While encapsulating all these elements, the twentieth-century theories through the prism of which I have analyzed Marryat's, Cooper's and Dana's novels, exhibit an orientation towards only one of them. Girard's model of triangular desire concentrates on the work, as it explores the mimetic nature of the relationships between literary characters. Pirandello's dichotomy, examining an antagonistic relation between form and life, focuses mainly on the reader's reaction to the depicted opposition. Abrams' famous metaphor, by contrast, investigates the artist holding a mirror which reflects both nature and his state of mind.

Although the three novels read through the lens of the above-mentioned theories differ considerably in their orientation towards the work, the audience and the artist, respectively, a closer examination clearly points to the conclusion that they are similar in many respects. All exemplify the concept of mimesis regarded as an imitation of reality, covering a wide spectrum of the possible ways of representing nature, from Marryat's symbolism, through Cooper's idealism, to Dana's realism. Hence, the novelists' use of mimesis may be generally described in terms of imitation, in Aristotle's, not Plato's, understanding of this term. Plato operates on three categories: the eternal Ideas, the world of sense, mirroring that ideal one, and, finally, a third one, reflecting the second, comprising not only images in water and mirrors, but also the fine arts (Abrams 8). In Plato's conception, the works of art occupy a lowly position in the order of existing things, as they imitate the world of appearance, not that of essence. Unlike Plato, Aristotle distinguishes only two categories: the imitable and the imitation. The world of unchanging Ideas is non-existent in his discussion of mimesis, which examines the reference of a work to the imitated subject matter (Abrams 8).

Still, the theories I have applied to examine Marryat's, Cooper's and Dana's works transgress the boundaries of Aristotle's *mimesis*. Characterized by a tension between mimetic, pragmatic, and expressive orientations, the texts transcend not only the generic boundaries of a Gothic novel, a romance, and a diary, respectively, but, above all, they may be regarded both as an imitation and an emanation of maritime life. Hence, the texts exemplify two kinds of mimesis: a repetition of a formula and a representation of reality. All three novels portray mimesis as a limiting category, arguing that sea fiction should be true not to the depicted object, be it the sailor, the ship, or the sea, but to the author's state of mind. In their seeking more ambitious goals than adhering to the established literary conventions in order to satisfy the public taste, the three novelists go beyond the pragmatic orientation; in their being torn between *mimesis* and *creatio*, they exceed the mimetic one. Imitation is, therefore, only instrumental in evoking an epiphanic experience at sea and stimulating "the post-epiphanic reflection," leading to a liberation from a limiting category. As has been indicated, in the examined novels the movement is from a more or less conscious imitation, through epiphany and reflection, to autonomy, spontaneity, and creativity, respectively.

Apart from the structure of the novels, their protagonists are also similar to one another. All three characters are focused on action, avoiding in their pride any kinds of self-examination. Captain Vanderdecken, the Red Rover, and the young Dana are presented as mere unconscious actors on the stage of the theatre of the world, who, having experienced epiphany, become ready for self-reflection. The epiphanic moment, stimulated by a maritime episode, occurs in all the novels that the study discusses. Perceived as a manifestation of meaning in the insignificant everyday existence, epiphany elevates the given individual from ignorance to awareness, contributing to the epiphanee's profound metamorphosis. It is the placid mirror of the sea that serves as an epiphanic instrument, uncovering the truth concerning the fragility of existence, and encouraging both reflection and self-examination.

In Marryat's *The Phantom Ship* sublimity, enhanced by the surface of the ocean, does not operate only as a source of moral elevation, but also of religious awakening, revealing both a philosophical and a spiritual dimension of existence. Looking at the undisturbed surface of the ocean, the doomed captain, no longer an agent of events, but their passive participant, becomes an incarnation of reflection. After the seventeen-year-long sea voyage, the *vita activa* of Captain Vanderdecken is transformed into the *vita contemplativa* of the Flying Dutchman, who may be regarded as a repentant Christian. The Captain's solitary pilgrimage at sea changes him so profoundly that after seventeen years he is able to categorically reject the slavery of Satan's external mediation. No longer a victim of triangular desire, he becomes an incarnation of autonomy.

In *The Red Rover* it is the moment of carnival that may be regarded as epiphany, revealing to the protagonist the truth concerning his existence imprisoned in form. Unlike in *The Phantom Ship*, in Cooper's novel epiphany no longer means the experience of *sacrum*. In *The Red Rover* it remains a literary device which suspends the meaninglessness of mimetic form and, uncovering meaningful, spontaneous life, introduces an existential dimension into the text. The epiphanic moment presented in Chapter XX of Cooper's novel is evoked by the carnival taking place aboard the Rover's ship. The Rover, no longer an incarnation of *actio*, but rather of *contemplatio*, resembles the passive Flying Dutchman, reflecting on his adventurous past. "The post-epiphanic reflection," which he has avoided out of vanity for many years, reveals to the protagonist that his apparently satisfying existence in the role of a rover is but death-in-life, leading to his choosing the spontaneity of life.

Likewise, Dana's Cape Horn episode, presenting his struggle with the sublime polar winter, may be regarded as an epiphanic experience. Unlike the Flying Dutchman, the protagonist of *Two Years Before the Mast,* having become fully acquainted with sublimity during his sea voyage, is neither morally nor religiously elevated. Nor does Dana resemble the Red Rover, who experienced epiphany after having watched and reflected on the performance presented aboard his ship. Although some of Dana's descriptions of an icy phantasmagoria are highly spectacular, they do not evoke any immediate epiphany. Both the awareness of the significance of the maritime episode for his future life and "the post-epiphanic reflection" occur much later. Hence, Dana's book, created after a profound self-examination, may be regarded as a magic mirror, revealing the truth concerning the author's two-year-long experience at sea.

On the basis of the above observations, it may be concluded that Marryat, Cooper and Dana present both imitation and emulation. What is the subject of the focus is no longer the adherence of a work of art to reality, but rather to the portrayed individual. In other words, it is not maritime reality that is imitated, but, paradoxical as it may seem, the emanation of the sailor's autonomy, spontaneity, and creativity. As the discussion of the selected sea novels has demonstrated, the subject of maritime experience is too broad to become exhausted only through the perspective of twentieth-century conceptions regarded as variations on mimesis. These theories exemplify solely one out of many possible approaches towards the interpretation of a relation between man and the sea. It would be interesting to conduct a comparative analysis of nineteenth-century maritime texts and Antoine de Saint-Exupéry's narratives, reflecting his experiences both in the air and in the desert. It is a possible avenue that can be investigated in the future, as the sea and the desert share a number of similarities. Both elements seem to be benevolent and approachable when they are calm, but it is not until a sea or a sand storm that their true nature and immense power are revealed. What is more, the overwhelming vastness of both the sea and the desert makes a human being more pensive and thoughtful regarding some existential issues: his or her position in the universe, the meaning of suffering, and the inevitability of death. Finally, the sea, as well as the desert, beautiful and awe-inspiring as they are, force people to struggle with their own physical weakness, extreme fatigue and complete exhaustion. The sea resembles the desert also in having the power to tear off a mask from a wanderer's face and to reveal his or her true nature. The undeniable power of these elements frequently serves as a source of epiphany, making a self-confident and courageous human being aware of his or her insignificance, vulnerability, and powerlessness.

On the whole, the analysis of mimetic relations in the examined novels reveals that the texts deserve a closer consideration than they have received so far, as Marryat, Cooper and Dana not only copy from nature, but also transcend the concept of *mimesis*. Although the three novels seem to function as mere copies of reality, imitating the then extremely popular literary conventions of the Gothic sea novel, the nautical romance, and the sea diary, respectively, this study has shown that the reading of these texts involves interpretations of symbols and analyses of epiphanies, as they enrich the imitation of maritime experience with an existential dimension, later masterfully developed by Melville and Conrad.

Bibliography
Primary Sources
Aristotle. *Poetics*. Trans. George Whalley. Eds. John Baxter and Patrick Atherton. Montreal: McGill-Queen's University, 1997.
Bunyan, John. *The Pilgrim's Progress*. With an Introduction by Hugh Ross Williamson. London –Glasgow: Collins, 1966.
Burke, Edmund. *A Philosophical Inquiry into the Origin of Our Ideas of the Sublime and Beautiful*. Ed. Adam Phillips. Oxford – New York: Oxford University Press, 1990.
Byron, George G. *Poems*, volume II. London: J. M. Dent and Sons, 1948.
Byron, George G. *Selections from Byron*. Moscow: Progress Publishers, 1973.
Camus, Albert. *The Stranger*. New York: Vintage International, 1989.
Conrad, Joseph. *A Personal Record*. London: J. M. Dent and Sons, 1946.
Conrad, Joseph. *Notes on Life and Letters*. London: J. M. Dent and Sons, 1949.
Conrad, Joseph. *Lord Jim*. London: J. M. Dent and Sons, 1989.
Conrad, Joseph. *Sulle mie tracce: autobiografia di Joseph Conrad* [*In My Footsteps: An Autobiography of Joseph Conrad*]. Ed. Maurizio Barletta. Rome: Robin, 2010.[5]
Conrad, Joseph. *The Collected Letters of Joseph Conrad*, volume I. Ed. Frederick R. Karl. Cambridge: Cambridge University Press, 1983.
Conrad, Joseph. *The Collected Letters of Joseph Conrad*, volume II. Ed. Frederick R. Karl. Cambridge: Cambridge University Press, 1986.
Conrad, Joseph. *The Mirror of the Sea*. London: J. M. Dent and Sons, 1946.
Conrad, Joseph. *Youth*. London: J. M. Dent and Sons, 1967.
Cooper, James Fenimore. *Czerwony Korsarz* [*The Red Rover*]. Trans. Kazimierz Piotrowski. Warszawa: Iskry, 1985.
Cooper, James Fenimore. *The Pilot. A Tale of the Sea*. With the Author's Preface to the 1849 Edition and Introduction by Susan Fenimore Cooper. London: George Routledge and Sons, without date.
Cooper, James Fenimore *The Red Rover*. The Project Gutenberg eBook. http://www.gutenberg.org/ebooks/ 11409
Dana, Richard Henry. *Pamiętnik żeglarza* [*A Sailor's Diary*]. Trans. Maria Boduszyńska and Tadeusz Meissner. Gdynia: Wydawnictwo Morskie, 1960.
Dana, Richard Henry. *Two Years Before the Mast*. The Project Gutenberg eBook. http://digital.library. upenn.edu/webbin/gutbook/ lookup?num=2055.
Defoe, Daniel. *Captain Singleton*. Gloucester: Alan Sutton, 1983.
Erasmus. *Praise of Folly*. Trans. Betty Radice. London: Penguin Books, 1971.

---

[5] All non-English titles have been translated into English for consistency.

Helsztyński, Stanisław, ed. *Specimens of English Poetry and Prose*. 2 vols. Warszawa: Państwowe Wydawnictwo Naukowe, 1973.
Hemingway, Ernest. "Monologue to the Maestro: A High Seas Letter." *By-line. Selected Articles and Dispatches of Four Decades*. Ed. William White. New York: Bantam, 1968.
Marryat, Frederick. *Peter Simple*. Gloucester: Alan Sutton, 1984.
Marryat, Frederick. *The Phantom Ship*. The Project Gutenberg eBook. http://www.gutenberg.org/ebooks/ 12954
Melville, Herman. *Moby-Dick; or, The Whale*. Ed. G. Thomas Tanselle. New York: The Library of America, 1983.
Melville, Herman. *White-Jacket; or The World in a Man-of-War*. New York: Literary Classics of the United States, 1983.
Pirandello, Luigi. *Il fu Mattia Pascal* [*The Late Mattia Pascal*]. Milan: Arnoldo Mondadori, 2001.
Pirandello, Luigi. *L'umorismo* [*Humorism*]. Milan: Arnoldo Mondadori, 1986.
Poe, Edgar Allan. *The Narrative of Arthur Gordon Pym*. London: Panther Books, 1964.
Smollett, Tobias George. *The Adventures of Roderick Random*. Oxford – New York: Oxford University Press, 1988.
Scott, Walter. *The Lives of the Novelists*. Ed. Ernest Rhys. London: J. M. Dent and Sons, 1928.
Shakespeare, William. *As You Like It*. Harlow: Longman Group, 1967.
Shakespeare, William. *Hamlet, Prince of Denmark*. Cambridge: Cambridge University Press, 1985.
Shakespeare, William. *King Richard II*. London: Methuen & Co., 1991.
Shakespeare, William. *Macbeth*. London: Methuen & Co., 1984.
Shakespeare, William. *The Tempest*. Oxford: Clarendon Press, 1987.
Thackeray, William M. *Vanity Fair*. London: Penguin Books, 2001.
The New American Bible. Washington, DC: United States Conference of Catholic Bishops, 2002.
Wagner, Richard. *Der fliegende Holländer* [*The Flying Dutchman*]. New York: Riverrun Press, 1982.

Secondary Sources

Abrams, Meyer Howard. *The Mirror and the Lamp: Romantic Theory and the Critical Tradition*. London: Oxford University Press, 1980.
Adamowicz-Pośpiech, Agnieszka. "'To follow the dream and again to follow the dream': Don Quixote, Almayer and Conrad as Multiple Reflections of the Dreamer." *Secret Sharers: Melville, Conrad and Narratives of the Real*. Eds. Paweł Jędrzejko, Milton M. Reigelman and Zuzanna Szatanik. Zabrze: M-Studio, 2011. 159–170.

Aste, Mario. *La narrativa di Luigi Pirandello: dalle novelle al romanzo Uno, nessuno e centomila* [*Luigi Pirandello's Narratives: From Novellas to the Novel* One, No One and One Hundred Thousand]. Madrid: Porrua Turanzas, 1979.
Auerbach, Erich. *Mimesis. The Representation of Reality in Western Literature.* Princeton: Princeton University Press, 1974.
Bachelard, Gaston. *The Poetics of Space. The Classic Look at How We Experience Intimate Places.* Trans. Maria Jolas. Boston: Beacon Press, 1994.
Bachelard, Gaston. *Water and Dreams. An Essay on the Imagination of Matter.* Trans. Edith R. Farrell. Dallas: The Dallas Institute of Humanities and Culture, 2006.
Baines, Jocelyn. *Joseph Conrad. A Critical Biography.* London: Weidenfeld & Nicolson, 1960.
Bakhtin, Mikhail. "Epic and Novel – Toward a Methodology for the Study of the Novel." *The Dialogic Imagination.* Ed. Michael Holquist. Austin: University of Texas Press, 1981.
Barker, Frank Granville. The Flying Dutchman. *A Guide to the Opera.* London: Barrie &Jenkins, 1979.
Błaszak, Marek. *Sailors, Ships and the Sea in the Novels of Captain Frederick Marryat.* Opole: Wydawnictwo Uniwersytetu Opolskiego, 2006.
Boulger, James D. *"The Rime of the Ancient Mariner* – Introduction." *Twentieth Century Interpretations of* The Rime of the Ancient Mariner. Ed. J. D. Boulger. New Jersey: Prentice-Hall, Inc., 1969. 1–20.
Buchholtz, Mirosława. *Canadian Passwords: Diasporic Fictions into the Twenty-First Century.* Toruń: Wydawnictwo Naukowe Uniwersytetu Mikołaja Kopernika, 2008.
Buczyńska-Garewicz, Hanna. *Miejsca, strony, okolice. Przyczynek do fenomenologii przestrzeni* [*Places, Directions, Surroundings. A Study in the Phenomenology of Space*]. Kraków: Universitas, 2006.
Castle, Terry. "The Carnivalization of Eighteenth Century English Narrative." *Publications of the Modern Language Associations of America.* Vol. 99 (1984): 903–916.
Christian, Lynda. *Theatrum Mundi: The History of an Idea.* New York: Garland Publ., 1987.
Cirlot, Juan Eduardo. *Słownik symboli* [*Dictionary of Symbols*]. Trans. Ireneusz Kania. Kraków: Znak, 2000.
Clark, Katerina, and Michael Holquist. *Mikhail Bakhtin.* Cambrigde, Massachusetts: Belknap Press of Harvard University Press, 1984.
Cuddon, John A. *The Penguin Dictionary of Literary Terms and Literary Theory.* London: Penguin Books, 1999.
Deathridge, John. "An Introduction to *The Flying Dutchman.*" *The Flying Dutchman.* New York: Riverrun Press, 1982. 13–26.

Delumeau, Jean. *Strach w kulturze Zachodu* [*Fear in the Culture of the West*]. Trans. Adam Szymanowski. Warszawa: Pax, 1986.

di Benedetto, Arnaldo. "L'eclissi del romanzo di formazione: falsa libertà e eticità nel *Fu Mattia Pascal*" ["The Eclipse of the Novel of Formation: False Liberty and Morality in *The Late Mattia Pascal*"]. *Lo strappo nel cielo di carta: introduzione alla lettura del* Fu Mattia Pascal [*The Rent in the Paper Sky: An Introduction to* The Late Mattia Pascal]. Ed. Nino Borsellino. Rome: La Nuova Italia Scientifica, 1988. 107–123.

Dobrzycka, Irena. *Kształtowanie się twórczości Byrona: Bohater byroniczny a zagadnienie narodowe* [*The Works of Byron: The Byronic Hero and National Issues*]. Wrocław: Zakład Narodowy im. Ossolińskich, 1963.

Domeracki, Piotr. "Meandry filozofii samotności" ["Meanders of the Philosophy of Solitude"]. *Zrozumieć samotność. Studium interdyscyplinarne* [*Understanding Solitude. An Interdisciplinary Study*]. Eds. Piotr Domeracki and Włodzimierz Tyburski. Toruń: Wydawnictwo Naukowe Uniwersytetu Mikołaja Kopernika, 2006. 15–25.

Drapella, Zofia. *Mity i legendy morskie* [*Nautical Myths and Legends*]. Gdańsk: Wydawnictwo Morskie, 1972.

Faenza, Vincenzo. *Silenzio della coscienza e gioco delle maschere: Letture psicologiche su* La nausea *di Sartre e* Uno, nessuno e centomila *di Pirandello* [*Silence of Conscience and Play of Masks: Psychological Reading of Sartre's* The Nausea *and Pirandello's* One, No One and One Hundred Thousand]. Ed. Paola Zamagni. Bologna: CLUEB, 2004.

Fleishman, Avrom. "*The Mirror of the Sea*: Fragments of a Great Confession." *Joseph Conrad. Critical Assessments*, volume III. Ed. Keith Carabine. Mountfield: Helm Information, 1992. 663–671.

Forstner, Dorothea. *Świat symboliki chrześcijańskiej* [*The World of Christian Symbolism*]. Warszawa: Pax, 1990.

Frenzel, Elisabeth. *Stoffe der Weltliteratur*. Stuttgart: A. Kröner, 1963.

Gale, Robert L. *Richard Henry Dana, Jr.* New York: Twayne Publishers, Inc., 1969.

Gekoski, Richard A. *Conrad. The Moral World of the Novelist*. Elek: London, 1978.

Gilmore, Michael T. *Surface and Depth*. New York: Oxford University Press, 2003.

Górnicki, Zdzisław. *Woda w duchowych przeżyciach człowieka* [*Water in the Spiritual Life of Humans*]. Kraków: Wydawnictwo M, 2008.

Guglielmino, Salvatore. Introduction to Luigi Pirandello's *L'umorismo*. Milan: Arnoldo Mondadori, 1986.

Heilman, Robert B. "Introduction to *Lord Jim*." *Twentieth Century Interpretations of* Lord Jim. Ed. Robert E. Kuehn. New Jersey: Prentice Hall, Inc., 1957.

Italia, Federico. *L'esistenza umana secondo Luigi Pirandello* [*Human Existence According to Luigi Pirandello*]. Rome: Scuole professionali Don Orione, 1968.

Jachimecki, Zdzisław. *Wagner*. Kraków: Polskie Wydawnictwo Muzyczne, 1973.

Janion, Maria. Introduction to the second Polish edition of Frederick Marryat's *The Phantom Ship*, published as *Okręt Widmo*. Trans. Maria Boduszyńska-Borowikowa. Gdańsk: Wydawnictwo Morskie, 1987.
Jędrzejko, Paweł. *Płynność i egzystencja: Doświadczenie lądu i morza a myśl Hermana Melville'a* [*Liquidity and Existence: The Experience of the Land and the Sea in Herman Melville's Thought*]. Sosnowiec: M-studio, 2008.
Kamiński, Piotr. *Tysiąc i jedna opera* [*A Thousand and One Operas*]. Kraków: Polskie Wydawnictwo Muzyczne, 2008.
Kamionka-Straszakowa, Janina. *Zbłąkany wędrowiec: Z dziejów romantycznej topiki* [*The Lost Wanderer. From the History of Romantic Topoi*]. Wrocław: Zakład Narodowy im. Ossolińskich, 1992.
Keyes, Homer Eaton. Introduction to Richard Henry Dana's *Two Years Before the Mast*. The Project Gutenberg eBook. http://digital.library.upenn.edu/webbin/gutbook/ lookup? num=2055.
Knapp Hay, Eloise. "Conrad's Self-Portraiture." *Joseph Conrad Colloquy in Poland 5–12 September 1972* – Contributions. Ed. Róża Jabłkowska. Wrocław: Zakład Narodowy im.Ossolińskich-Wydawnictwo, 1975. 57–71.
Kotarska, Jadwiga. *Theatrum mundi*. Sopot: Wydawnictwo Uniwersytetu Gdańskiego, 1998.
Köhler, Joachim. *Richard Wagner – ostatni Tytan* [*Richard Wagner: The Last Titan*]. Trans. Robert Reszke. Warszawa: KR, 2004.
Krajka, Wiesław. *Izolacja i etos – studium o twórczości Conrada* [*Isolation and Ethos: A Study of Joseph Conrad*]. Zakład Narodowy im. Ossolińskich: Wrocław, 1988.
Krajka, Wiesław. "The Multiple Identities of Yanko Goorall." *Joseph Conrad: East European, Polish and Worldwide*. Boulder: East European Monographs; Lublin: Maria Curie-Skłodowska UP; New York: Columbia UP, 1999. Vol. 8 of *Conrad: Eastern and Western Perspectives*. Wiesław Krajka, gen. ed. 12 vols. to date 1992–. 131–164.
Królikiewicz, Grażyna. *Terytorium ruin: Ruina jako obraz i temat romantyczny* [*The Territory of Ruins: Ruins as a Romantic Image and Issue*]. Kraków: Universitas, 1993.
Künstler-Langner, Danuta. *Idea vanitas: Jej tradycje i toposy w poezji polskiego baroku* [*The Idea of Vanitas: Its Traditions and Topoi in the Poetry of Polish Baroque*]. Toruń: Wydawnictwo Naukowe Uniwersytetu Mikołaja Kopernika, 1996.
Lawrence, David Herbert. *The Symbolic Meaning: The Uncollected Versions of Studies in Classic American Literature*. Ed. Armin Arnold. Fontwell: Centaur Press, 1962.
Macchia, Giovanni. *Pirandello o la stanza della tortura* [*Pirandello or a Chamber of Tortures*]. Milan: Arnoldo Mondadori, 1992.
Manotta, Marco. *Luigi Pirandello*. Milan: Bruno Mondadori, 1998.

Masiello, Vitilio. "La mosca nella bottiglia. Introduzione alla lettura del *Fu Mattia Pascal*" ["The Fly in the Bottle. An Introduction to *The Late Mattia Pascal*"]. *Lo strappo nel cielo di carta: Introduzione alla lettura del* Fu Mattia Pascal [*The Rent in the Paper Sky: An Introduction to* The Late Mattia Pascal]. Ed. Nino Borsellino. Rome: La Nuova Italia Scientifica, 1988. 67–82.

Matthiessen, Francis Otto. *American Renaissance. Art and Expression in the Age of Emerson and Whitman*. London – Toronto – New York: Oxford University Press, 1962. 69–80.

Matthiessen, Francis Otto. "The Fate of the Ungodly God-like Man." *Ahab*. Ed. Harold Bloom. New York: Chelsea House Publishers, 1991. 69–80.

Mazzali, Ettore. *Pirandello*. Florence: La Nuova Italia, 1973.

Mitosek, Zofia. "Mimesis i religia" ["Mimesis and Religion"]. *Mimesis w literaturze, kulturze i sztuce* [*Mimesis in Literature, Culture and Art*]. Ed. Zofia Mitosek. Warszawa: Wydawnictwo Naukowe PWN, 1992. 173–192.

Mroczkowska-Brand, Katarzyna. *Overt Theatricality and the Theatrum Mundi Metaphor in Spanish and English Drama 1570–1640*. Kraków: Universitas, 1993.

Mstowska, Joanna. "Inner Sea Space in Joseph Conrad's *Youth* and *The Mirror of the Sea*." *Exploring Space: Spatial Notions in Cultural, Literary and Language Studies*, vol. 1. *Space in Cultural and Literary Studies*. Eds. Andrzej Ciuk and Katarzyna Molek-Kozakowska. Newcastle: Cambridge Scholars Publishing, 2010. 58–65.

Mstowska, Joanna. "The idea of Vanitas In *The Mirror of the Sea*." *Secret Sharers: Melville, Conrad and Narratives of the Real*. Eds. Paweł Jędrzejko, Milton M. Reigelman and Zuzanna Szatanik. Zabrze: M-Studio, 2011. 185–204.

Ortega y Gasset, José. *Man and People*. Trans. Willard R. Trask. New York: W. W. Norton and Company, Inc., 1963.

Percival, M. O. "A Reading of *Moby Dick*." *Twentieth Century Interpretations of Moby-Dick*. Ed. Michael T. Gilmore. New Jersey: Prentice-Hall, Inc., 1977. 110–111.

Philbrick, Thomas. *James Fenimore Cooper and the Development of American Sea Fiction*. Cambridge, Massachusetts: Harvard University Press, 1961.

Pociej, Bohdan. *Wagner*. Kraków: Polskie Wydawnictwo Muzyczne, 2004.

Ratajczak, Wiesław. "Jak w świecie *Lalki* ludzie patrzą na siebie?" ["How Do People View Each Other in the World of *The Doll*?"]. *Bolesław Prus: Pisarz nowoczesny* [*Bolesław Prus: A Modern Writer*]. Ed. Jakub Malik. Lublin: Wydawnictwo KUL, 2009.

Ricciardi, Mario. "*Uno, nessuno e centomila*: il romanzo della scomposizione della personalità" ["*One, No One and One Hundred Thousand*: A Novel of Disintegration of Personality"]. *Nuvole e vento: Introduzione alla lettura di* Uno, nessuno e centomila [*Clouds and Wind: An Introduction to* One, No One and One Hundred Thousand]. Ed. Stefano Milioto. Agrigento: Centro nazionale di studi pirandelliani, 1989.

Rosenfield, Claire. *Paradise of Snakes: An Archetypal Analysis of Conrad's Political Novels*. Chicago: University of Chicago Press, 1967.
Santeramo, Donato. *Luigi Pirandello: la parola, la scena e il mito* [*Luigi Pirandello: The Word, the Stage and the Myth*]. Rome: Neu – Nuova Editrice Universitaria, 2007.
Said, Edward. *Joseph Conrad and the Fiction of Autobiography*. Harvard University Press: Massachusetts, 1966.
Shapiro, Samuel. *Richard Henry Dana, Jr., 1815–1882*. East Lansing, Michigan: Michigan State University Press, 1961.
Sherry, Norman. *Conrad's Eastern World*. Cambridge: Cambridge University Press, 1971.
Skutnik, Tadeusz. "O semantyce kompozycji *Zwierciadła morza*" ["On the Semantics of Composition in *The Mirror of the Sea*"]. *O kompozycji tekstu Conradowskiego* [*On the Composition of the Conradian Text*]. Ed. Andrzej Zgorzelski. Gdańsk: Wydawnictwo Morskie, 1978. 7–28.
Stala, Marian. *Trzy nieskończoności. O poezji Adama Mickiewicza, Bolesława Leśmiana i Czesława Miłosza* [*Three Infinities. On the Poetry of Adam Mickiewicz, Bolesław Leśmian and Czesław Miłosz*]. Kraków: Wydawnictwo Literackie, 2001.
Stape, J. H. *The Cambridge Companion to Joseph Conrad*. Cambridge: Cambridge University Press, 1996.
Świontek, Sławomir. *Norwidowski teatr świata* [*The Norwidian Theatre of the World*]. Łódź: Wydawnictwo Łódzkie, 1983.
Thwaites, Sarah. "Melville and the Magic Mirror." *Secret Sharers: Melville, Conrad and Narratives of the Real*. Eds. Paweł Jędrzejko, Milton M. Reigelman and Zuzanna Szatanik. Zabrze: M-Studio, 2011. 209–224.
Twain, Mark. "Fenimore Cooper's Literary Offences." *The Norton Anthology of American Literature*. Ed. Nina Baym. New York – London: W. W. Norton, 1999. 1457–1465.
Vaughan, William. "Loneliness, Love and Death." *The Flying Dutchman*. New York: Riverrun Press, 1982. 27–32.
Walker, Warren S. *James Fenimore Cooper. An Introduction and Interpretation*. New York: Barnes and Noble, 1963.
Warren, R. P. "A Poem of Pure Imagination: An Experiment in Reading." *Twentieth Century Interpretations of* The Rime of the Ancient Mariner. Ed. J. D. Boulger. New Jersey: Prentice-Hall, Inc., 1969. 21–47.
Wilczyński, Marek. *The Phantom and the Abyss. The Gothic Fiction in America and Aesthetics of the Sublime 1798–1856*. Frankfurt am Main: Peter Lang, 1999.

**Dis / Continuities
Toruń Studies in Language, Literature and Culture**

Edited by Mirosława Buchholtz

Volume 1 Mirosława Buchholtz / Grzegorz Koneczniak (eds.): The Visual and the Verbal in Film, Drama, Literature and Biography. 2012.

Volume 2 Mirosława Buchholtz: The Beautiful and the Doomed: Essays on Literary Value. 2013.

Volume 3 Joanna Mstowska: Various Aspects of Mimesis in Selected Sea Novels of Frederick Marryat, James F. Cooper and Richard H. Dana. 2013.

www.peterlang.de